AGAINST ALL ODDS

Statement of Purpose

The Holocaust spread across the face of Europe just a few decades ago. The brutality then unleashed is still nearly beyond comprehension. Millions of innocents—men, women and children—were consumed by its flames.

The goal of Holocaust Publications, a non-profit organization founded by survivors, is to publish and disseminate works on the Holocaust. These will include survivors' accounts, testimonies and memoirs, historical and regional analyses, anthologies, archival and source documents and other relevant materials that will help shed light on this cataclysmic era.

These books and studies will be made available to the general public, scholars, researchers, historians, teachers and students. They will be used in Holocaust Resource Centers, libraries and schools, synagogues and churches. They will help foster an increased awareness of the Holocaust and its implications. They will help to preserve the memory for posterity and to enable this awesome time to be better understood and comprehended.

Holocaust Library
216 West 18th Street
New York, NY 10011
212-463-7988

AGAINST ALL ODDS

A Tale of Two Survivors

Norman Salsitz
and
Amalie Petranker Salsitz

Holocaust Library
New York

Edited by Dr. Mortimer Gross and Robert Skolnik, Ph.D.

General Editor, Sol Lewis

Library of Congress Cataloging-in-publication Data

Salsitz, Norman, 1920-
    Against all odds: a tale of two survivors / Norman Salsitz and
Amalie Petranker Salsitz.
        p.   cm.
    ISBN 0-89604-148-4: $24.95.—ISBN 0-89604-149-2 (pbk.): $12.95
    1. Jews—Poland—Persecutions. 2. Holocaust, Jewish (1939-
1945—Poland—Personal narrative. 3. Salsitz, Norman, 1920-   .
4. Petranker Salsitz, Amalie, 1922-   . 5. Poland—Ethnic relations. I. Petranker Salsitz, Amalie, 1922-   . II. Title.
DS135.P63A16   1990   90-20281
                                                              CIP

Cover Design by The Appelbaum Company

Printed in the United States of America

Dedicated
to
Our Beloved Grandsons

Dustin Issaac
Aaron Richard
Michael Freed

and to Our Nephew

Dr. Edwin Arnold Salsitz

"I shall not die but live,
to recite the deeds of the Lord.
The Lord has soarly afflicted me,
but He did not abandon me to death."
Psalms 118: 17-18

Acknowledgements

We wish to acknowledge with gratitude the invaluable help and encouragement of Dr. Mortimer Gross and his wife JoAnn, Dr. Samuel Gross, Richard Skolnik, Ph.D., Dr. Martha Shapiro, Dr. Elijah Bortnicker and his wife Clair and, Sol Lewis, General Editor, for his patience and understanding.

Foreword

Both Norman and Manya now speak of their lives in war ravaged Poland without hesitation, without much visible emotion. Though many of the events they recall took place 50 years ago or more, time is not the enemy. Their recollections remain sharp, their reconstruction of events richly detailed and textured. Norman, it is true, is blessed with a memory of awesome acuity in its ability to coax forth small details about which one almost forgets to ask. Manya also remembers, because she's never been able to forget.

They must tell their stories; as survivors it is an obligation both accept. They were spared and so they must speak. They must leave their accounts because soon, all too soon, their generation will pass on. They must set down their stories, place additional indisputable evidence on the record, because there are still those who question, and some who even deny the events of which they speak.

Each reviews the manuscript with microscopic precision. Every detail must be as it was. A decision to omit a piece of information here or there is troubling at first until I assure them that nothing essential has been removed. Names, every one must be recalled. These people may still be alive. Their children, other relatives too, must be assured that they have not been forgotten, that once they lived in community with others. Their memory must be sustained by more than tributes to their collective sacrifices.

And so a manuscript emerged as his story is told and her account unfolds. Both are similar—ghetto confinements, false identities, tales of brutality, miraculous, nimble-witted escapes—yet different in striking ways. Manya was a young woman, raised in a cosmopolitan city yet sheltered and innocent in many respects. For her to survive all alone, her immediate family—mother, father, sister, all killed early on—seemed beyond all probability. Her only chance to stay alive, Manya calculated, was amidst the anonymity of a large city, its population swollen by the influx of outsiders. Still, this meant a daily ordeal, agonizing efforts to avoid discovery and betrayal in the midst of the enemy camp with its elaborate identification procedures and spy networks. At any moment, a misstep, a false friend, an inadvertent remark, and the masquerade would be over, the end swift and certain.

Norman was a product of a world quite different from the one Manya inhabited. The small town, the countryside and its peasant population—all this he knew intimately. Here backwardness, suppressed improvements, and tradition discouraged innovation. Yet Norman was a young man sheltered, it is true, subject to the restrictions that religious orthodoxy imposed, yet unfettered by his own rebellious nature and the opportunities for worldly experience gained through involvement in his family's thriving business. Uncommon physical endurance enabled him to withstand the work details, beating and shootings perpetrated by the Germans. Then he fled into the woods where the challenge to remain alive assumed a form quite different from that which Manya faced in the city. Although Norman was in the company of other fellow Jews, including his brother, the odds against survival were formidable. Unfamiliar surroundings, exposure to the harsh elements, reliance for food and supplies upon the surrounding population which betrayed and butchered as often as it befriended them—all this made their existence ever so precarious. In the end only a handful left the woods alive.

Even as Manya and Norman fought so bravely to survive, they attempted, at the same time, to strike back at the enemy. Each, in his own way, succeeded, their wrenching encounters and exchanges of vital information toward the close of the war serving as the most striking example of such instances. Each will tell you, however, that there was no greater revenge for them than their individual survival coupled with the defeat of the Germans. Somehow, though suffering indescribable losses, they withstood the mighty forces arrayed against them, survived the systematic efforts to exterminate all Jews, and saw the enemy, once so confident and convinced of its superiority, humbled and defeated. This volume thus represents their final lasting triumph, the fulfillment of sacred obligations to family, friends and fellow Jews swallowed up by the Holocaust. They will at last have added their voices to those of many others who have borne true witness to the events of those years so that the world does not forget the true face of barbarism nor ignore the fact that such forces ever threaten the painful progress mankind has achieved.

Richard Skolnik, Ph.D.

Introduction

"I must bear witness to what was perpetuated. . . . I want to heal, or at least try to reduce the pain." These words, written by Amalie Salsitz, are as much the survivor's story as the painful reconstruction of terrible events. Amalie, and her husband Norman, authors of this double memoir (it's really a conversation we're allowed to overhear), write in a vein survivors have been writing for decades: To *proclaim* their survival, again and again, for now and posterity. The repetition, something Norman Salsitz calls his obsession, is characteristic, for the urge to live is always in conflict with the shadow of death. To heal, like their determination just to stay alive, is a quest "against all odds."

It's the subtitle they've chosen for their luminous memoir which suggests the memoir's distinctive voice. When I first thought about what "The Tale of Two Survivors" meant, I wondered if, on some level, it might be a play on Dickens's "tale of two cities": The Salsitzes appeared to transform "the best of times, the worst of times" into an account of the worst of times . . . the very worst of times. "The world had become unbearably grim," writes Norman Salsitz. It had become "consistently gray." But as I read their stories I realized they were describing two faces of survival, one affirming life, the other showing a world forever changed.

The Salsitzes' world had surely "turned upside down." Their traditional Jewish values, such as faith in God or family ties, had become sources of weakness during six dreadful years coinciding with World War II. If they were to endure, they had to become fighters and fiercely independent. Just thinking about the cumulative impact of their daily torment in the ghettos and their corrosive fear of betrayal, not to mention the murder of their loved ones and friends, explains why everything they once revered and cherished "had come to an end."

In one particularly poignant episode, Norman Salsitz recounts the days just after the Germans were finally forced out of Kolbuszowa, the small Polish town where he grew up. Having been away for so many years, would he long to return? Hardly. Of the 2,000 people who lived there, only nine survived. There would be no turning back for another reason: Many neighbors, "among whom we had lived for centuries," revealed their dark side. Their "treachery" destroyed his ability to trust others. It also destroyed a worldly innocence. In spite of the documented historical Polish and Jewish rapport, for someone like Norman Salsitz, who touched fire, nothing could convince him that Jews were *ever* accepted by Poles.

Simple, everyday matters could never be experienced the same way. Children playing reminded him of his niece who was taken away and killed with her mother and her playmates. Romantic stirrings always evoked sad memories of a girl he longed to hold: "The one I had loved lay dead." A trip to the barber was a parlous undertaking. ("Would he cut my throat?") He wanted desperately "to get back to normal living," but wouldn't even let the barber finish cutting his hair.

"For what did we survive, then?," we hear the Salsitzes lamenting. One answer, inevitably, was to seek revenge, to fight the Germans in retaliation for years of being hunted by them and their collaborators. They recognize that revenge offered no real satisfaction, but for a while, while fighting with the partisans, Norman Salsitz "felt like a lamed one who learned to walk again."

I believe a better answer can be found, paradoxically, in their references to Poles who helped them survive. When reading their reenactment of dramatic escapes, close calls, and innumerable desperations, it becomes clear how dependent their survival was on friendly, always courageous gestures of assistance. Luck surely played a role, as survivors commonly note. If the liberating Russian partisans didn't believe Norman Salsitz was on their side, if Amalie Salsitz didn't look "gentile," their chances of survival would have been slim. Sheer determination also counted measurably. But the Salsitzes warn us not to overlook the people who gave them false identity papers, hid them, nursed them back to health, and provided them with food and crucial contacts. How dreadfully "rare" these people were, they say. How fickle they could be: one peasant betrayed Norman Salsitz and his friend after harboring his friend for weeks. Still, we almost get a sense of reassuring gratitude in their discussions of the men and women who saved their lives.

A different memoir would make scant reference to rescuers. Indeed, stories of survival often seem like 20th century morality plays, excoriating villains. The Salsitzes give us a different, more complicated picture— two faces of survival. Nothing in their story even suggests that there was anything like a triumph after the Holocaust. Yet, we learn about Poles who risked their lives for them. For the Salsitzes to say this about a people whom they also spurn for turning against them indicates how scrupulous they have been in recalling so difficult a past.

Abraham H. Foxman

Part One

OUR FIRST ENCOUNTER

Chapter 1

Mass confusion reigned as the liberation of Poland began. Ordinary feelings receded, insufficient for the emotional upheaval at hand. All about people cried disconsolately for joy, and laughed dementedly from pain. Love and hate, joy and sorrow, reality and fantasy, alternated in rapid wrenching confusion. Survivors pinched themselves to make sure they were yet alive, insisting all the time that the dead too still lived. How could it be that they had all been taken from us?

The Germans had not yet lost the war, but now were on the run. Having already retreated from Russia, they were about to be driven from Poland. At last they had met their match; total defeat was just a matter of time. But my mother, my father, my sisters and their families, almost everyone else I knew would not be there to witness the end of the "master race."

My mother had at the outset assured us this would happen, that Hitler would not triumph. Six years ago—or was it six eternities ago—the Germans had marched into our town. All Jews, they ordered, were to wear a white armband with a blue Star of David. "Take good care of these armbands," I heard my mother tell a neighbor. "When this war is over and the Germans are beaten, we'll edge these bands with gold thread and wear them on every Jewish holiday."

3

Such was her faith, her conviction of ultimate triumph. With it I was able to endure. "Naftali, you are my ninth, my youngest. You are young, strong and bright—go on living, my son. Don't despair, it is your duty to survive and let the world know what is happening to us." These were her very words, spoken to me just before she was taken away. Clinging to them I stayed afloat, did not sink into the abyss, or surrender to those who shattered our world into useless pieces.

For six years I lived like a hunted animal. Around me almost everyone died, but somehow I stayed alive. I survived even though a marked man. Both Germans and Poles had determined to kill me and exterminate all my people. How hard they tried; how very close they came to succeeding. Few would have lifted a finger to save me, me, Naftali Ben Yitzhak, son of an orthodox Jew. But when posing as Tadeusz Zaleski, offspring of Polish Roman Catholics, my prospects improved dramatically. My high Slavic cheekbones, eager eyes under bushy eyebrows and snub nose would not betray me. And passing for a Pole was no great challenge given my fluent Polish, uncommon among the mainly Yiddish speaking Jews in our area. As a "Pole" I succeeded far beyond what a Jew would ever have imagined, becoming an officer in the Polish army. In that capacity I controlled the lives of countless others, was in a position after the war to secure all that I might need. But my thoughts were elsewhere, preoccupied as I was with the staggering pain, the open wounds from a very recent past.

While my Polish military comrades made plans for their futures in liberated Poland, such preparations were for me impossibly irrelevant, haunted as I was by the memory of all those who had been part of my life but who were no more. Everything I had revered and cherished had come to an end. Nearly everyone I loved was gone. What plans could I have? My world had vanished, my home town reduced practically to rubble, my fellow Jews removed from the face of the earth in one unrelenting wave of violence. (Of the 2,000 Jews who once lived in my town only nine remained alive at war's end.) Across all of Poland the story was the same, a Jewish population of 3.5 million reduced to 50,000, a murderous irrevocable end to centuries of Jewish culture.

The world had become unbearably grim, consistently gray, much like the negative of a photograph. The sunniest of days appeared dark and somber, the very brightness a grotesque mockery to all who were no longer alive to enjoy it. To watch a cluster of happy Polish children at play produced immediate pain, reminded me of so many beautiful youngesters, especially my niece, Blimcia, an angelic child who was taken away, then killed along with her mother and her playmates. A girl's earnest invitation for me to kiss her evoked only sadness; the one I had longed to hold, the one I had loved lay dead, savagely killed. Revenge brought little satisfaction. I too would end up killing, but even when I did I felt keen disappointment; it did not bring anyone back. Still I had survived and at 24 faced the challenge of learning to begin life again.

While waiting for hostilities to end my comrades devoted most waking hours to drinking vodka and amorous pursuits. I could not. My work, always my work. It became an obsession; continued promotions only drove me to greater efforts. Work was my antidote for gloom, my escape from the void of loneliness, so completely cut off was I from the life I had once known. In this way the days passed. A sense of responsibility replaced a sense of purpose. Though I befriended several of my comrades no one seemed interested in my woes, or for that matter, in talking about their own. Take your pleasure while you could, put on a happy face, no matter what your real feelings — such was the prevailing code of conduct. No one exemplified this better than one fellow officer with whom I became fairly friendly. His name was Yanek. He too was a Jew passing for a Pole. A native of Cracow, he had escaped to Russia at the outbreak of the war. Now he had returned to Poland with the advancing Russian army, and was attached to our unit. Yanek was a dapper, dashing, wiry fellow, aware of his good looks, and forever preening his David Niven mustache. He had no equal in our unit as a ladies' man. Unlike the rest of the men, he did little talking about his romantic conquests. While others talked, Yanek was busy.

In late December 1944 Yanek and I were selected for a special mission to Cracow. We were then stationed in Rzeszow, a town halfway between Cracow and Lvov. Rzeszow I knew quite well since it lay but a few miles to the south of my home town, Kolbuszowa. I had been there many times before the war in connection with the family business. Rzeszow had been liberated by the Russians six months before, when their general offensive advanced across Poland towards Germany. With Warsaw in ruins after the ill-fated uprising against the Germans, the provisional Polish government established its headquarters in Lublin in central Poland. It was this new government that directed a task force be sent westward to Cracow. At the time the enemy was still in control of the region and fierce fighting between Germans and Russians raged. Still the Polish government wished to establish its presence in Cracow. Having served as the center of the German occupation government and as the ancient historical capital of Poland, it symbolized Polish sovereignty. It was important that the Polish army be able to claim some credit for its liberation and be present to assist in administering the city until the formation of a permanent post-war Polish civilian government. Cracow to the Russians was simply another city, just one more pocket of German resistance on their road to Berlin. To our army unit, glowing with Polish patriotism and fired up by the imminent downfall of Poland's worst enemy, Cracow was a hallowed name. All of us on this assignment felt enormously proud for having been chosen, were eager for the upcoming mission to begin.

Our task force, about 100 men and 10 women, largely officers, set out for Cracow. Traveling mostly at night in a small convoy of army trucks and jeeps, we followed on the heels of the advancing Russian army. The first days were uneventful except that it kept getting colder. Staying warm became our main concern. In between we smoked, joked, drank and dozed off periodically. Yanek and I rode in a jeep with a young Pole from Lvov named Roman. By the third day we had run out of jokes. Then quite unexpectedly the ingredients for one materialized when we spent a night in a building once a Jewish-owned flour mill which the Germans had just recently abandoned. Upon entering we immediately began a search for souvenirs and in short order discovered a Victrola. Records were also uncovered and to kill time we began playing them, mostly classical pieces along with some popular Polish tunes. But then someone put a record on that in an instant penetrated to my very core. It was the *Kol Nidre*, the sacred prayer of the Day of Atonement. I was stunned; it had been years since I had heard this mournful, awe-inspiring prayer. Naturally the Polish boys had no idea what it was; they didn't like it, called for it to be tossed out.

"Wait a second," I said, "don't throw it out. It's a classical Spanish opera, an ancient Castillian aria." This came to mind, I think, because *Kol Nidre* was in fact created in Spain by the Maranos. The ploy worked and some of the more cultured fellows, ashamed of their ignorance, suddenly recalled that indeed it was a Spanish opera. In this way I was able to rescue the record and take it with me to Cracow.

Mostly we managed to entertain ourselves by singing, accompanied by Roman's harmonica. Roman had taken a liking to Yanek and me and had attached himself to us shortly after we had left Rzeszow. He was the youngest and tallest man in the unit, and his lean body swayed like a birch sapling when he walked. His thatch of light golden hair was never combed, and his long boyish face was a bright field of freckles in which his eyes, nose and mouth all but disappeared. Roman was a typical Polish youth who came of age during the war. He was a young boy acting like a man. He was good company; Yanek and I did not mind having him along.

Chapter 2

On the fifth night we reached Tarnow, a city east of Cracow. The Germans had evacuated the city only a few hours before; we met no one during our "triumphal" entry. Instead we drove through dark, silent streets, seemingly a ghost town. The townspeople remained inside assuming, no doubt, we were yet another German column. Near midnight we reached the center of the city where we stopped, uncertain of where to go or what to do. As a youngster I had attended the Yeshiva[1] of the Dzikiver Rebbe in Tarnow and remembered that the best hotel had been Hotel City located on Walowa Street, owned then by a Jew named Weiss. If it still stood, there would be a good place to spend the night. Sure enough we found Weiss's hotel and parked our vehicles along the curb. Stopping before the gate I recalled how I had stood there years before with my father. Then I was a young Yeshiva student dressed in the traditional manner with long brown earlocks and wearing the traditional long black coat and my father the graybearded patriarch proudly and hopefully entrusting his son to the care and tutelage of his revered Rebbe. That was ages ago.

No one answered as we pounded on the gate. As for signs of life in the hotel—there were none. The only

---

[1] School for Rabbinical studies

sounds were off in another section of town where one could hear the roar of tanks, and short bursts of *pepeshas*[2], and off in the distance the continuous booming of cannons. But around us the streets were silent and it was cold—a bone chilling night, probably some 20 degrees below zero. A full moon cast a silvery light on the snow, revealing the silhouettes of our men and outlines of the houses.

As we loitered restlessly outside the hotel our patrol jeep pulled up alongside and a Russian colonel stepped out. The news was good. Enemy pockets of resistance were crumbling, he said. The Germans were in full retreat to the west, the Russians in pursuit along the entire front. He suggested we remain in Tarnow for the night, and then proceed toward Cracow the next day. That made sense; still we had yet to find a place to stay.

All around were dark windows, most lined with black paper and draped with curtains as a precaution against air raids. We lit cigarettes, and then spontaneously began to sing Polish folk and military songs. Perhaps someone would hear us and realize that the Germans were gone and liberation was at hand. Minutes passed. A window in a house nearby parted; then quickly shut. Again it opened, this time a little wider. In the narrow opening a head appeared, looking down at us with wide, bewildered eyes. A few seconds later a second head joined the first in the window. Another window then opened partially. Close by a flickering candle appeared. Additional people in the surrounding houses parted their windows to gaze down at the strange sight. What soldiers were these standing in the snow in the middle of the night singing Polish songs?

---

[2] Russian machine guns

The hotel gate now opened and the night watchman, half asleep, bearing a candle, approached. The Germans had been driven out, and we were the Polish Army, liberating the town. He seemed to understand. Without saying a word he went back into the hotel, returning quickly with a group of nightgown-clad people, some of whom opened the gate and put on the lights while a few continued to look on in amazement, not believing their eyes. One elderly man with a long upturned mustache came forward holding out a bottle. He spoke in a trembling, halting voice, almost a whisper, as if afraid that if he raised his voice the spell might be broken. He had kept that bottle of the best vodka, he told us, since 1939, and had vowed not to open it until the day Polish soldiers returned to Tarnow. His voice choked with emotion as tears rolled down his cheeks. He uncorked the bottle and passed it around.

Now lights appeared in windows all about, and soon a small crowd had gathered. I was freezing even in my bearskin army coat, but the townspeople seemed oblivious to the cold. Out onto the street they came in night clothes and flimsy slippers, some with blankets draped over their shoulders. For reassurance young and old began to touch us, many eyes wet with tears of joy, kissing the insignias of our uniforms. They dragged out their children, half naked, mostly asleep, and pointed at us, saying: "Look, these are Polish officers— we are free!"

More vodka, mostly the home-made Samogonka-Bimber, made the rounds. Then a few plates of bread and kielbasa appeared, carried by women who pushed their way through the crowd that surrounded us. Several young girls threw their arms around our necks and kissed us.

At the moment how easy it was to see myself as
Tadeusz Zaleski, an ardent Polish patriot, the liberator
of Tarnow. A middle-aged woman took my hand. "Let
me touch you," she said, "let me feel the pulse and life
of a free Pole." She burst into tears. "I am happy to be
here at this moment; but I'm not sure I have the right
to be happy, when my son cannot be here to share this
happiness. He was arrested by the Germans for belonging to the A.K.[3] and he was taken to Auschwitz
and executed." She held out a tin box. "This is what's
left of him. The Germans sent back his ashes. He would
have been 24 years old today." "My age," I thought to
myself as the woman caressed the tin box with her
bony, shaking fingers.

I was swept back into the crowd again by some of my
comrades, who were laughing and cavorting, each with
a bottle of vodka in one hand and a girl in the other.
Everyone, it seemed, had found a partner and was preparing for further celebration. But my momentary elation had passed. I felt unable to join in with them. For
me there was no escaping that bereaved mother's
question. What right did I have to be happy? Who had
been liberated here in Tarnow? Certainly not the
30,000 Jews who once lived here. Nearly all of them,
like that woman's son, had been turned to ashes. Not
Alter Horowitz, the martyred Dzikiver Rebbe of
Tarnow, with whom I had years ago studied and
learned the laws and lore of my people. Not Dr. David
Rabinowicz, the great surgeon of the city, who during
the war, under almost impossible circumstances, had
saved my life here. Nor those lovely girls who had
been his assistants—Eda Brana, Giza Flor, Hanka
Israel, whom I came to know at the hospital, who cared

---

[3] The Polish underground

for me most tenderly after my surgery. Recognizing this, what pride was there being Tadeusz Zaleski?

Someone tapped me on the shoulder. I turned around and saw my friends, Yanek and Roman. Roman, as usual, was looking over Yanek's shoulder, like a bodyguard protecting his charge. Both of them were in high spirits. "I just got the word," Yanek announced ceremoniously, imitating a pompous officer. Then he jutted out his chin and flashed a broad smile. "There is an apartment next door and in that apartment are five beautiful girls. What do you say we go up there and show them a good time?" Without waiting for an answer Yanek put his arms around our shoulders and steered us out of the crowd. Bottles of vodka and packs of cigarettes were passed from hand to hand. We three helped ourselves to as much as we could stuff into our overcoat pockets. We had no trouble finding the apartment, where we were welcomed as enthusiastically as we had just been in the street.

The apartment, modestly furnished, was spacious and well heated. Yanek and Roman quickly selected partners; I refrained and instead made small talk with the other three girls. Soon all of us were drinking and smoking. I forced the vodka down and puffed awkwardly on my cigarette. Still the warmth and conviviality of the room was real; I began to relax, even enjoy myself. Before long I noticed something different about one of the girls—that she was strikingly beautiful, blue-eyed and blonde was obvious, but like me she seemed only to be going through the motions. There was something forced about her drinking and smoking. The war had sharpened my ability to interpret outward gestures and expressions as the reflection of inner feelings and thoughts. There was in this girl's eyes a deep sadness, completely out of keeping with the occasion. It suddenly occurred to me—could this girl be Jewish? But how to find out? I myself was masquerading as a Gentile. If I asked her outright, even in private, she might well take offense. If I was wrong it would doubtless ruin the entire evening. I had all but given up when an idea hit me. Strolling around the room I stopped behind the girl and softly I whistled the *Hatikvah*, the Jewish national anthem. After a few bars, I stopped. She had not reacted. I was mistaken. I walked past her and sat down. At that point I felt a hand on my shoulder. I looked up and she was standing there behind me, her sad eyes staring down into mine, with an unmistakable message. No words were uttered. How in the midst of all this joy and laughter could we commiserate with each other, talk about suffering and death?

We pretended nothing had happened. Two hours passed. By now Yanek and Roman and the other girls had consumed more than a little vodka. Even after coffee had been served they continued downing drink after drink. It now seemed safe to talk to this girl without being noticed. I followed her into the empty kitchen, and when she turned to face me I spoke the secret password, *"Amchu,"* the word which both identified and linked Jewish survivors. "Yes," she replied. I felt an intense rush of joy. Here was a miracle, finding a Jewish girl alive and well in Tarnow, and on the very night of liberation.

At that moment Yanek came into the kitchen. "We must get along," he said. Word had just arrived that our unit had been ordered to move on Cracow at once. We put on our coats and walked down to our jeep accompanied by all the girls. My two friends, rather drunk, kept up their hugging and kissing, and I stood there next to the beautiful blonde girl, neither of us saying a word. I hadn't even learned her name. As we climbed into our jeep, my friends teased. "What are you staring at her for? Why don't you kiss her good-bye? Go ahead, kiss her. Today we live, tomorrow we might die." I got out of the jeep, approached, and barely brushed my lips against her cheek. The jeep began to pull out; I jumped in and waved to her. Hesitantly she waved back. She remained in the middle of the street watching me disappear into the night. I would never again see her though long after-ward I would remember her beautiful blue eyes, full of tears as she stood there.

Chapter 3

The liberation scene at Tarnow was replayed in many towns and villages on the way to Cracow. Each time there was the mingling of disbelief, joy, sorrow, an outpouring of tears, laughter, dancing and singing. Always the same hero's welcome. No matter that the fighting had been done by others, we merely following in their wake. Greeted as liberators we were swept up by the wild enthusiasm. Times like this called for heroes, and gladly we played our parts. It was our moment of glory.

But there was no way to liberate the dead. Again and again Naftali Ben Yitzhak reappeared. No matter where we went I sought out, usually in vain, my own people. One person here, one family there—that was all that remained of Jewish communities that once covered the face of Poland.

One such experience reflected tens of thousands of others. About 20 miles west of Tarnow we were forced to detour to a small town freed by the Russians the day before. It happened to be the home town of one of our officers, a Jew named Leon. While our comrades were going through the typical scene of liberation—hugging and kissing the townspeople while keeping an eye out for the prettiest girls in the crowd—Yanek and I took off with Leon to find out what had become of his family. His home still stood, but we found a strange Polish family living there. They had, they claimed, no idea where the former occupants might be. Neither could neighborhood people offer us any useful information about Leon's family or of other Jewish families who had lived there. All the Jews were deported; none had returned—everywhere the same answer. Finally we found a man and his wife who had transacted business with Leon's father before the war. When Leon introduced himself, their faces lit up, but they said nothing. Poor Leon did not know what to make of this. He stopped questioning them. He just stood there hoping they would say something. The woman left the room, and a moment later returned with a young girl, perhaps eighteen years old. She stood there with downcast eyes, visibly frightened. "Say hello to your cousin," the woman said to Leon. "We kept her here since the Jews were deported two and one-half years ago," her husband said. "We promised her mother we would save her, and we did. In our family we have never broken a promise."

"Have any other Jews survived?" asked Yanek. The man's face clouded. "The Germans killed them all." Leon's face twitched but he said nothing. For a moment we stood there, heads bowed as though observing a ceremonial moment of silence in memory of the dead. Then in a clear, solemn voice such as one might have imagined coming from the prophets of the Bible, Leon declared: "I am taking this girl with me. She and I are all that are left of the entire Jewish community. I will marry her and we will rehabilitate this community. It may take a long time, but as God is my witness, nothing will stop me!" Leon's cousin accompanied us to Cracow. True to his word he married her. Sadly, though, she contracted tuberculosis and died six months later.

Traveling all morning, we reached the outskirts of
Cracow in the late afternoon and stopped to await
further orders. The distinction of being the first Polish
unit to enter the city was ours. As usual the reception
was tumultuous. Yanek and Roman had already begun
to look for female company when a distinguished
looking gray-haired gentleman approached and with
a bow, told me that he would be greatly honored if I
agreet to be his guest for the night. I would, I told
him, if he would also invite my two dear friends, which
he did promptly. He escorted us to his apartment,
where we were greeted by a timid looking, neatly
dressed wife, and by two attractive, smiling daughters,
who kissed all of us when they learned who we were.
The father had been a gymnasium professor before
the war and lost his position after the Germans arrived.
The two girls supported the family by doing office
work. They did not earn much, and the family barely
managed to survive. The professor apologized for a
repast he considered inadequate for the occasion.

We ate the austere but tastefully prepared dinner of
beet soup and potato pancakes, repeatedly praising
the food after each mouthful. The professor's wife kept
blushing, his daughters continually giggled. After
dinner the girls invited their friends in the building to
meet us. In short order the apartment was buzzing
with people who wanted to see the Polish officers who
had come to liberate Cracow. Some brought the usual
bottles of vodka, mostly home made Samogonka. After
a few toasts we all began to sing familiar Polish songs.
Once having exhausted the standard repertory, we introduced some new Polish and Russian songs, songs
from the battlefields and the forests probably being
heard in Cracow for the first time. After some prodding

I agreed to sing the latest ballad and song about Warsaw in ruins, one that had become quite popular.

> *Warszawo Ty Moja Warszawo*
> *Warsaw, my beloved Warsaw,*
> *You are ever in my dreams,*
> *You are ever in my longing,*
> *Not only songs and words I offer you, Warsaw,*
> *I will gladly lay down my life for you.*

All listened in rapt silence, tears streaming down the cheeks of the girls, some of the men sniffling and clearing their throats. Thunderous applause and shouts of "Encore" followed. Again and again I sang the song until everyone knew it. Then one of the professor's daughters sat down at the piano and played the melody. We sang, we harmonized late into the night.

That evening I outdid even my companions in downing vodka. I felt nothing, I remembered little of what followed. I must have passed out because when I first became conscious I felt someone shaking me, telling me about having to leave for Cracow. Opening my eyes I saw Yanek; I also saw where I was in bed with both the professor's daughters. I had, so I was told, fallen asleep on the couch in the drawing room and then had been carried upstairs, undressed and put to bed. Why, I asked, had I ended up in the girls' bed? Both burst out laughing. "We wanted to make sure nothing happened to you during the night," one said, winking at her sister. "After all, we have to take good care of a Polish officer who is about to liberate Cracow." As she spoke, the two of them got up and tiptoed out of the room. I struggled up, looked for my clothes, but couldn't find them. I stood there, uncertain about what to do, when the girls returned carrying my clothes. During the night they had pressed my uniform and polished my boots. I got dressed with great difficulty, then staggered into the dining room where I found Yanek and Roman drinking black coffee to dispel the cobwebs. My head was pounding; I could not see straight. It was the first time in my life I had ever gotten drunk. I felt ashamed. When the professor came into the dining room, I couldn't look him in the eye. "I am sorry if I made a spectacle of myself," I told him when he offered his hand to bid me farewell. "I don't know what came over me; it never happened to me before." "Oh, it was nothing," he remonstrated, taking my hand in both of his. "You were entitled to let yourself go. You did us a great honor by spending the first night of the liberation with us. Our daughters will never forget that they had the privilege of pressing the uniforms and cleaning the boots of the liberators of Cracow."

On January 16th a few miles from Cracow a Russian patrol stopped our convoy.[1] It was, we learned, a battle zone; it was not safe to proceed, as the situation remained fluid and uncertain. After some discussion, we were advised to travel north, bypass the city and to prepare to enter it from the northwest, from which direction the Russians, in a surprise move, had attacked the city. We knew of the Germans' savage destruction of Warsaw. Rumors circulated of secret orders from Hitler to level all the cities which the Germans had to abandon. Had Cracow already met the same fate? Why

---

[1] At this time our unit was attached to the 22nd Brigade of the 59th Army of the first Ukrainian Front commanded by Marshal Ivan Koniew.

should this living symbol of historical Poland be spared by the Germans?

Over the next two days with the Russian attack in full swing, the destruction in and around Cracow accelerated. Much of it originated with the Germans who began detonating their ammunition depots and setting fire to warehouses containing military equipment and material. Meanwhile Russian airplanes attacked the retreating columns of military and civilian personnel and the Russian army poured across the frozen Vistula River to do battle with the Germans (joined in this struggle by Russian soldiers under the command of General Wlasow, who had, some time back, switched sides and along with his men joined the German forces).

While the liberation of Cracow was under way (official date January 19th) our orders arrived from the Russians. The Germans, it seemed, had constructed hollow columns throughout the city and filled them with quantities of dynamite powerful enough to level substantial sections of that city. (This they had done not only to thwart an expected Polish uprising in the city but to stymie the Russian invasion forces and, in the end, to destroy much of Cracow itself.) Important historical buildings were also, we were informed, wired with explosives. Working along with units of the Russian intelligence (in charge of the dismantling operation was Colonel Kostenko of the 59th Army) our principal objective would be to neutralize these columns and prevent further destruction.

Chapter 4

During the war the Germans naturally had chosen the new section of Cracow as their base of operations. They had taken over many large buildings and there set up headquarters for the Gestapo, S.S., CRIPO, municipal police, Sonderdienst[1] and other administrative offices. The offices of many German firms working on contracts for the German government were also housed there. By now hundreds, probably thousands of German nationals who lived and worked in the area were fleeing west to Germany. Our task was to clear the liberated parts of the city of the remaining Germans and collaborators and to assume control of all facilities, ensuring law and order and administering the city. Our unit chose a large building as its headquarters, our offices on the main floor, the upper level set aside for temporary living quarters.

Riding through the city in our jeep, dressed warmly against the January wind, we saw more and more of the grotesque, ugly monuments, concrete columns about one story high and about three feet square. The Germans, we learned, had constructed similar structures at practically every major intersection of the city,

---

[1] The auxiliary SS unit whose troops were recruited from citizens of German descent (*Volksdeutschen*) in countries neighboring Poland.

each hollow and filled with dynamite. German intentions seemed clear enough—to blow up as much of the city as possible should they have to evacuate. The Russians had dismantled several of the columns but because it was such slow, dangerous work most were still intact. "There must be a master plan for these columns, we've got to get that information somehow," I said. "The whole city could still be blown up."

Yanek for some reason kept insisting that in the end it would be a woman who would help us neutralize the German explosives throughout Cracow. Yanek and women! I laughed and said teasingly, "You don't care about Cracow; what you really care about is finding women." As it turned out Yanek was right. We learned that in the building across the street from the M & K Construction Company[2] there lived eight Polish girls who had worked as maids for the Sonderdienst, which had occupied the building before the Russian assault. Wasting no time we put on civilian clothes, armed ourselves with Bimber—homemade vodka—and cigarettes, and went to see them. Without hesitation they opened the door. We were, we told them, Polish officers on leave, with presents for them. In no time we were enjoying ourselves, laughing, drinking, flirting, almost to the point of forgetting why we had come. The girls were uncommonly affectionate and with vodka in them unusually talkative. Our "efforts" yielded important information.

A German girl had apparently been left behind in the offices of M & K. She was German, they explained, because they had watched her from their apartment windows, coming and going during curfew hours. At such times no one except Germans were allowed on the streets. They saw her for the last time the day after

---

[2]Meyereder & Krauss

the departure of the entire staff; she was therefore probably still there.

Fighting our way through a blizzard, we returned to our office and informed our superiors of this discovery. Why a German girl would be left behind at risk to her life puzzled us. Why didn't the Germans blow up the columns before they left? The German girl might just have the answers.

We sent three men with orders to apprehend her. Within an hour they returned.

"Well, where is she?"

They looked upset. "We couldn't get into the building."

"What do you mean, you couldn't get in?"

"We couldn't. The only entrance was protected by an iron gate with a concrete bunker in front of it. We pounded and yelled for someone to let us in but no one came. With your permission we'll use force. There's no other way."

"Okay, fellows, you can go," Yanek said to the three. "We'll take care of it."

"Well, Yanek," I said, "What now?"

"Let's go there ourselves. We'll find some way to get in."

Buttoning my coat, I said, "You know, I don't like this. If the girl's inside and heard all the knocking and yelling she's more likely to have alerted someone. It may be too late."

"What choice is there?" Yanek asked.

"It may end up a bad situation," I grumbled. "Anyway, let's go."

Roman joined us. A few minutes' walk and we were at the address—19A Juljusza Lea Street.[3] We knocked

_____

[3] If somehow we managed to get the plans for the explosives, we agreed it would be necessary instantly to kill whoever it was

and waited. A cold, wet wind made me shudder. What does a German girl look like, I wondered. With all my experience during the war I had come in contact only with German men. I tried to picture mothers and wives of German soldiers, back in Germany, enjoying the goods stolen from my people. No doubt they worshipped their Fuehrer just as their men did, despised Jews as intensely as the German soldiers.

Yanek wanted to force the lock by shooting it off with his revolver, but I cried out, "Wait!" I had observed a girl peeking out of a window just above us. Then suddenly a man in working clothes appeared behind the gate. He seemed frightened and remained silent. I stepped up as close as I could and asked whether this was the M & K Construction Company.

"Yes, it is," he answered hesitatingly.

"Do you work here?"

"I'm the custodian."

"We must talk to someone in charge."

"Sorry, they're all gone."

"That can't be; I saw someone at the window," I said pointing up to it.

He looked from one face to another, apparently sensed we were determined, and mumbled, "I'll get the key." He turned and went inside, returning a moment later to unlock the gate and let us through. We followed him to an apartment on the first floor, where we saw a woman, who looked to be in her early thirties, approaching us. She led us into a larger room farther down the hall.

I could scarcely believe my eyes. It was the most beautifully decorated apartment I had ever seen.

---

who disclosed that information to us. Otherwise should the Germans learn of our discovery surely they would destroy the city in short order.

Crystal chandeliers, brass wall sconces, and brass floor lamps were all lit, shedding a light which was dazzling to us who had just come in from a dreary overcast day. Paintings in gilt rococo frames were hung all about the high-ceilinged rooms; the furniture was elaborate and obviously very costly.

What a contrast! Jews in rags burned out of their homes living like wild beasts until tracked down and killed and these murderers living like this. So busy was I concentrating on the furnishings I hardly noticed the three young women standing in a corner staring at us. Two of them, rather young, wearing cotton dresses and heavy shoes, seemed nervous. Their broad Slavic faces showed panic. Standing a foot or so behind them was a woman a few years older. She was obviously the German. Her beauty stunned me. Long blonde hair flowed loosely over her shoulders, framing a delicate face. In a glance I took in her berry-brown eyes that radiated a strange glow, her petite figure, her elegant clothes. A brown turtleneck sweater matched a fashionable tweed skirt. I stood transfixed. Then I thought, my God, was I so starved for a woman that I could be fascinated by a German? My rage returned. Control yourself, you have a job to do, information to uncover; there will be time later . . .

"Who are they?" I asked the woman who had taken us in, pointing to the two Slavic-looking girls.

"They are maids," she replied.

"Do you live in this apartment?"

"Yes, I am the daughter-in-law of the owner of this building."

"Do all Germans live in this kind of luxury?" I asked, trying unsuccessfully to conceal my bitterness.

"This apartment belonged to the manager of the firm, and when he went back to Vienna I moved in."

I turned to the German girl. Her smile infuriated me. What a bitch, I thought, calm as can be with three armed men whose intentions she would have no way of fathoming.

"What is your name?" I asked her.

"Felicia Milaszewska."

"Isn't this a Polish name and you're German?"

"No, I am Polish."

I felt my face flush. "Don't lie, we have information that you are German."

"You are wrong, I am Polish, I tell you," she said, looking directly into my face.

"Where were you born?"

"In Wilno."

"Isn't this the office of M & K Construction Company?"

"No, these are the living quarters for the company's personnel. The offices are across the hall."

"Who is in charge here?"

"I am, or rather I was," she responded with a polite smile.

"What are you talking about? How are you in charge? Do you think I'm going to believe that such responsibility was given to a Polish woman?"

"I was told by my boss that they would all return in a few weeks and I was ordered to manage the office until then." Lowering her head for the first time, she said, "I thank God that the Germans seem to be losing the war. I will no longer be in their employ."

I was furious. "How well you have rehearsed your part in this operation! Ha, you are glad your people are losing the war! You're not fooling me. Why would Germans put a Pole in charge of a German concern engaged in military operations? Go ahead, clever one, let's hear your practiced answer."

Her smile vanished. "If you don't believe me, here is my Kennkarte." With quivering hands she removed a purse from a closet and pulled out a card. "Here is my most valuable possession, my identification card. See my name on it?" Lowering her voice to a whisper, she said slowly, "If there is anything you would like to know, please take me to your superiors. I will explain everything."

"You will explain everything to me. Maybe your beauty brought you favors in your lifetime, but just this once it means nothing. I can see through you as clearly as I can see out of that window. So if you know what's good for you, start cooperating. My patience is short. Admit you're German and let's get on to other matters."

No one spoke. Yanek's eyes were riveted on me; Roman's freckled face was red and glistening with perspiration. Both were waiting for my next move. I unbottoned my coat, fully aware that my revolver would show. Let her know I mean business.

Beads of perspiration appeared on her face now; otherwise she appeared calm and defiant. I couldn't help but admire her courage. Admiring—hating, filled with disgust—impressed by her beauty—such a confusing mix of feelings.

"Please," she said, pointing to Yanek, "let me speak to him in private." Yanek gave me a questioning look; I hesitated, then nodded. She motioned for him to follow her into an adjoining room. As the door closed, I slumped into a chair, exhausted. I then realized that all through this questioning I had been clenching my jaws so tightly that they ached. The girl was exasperating!

My eyes traveled around the exquisite room, settling on an oil painting of a beggar. My mind wandered to

Rabbis, writers, the revered educated people of my community, reduced to begging for bread or for another moment to live.

The door opened with a bang. Startled, I jumped up and walked over to Yanek, who was standing there beaming. Did she have time to make love to him—is that why he looks so pleased? This is getting bizarre, I thought. Yanek excitedly asked me to follow him, insisting he had something important to tell me in private. In a corner of the room, he whispered, "This girl is not German, she's Polish; not only that, she's a Jew! Do you hear, she is Jewish!"

"You're crazy, my friend."

"I know it sounds crazy, but it's true!"

"You know, Yanek, when it comes to women, you amaze me. If you met Eva Braun[4] you'd make a Jew out of her just to get something out of her."

He laughed. "Seriously though, she showed me proof."

"Proof? That she was circumcised?"

"Look," Yanek said, "go over and talk to her yourself. You'll see."

I called the girl over. She seemed calmer now; she stayed close to Yanek, as though there was something between them.

"Tell me, did you make up your mind what nationality you are?"

She said nothing, but her gaze stayed on Yanek. "Do you speak any other language?" I asked.

"Yes, German, Russian, English, and . . ."

"English? Good," I said, thinking it best that the others in the room should not understand our conversation.

---

[4] Hitler's mistress

In broken English, I asked, "From what nation do you come?"

"I am Jewish," she said, "and I can prove it."

"How?" I asked. "Like you proved it to my friend in the next room?"

"I don't know what you mean, but I can speak Hebrew."

"Say something."

"Why? You won't understand. It shows on your face that you have no love for Jews."

"Never mind, say something."

Pronouncing each word clearly, she said in Hebrew, "You are a fool, and I wish you would stop questioning me."

"You are very clever. No Jewish girl can speak Hebrew so fluently. Where would you have learned it? Obviously the Germans got someone to teach it to you so you could mingle among Jews and spy on them."

In English she said, "You are mistaken. How can I convince you? What if you don't believe me and kill me? How will you live with yourself when you find out I am a Jew?"

"All right," I said, trying to trap her. "When do Jews pray Kol Nidre?"

"On Yom Kippur," she quickly responded.

Suddenly her face broke into a wide smile, her eyes glistened with tears. "You, you, how do you know about Kol Nidre? Oh, my God, can it be that you too are Jewish?"

I swallowed hard; my head pounded; the tears welled up in my eyes. "Yes, I am Jewish." I could hardly believe it, a Jew in charge of a German firm!

I regained my composure, and we all relaxed. Then I remembered the real purpose of my visit. Speaking

Polish, I told her that we had information that the
M & K Construction Company had built the dynamite-
filled columns that were all over Cracow, and that our
orders were to uncover the plans for these columns.

"Oh," she grinned, "why didn't you tell me? Do you
know how I have prayed for this day when I could put
those plans into Polish hands? I notified the A.K. days
ago that I had the master plan in my possession."

I followed as she walked into the handsome offices
across the corridor. Opening the wall safe, she removed a set of blueprints. "With my compliments,"
she whispered, handing them to me. Looking at her
remarkable brown eyes, they looked like the huge
brown shiny berries I used to pick as a boy.

"Thank you. This is a very important moment."

She became pensive, and looking up at me for a few
moments, she finally said, "How strange life is. We
pray for something, hope, work, even endanger our
lives for it, and when the dreamed-of moment comes,
we are calm. No trumpets go off in our heads."

"What you say is true, but this is no time to be philo-
sophical. There is much to do; we must study these
prints and somehow make sure these columns are not
detonated."

"Don't worry, they won't be."

"How can you say that with such assurance?"

"I will tell you, but first I must say how happy I am
that you are a Jew and that I can sit here without fear
and explain everything. When things started to go
badly for the Germans, the M & K Company was
ordered to build the columns you know about on all
the major streets of Cracow. I know you're curious
how I, a Jewish girl, was put in charge of a German
firm. But that is a long story, perhaps another time. I
survived the war because I was able to pass as a Pole,

and even as a *Volksdeutsche*.[5] I was employed as a personal secretary to the manager here in Cracow. This branch was opened so that the construction of bridges and fortifications along the Russian front could be closely supervised.

"When it became obvious that the office would have to be evacuated, my boss asked me to go back to Vienna with him to work in the main office. Explaining that Poland was my homeland, I begged off. He called me into his office the day before he left and handed me a check for two months' salary in advance. He then assured me that he would return long before then—'as soon as the German army launched its counteroffensive and retook the city.' Until then I was to be in charge of the office. For that reason he gave me the combination to the safe and explained that a call would be coming in from the military commandant.

"In a few days we did get a call from the headquarters of the commandant of the German combat forces in the Cracow area. I heard this clipped military voice: 'Oberfeldkommandatur spricht! Ist das das Büro M & K Gesellschaft?'[6] 'Jawohl,' I answered. Then he said, 'Springen Sie die Säulen!'[7] and he hung up. As I lowered the receiver into the cradle, I realized what I had done. I neglected to tell the Kommandant that all Company officials had left and that the German army would have to blow up the columns. I felt frightened but I was overjoyed. The Germans were on the run, desperation setting in. Otherwise why blow up so beautiful a city as Cracow."

---

[5] An ethnic German

[6] "Combat Commander speaking. Is this the office of M & K Company?"

[7] "Blow up the columns."

I stood up and walked over to her, putting my arm on her shoulder. "So you, a Jewish girl, saved Cracow. My God, what tricks life plays—it's like something out of a novel. But I'm sorry for interrupting. Please go on."

"I realized that the Oberfeldkommandatur didn't ask my name, and if I were to be questioned, I could deny having talked to him. Then I telephoned my contact in the underground and told him what had happened."

"You deserve a medal," I told her. "You're a real hero, I mean heroine." Embarrassed, she shrugged. "You seem very tired, but please, if you don't mind, I would like to ask two questions."

She smiled and said, "I'll be glad to answer your questions."

"I've been curious as to why we were allowed in, when several of our men earlier got no response when they tried to get in the building."

"The first time I instructed the custodian not to let anyone in, but when you and the other two came later, I watched you from the window; I studied Yanek's face and I was absolutely sure that he was Jewish. I felt somehow I could trust him, and I simply waited for the opportunity to talk to him alone. When he asked where I was from I told him Stanislawow, and he said he was from Cracow. We talked about people we had known, and it turned out that his cousin Oskar Margules, a refugee from Cracow, was my classmate in the Jewish gymnasium in Stanislawow in 1939-1940. I guess I took an awful chance revealing my identity, but I never really doubted I was right about Yanek."

"Now the last question. How did you know how to reach the underground?"

"The A.K. had gotten in touch with me before and I

agreed to join them (I was assigned to the 19th platoon of "Zelbet") and to give them whatever important information came my way. My contact was a fellow named Tadek or Przemyslaw. I assume he immediately got in touch with you."

"No," I replied. "The A.K. takes orders from the old Polish government in exile in London. They work against us in a sense. We represent the new Polish government in Lublin, supported by the Russians. So you see, the A.K. never told us about your call. They consider themselves great Polish patriots, but they wouldn't put politics aside to help save a city, even a city of such historical importance. It's ironic; it took you, a Jew . . ."

"It is ironic. To save Cracow, but not be able to save my own people, not even one, not even one person. I feel like a traitor in a way. I have nightmares that Jews scream from inside the columns—'save us, save us!' If only I could."

"If only," I said. "How often do we say that, we Jewish survivors. Here we are, trying to save a major Polish city, two Jews. Yet whatever we do the world seems to hate us."

I had to leave. As I extended my hand, she got up from the sofa. Looking directly into my eyes, she shook my hand, her hand lingering in mine. I grew weak, excited; it was not easy to reply.

"I beg you," I finally said, "forgive me for my harsh questioning. Thank God I didn't hurt you."

She laughed and said, "I'm grateful that you didn't. When you entered the apartment I thought, 'Now there is a real anti-Semite.' I'm sorry, but your face, your snub nose, hah, we all make assumptions, don't we?" She grew silent and looked into my eyes for a few more moments, then, almost whispering, she said,

"Meeting you has been like . . ." Her voice trailed off and her words became inaudible. Then she asked me, "By the way, what is your name? We've talked so long and neither of us knows the other's name."

"Tadeusz Zaleski."

"That's not your real name, is it?"

"No. With my position in the army it isn't wise to have a Jewish name. My real name is Naftali Saleschutz."

"Naftali, what a beautiful name. Mine is Felicia."

"All right, but I ask you now, what name were you given at birth?"

"Manya Petranker, daughter of David and Frieda, sister of Celia. Forgive me, I haven't used my real name so long it has become automatic to say 'Felicia.'"

"I understand. Felicia, may I come to see you again? . . . Felicia, what is the matter?" She was staring out of the window, as though she had forgotten I was there.

Slowly turning around and facing me, she said, "I'm so sorry. I was just thinking of my parents and how much it meant to them that I get a good Hebrew education. You see, it was my family's dream that some day we would all go to Palestine. You know, when I was older, when my sister finished school, when my father had enough money . . . To think that my knowledge of Hebrew and of Jewish holidays might have saved my life . . . isn't it all so strange?"

With the plans in hand we returned promptly to headquarters, so that preventive measures to neutralize the explosives could begin. Collaborating in this effort were Colonel Kostenko of the 59th Army and Colonel Svinchenko, head of the 42nd independent brigade of engineers and Colonel Muranow of the 22nd brigade.

Lying in bed that night, Manya's face drifted through my thoughts. Feelings had been stirred, feelings of . . .

Chapter 5

Back at headquarter we were interrupted by a commotion outside. From an orderly we learned that bands of peasants were looting buildings in our area, carrying out everything and anything. With their horsedrawn wagons lined up along the curb they were liberating desks, lamps, cabinets, chairs, etc. I ran downstairs, drew my gun and ordered them to put everything back. Cursing under their breath, they obeyed. "Where did you get the idea you could loot buildings belonging to the Polish government?" I asked. "Polish government?" They seemed shocked. "We were told the Germans had left and that we could have what was left behind."

Soon after, a dark, gaunt middle-aged peasant approached me. He took off his matted fur cap and clutched it to his chest, waiting for me to acknowledge his presence. His wagon was standing nearby. On it a squat, round-faced woman sat, reins in her hand as if ready to move quickly. I nodded at him and asked him what he wanted.

"You are a pretty important person around here, eh?"

"Perhaps," I replied.

"Then maybe you could answer my question. What will happen to the Jews who managed to escape the Germans? Is it true that this army will kill them?"

"Why do you ask?"

"Well, I was told that the few Jews who are left are going to be killed off by this new army that is coming in. If it is true I have something important to say."

I sensed something which froze my blood, but I maintained a casual air. "Yes, it is true," I said. "We are finishing off the job which the Germans started."

"In that case," he said eagerly, "I know this one Jewish family still alive in my village. I can take you to them so you can finish them off. All I ask is that you give me their "ich lachy" (their rags)."

I nodded, knitted my brow, pretending to weigh his offer in my mind.

"In fact," he went on, "I think you should also kill the Poles who were hiding those Jews during the war. Hiding Jews! What kind of Pole would hide Jews?"

"It takes all kinds to make a world," I replied.

"It certainly does! Where I come from we had more Jews than we knew what to do with. The Germans got rid of most of them, but many got away and hid in the woods outside the village. We went into the woods a few times, a whole group of us, and each time we killed off a few. I killed one with my own hands. One time we surrounded the woods . . ."

I no longer heard what he was saying. A violent surge shot through my body, and in an instant I was reliving my years of hiding out in the woods, always fearful of being attacked by mobs of peasants. I could see them coming, I could feel myself running for my life. A moment more and I knew I would no longer be in control of my actions. Calm down, I told myself, calm down, and try to stay composed.

"You have come to the right person," I told him. "We are all very busy now; we really don't have time to deal with this matter at the moment. But you can count on me. I can see that you are a Polish patriot, and I won't let you down. Come with me."

I took him inside and asked Yanek and Roman to join us. "This man has come to the right place," I said, giving them a long look. "He has something very important to tell us." I asked the peasant to repeat what he had told me. He became more expansive and related that he had found out about this family—a father, mother and two young boys—who had a prosperous drygoods store in the village before the war. They survived, he said, by paying off a peasant family. The other day when the Russians overran the village, this family came out of hiding. This is how he learned about them. He was sure that he would be killed by the villagers, who had their eyes on all the merchandise presumably hidden there. So, the peasant reasoned, we might as well be the ones to lay claim to all that bounty; and, of course, he wouldn't mind having a little share of it himself. It would only be right, he thought, to kill the Polish family which had harbored these Jews.

I was afraid Yanek or Roman might shoot this man on the spot. I kept signaling to them to play along. When he had finished, I told Roman to wait outside in the hall; I was going to type a letter which I wanted him to deliver to the mayor of the village. The letter ordered the mayor to deliver this Jewish family to Roman, emphasizing that I made him, the mayor, personally responsible for their safety. I then asked Yanek to find Canarek. Canarek was our orderly, a simple soul, among whose duties was to act as warden, in charge of all prisoners we rounded up.

Just after Roman had left with the letter, Canarek came in. I told him we wanted the peasant waiting in the hall taken into custody, that we learned he had worked for the Gestapo. Canarek needed no further explanations. He went into the hall and ordered the peasant to come along with him. A few hours later Roman returned. He had found the family, and brought them to a safe place in Cracow. With that problem no longer on my mind, I went down into the basement, followed by Yanek, to make a final disposition of the peasant. We found him sitting in the corner on the floor, covered with blood, one eye blackened and swollen shut.

"What happened to you?" asked Yanek.

"I don't know," he groaned, glaring at us through his good eye. "I was beaten up because someone said I worked for the Gestapo, but I had nothing to do with them, honest to God. If it pleases you, officers, my wife has been waiting for me outside on the wagon for hours, and I have to get back to her."

"Don't worry about your wife," said Yanek. We gave her some food and sent her home with the wagon. Now you come along with us and show us where these Jews are."

The man sensed something was wrong. "Why don't we forget about it. I really don't want anything."

"Sorry, friend," said Yanek. "We have made all the arrangements and now we have to go through with it. We will take you with us in the jeep. It shouldn't take long."

We dragged him to his feet, pushed him out into the street and into the jeep next to Yanek. I climbed into the back seat. Yanek raced down the street toward the river. It was late afternoon, already getting dark. The Vistula was frozen, a solid sheet of ice. Over the river was a temporary wooden bridge built by the Russians

—for the Germans had blown up all the bridges over the Vistula. In the gathering dusk we could see the Wawel Castle high on the hill.

Yanek stopped the jeep before the wooden bridge. He ordered the peasant to get out and walk with us to the other side, but he refused. Yanek ordered him again, but he would not until I nudged him in the back with my revolver. He started to shake.

"What are you going to do with me?" he asked, getting out of the jeep.

We realized that the Russians were checking every vehicle on the temporary bridge, so we decided we would cross the frozen Vistula on foot. We started across the river; the peasant made no protest. When we were halfway across we finally let our fury erupt.

"You miserable son of a whore," I shouted. "Do you know who we are?"

"Yes," he said, "Polish officers."

"Yes," I said, "Jewish Polish officers."

"What are you going to do to me?" he wailed.

"You bastard, we are going to shoot you," answered Yanek.

"But why? I am a good Pole. I love my country."

"We are good Poles too," Yanek said, "but we are also Jews. According to you not only are we not good Poles but we have no right to live."

"Please, please, let me explain. Please don't kill me. You Jews, you are good, God-fearing people, not like the bloody dogs the Germans. Please, my God is the son of your God!"

"Tell me the truth," I said to him. "How many Jews did you kill in the woods?"

"Not as many as some of the others in the village. I only went out to hunt Jews because my neighbors and friends did."

"How many? How many did you kill?"

"Only three. But I could find you some peasants who killed a lot more."

"Do you have any children?"

"Yes. Two."

"You son of a whore! So you have a wife and two children just like that Jewish family. You have a right to live, but this Jewish family, who spent the whole war in hiding and were lucky enough to survive, now have to die? Why should you live, why should your wife live, while this Jewish man and his wife should be killed?"

"I just wanted to help out, that's all. They said the Polish army was going to kill the Jews who were still alive, to clear Poland of all of its Jews."

"Let's finish him," Yanek said to me. He took out his revolver. Two shots ran out like thunderclaps on the hard frozen surface of the river. We drove back to headquarters without speaking.

Part Two

UNDER THE OCCUPATION

Chapter 6

My name was Amalie Petranker when the war broke out. It feels so strange pronouncing my real name. Actually my friends called me Manya. You are right. It wasn't six years ago; it was six million eternities ago. This is how far removed in time I feel now from that seventeen-year old girl, Manya Petranker.

We were three sisters. People spoke of us as "those three beautiful Petranker sisters." And I hope I'm right in saying the compliments did not make us vain. I was the middle one. The oldest, Pepka, was blonde, tall, blue-eyed under dark eyebrows and eyelashes. She had a snub nose. She looked Gentile. Celia, the youngest, was of medium height, slightly chubby, with green eyes, chestnut brown hair, and a lovely, creamy complexion. The prettiest of all, her beauty, openness, friendliness always attracted attention. We were all close in age, about a year and a half apart. While Pepka was my mother's favorite, I was father's, an unenviable position for Celia. Because of this, I always felt a need to support her. I spent much time with her, listening to her problems, helping with her homework, telling her about those things a growing girl ought to know and which I was just beginning to find out.

We were a happy, close-knit family then. My parents, David and Frieda Petranker, were modern, liberal Jews. My mother was a worldly outgoing woman who

lavished love and attention on her daughters and
always greeted everyone with a smile. My father was
outwardly placid, looking out on the world through
rimless glasses, a scholarly looking man who at forty-
five could pass for twenty-five. He was a strict discipli-
narian who set high standards for himself and his
family. Yet he was fair when we found it hard to meet
his expectations. He went into the lumber business,
and later became an assistant director of the government's Agency of Forestry (PAGED) in our region.
But at heart he was always a scholar, given to quoting
Goethe and Heine with the same ease as the Bible and
the Talmud.[1] Both he and my mother displayed a deep
love for Jewish learning and Jewish traditions. They
sent all of us to private Hebrew primary and secondary
schools and saw to it that we were all well acquainted
with the Bible, Hebrew Literature, Jewish history, the
Hebrew language, likewise the subjects taught in the
Polish schools. Highly motivated, always encouraged,
we all were good students. I remember my high school
days as the happiest time of my life.

The greatest passion of my father's life was *ahavat
tzion*, the love of Zion. He was an ardent Zionist, much
involved in all the Zionist activities in our town. It was
the great dream of our family to settle one day in
Palestine, and there help build a Jewish national
homeland. "Some day" that dream would, we prayed,
become a reality for us. Just one week after the war
began it became true for my older sister, Pepka. In
August 1939 Pepka met and fell instantly in love with
Lonek Eigenfeld, a former resident of Stanislawow,
who had left for Palestine in 1934 and had returned for
a visit. Lonek wished to be married immediately and
take his new bride with him back to Palestine. He

---

[1] A commentary on the Jewish civil and religious law.

understood, however, that to act with such haste might be troubling to Pepka and to my parents. He therefore offered her the alternative of first becoming engaged, then afterwards joining him in Palestine. My parents preferred, naturally, that Pepka not rush into marriage, but as the political situation darkened and with Pepka so eager to marry, they yielded.

It was a great shock to all of us. Here was Pepka, all of 18 and so very innocent and sheltered, about to marry and then leave us. The day that she left Celia, altogether heartbroken, started to bleed through her nose, then fainted. Predictably my mother did not stop crying. Lonek and Pepka left a week after war had been declared and in the midst of a German bombing attack upon Stanislawow. How we feared for them as they set off in a horse-drawn wagon on their treacherous journey, first to Rumania and from there to Palestine. Who knew then of the horrors that awaited us.

My home town, Stanislawow, was a prosperous and happy place when I grew up. A rapidly growing, cosmopolitan center located at the foothills of the Carpathian Mountains close to Russia, Rumania and Hungary, it was a city of about 100,000, 40,000 Jews, 40,000 Ukrainians and 20,000 Poles. The Jews brought a great deal of commerce and industry to Stanislawow, enabling it to become an important city. Who knew we were living in a fool's paradise? The ground trembling beneath our feet went unnoticed. But then what could have prepared us for the approaching catastrophe?

In September 1939, the Germans invaded western Poland, while the Russians overran the eastern portion. I remember coming home Friday, the first of September to discover that war had broken out. We were living at the time on a main avenue, 35 Sapiezynska St., in a spacious apartment. It was a bright, sunny day; the leaves of the oaks and beeches glistened in the sun. It was the end of summer, a beautiful time of the year, and I felt lighthearted and gay, so enchanted with the world around that I thought I might write a poem about it when I got home.

My sister, Celia, greeted me with a hug and a kiss when I walked in. I went to the kitchen to see my mother, who was busy preparing the Sabbath meal, and to find out if I could be of help. My mother, wearing a white apron, was stirring the soup. She turned around with a somber face, a look most strange I thought. Pepka's departure for Palestine, I assumed, must still be troubling her.

"Where have you been so long?" my mother asked in a quavering, impatient voice.

"Why, I'm not late, am I?"

"Haven't you heard the news?"

I shook my head.

"The Germans have invaded Poland. They have been bombing all over. A few bombs fell right outside Stanislawow."

At that moment my father walked in the kitchen. Visibly agitated, he muttered an almost inaudible greeting. He took off his glasses and wiped his brow. "This is very bad news, Frieda. It's the beginning of an all-out world war."

The Sabbath meal, always a happy occasion, this time proceeded under a cloud of anxiety and tension. Hoping to hear the latest news, instead we listened as the radio played Chopin's Military Polonaise again and again. So was popular morale bolstered. "Either the Germans or the Russians are going to be here shortly," my father said. "I don't know which is going to be worse."

Over the next two weeks the news grew more and more ominous. Initial fears turned to panic. Outside most stores were people waiting in long lines for hours buying up all the food, clothing and whatever necessities still remained. Each evening my father brought us word of the latest events. Then the first waves of Jewish refugees began arriving in Stanislawow with grim accounts of German fighter plane attacks. The pilots, guns blazing, had taken to diving within a few yards of the refugee throngs, then laughing uproariously as their victims scattered, desperate for shelter along the roadside.

"We are in for some very bad experiences," my father predicted. And as if to confirm his grim prophecy, the very next day a few German bombs hit the center of Stanislawow. One exploded in the old market on Halitzka Street. Another hit the lumber yard of Mr. Schleimer, an acquaintance of my father. He had been standing outside watching the planes. Caught in the open, a wall fell on him, killing him instantly.

On the 16th of September rumors circulated of Russians approaching Stanislawow. Would our fate then be placed in their hands? Our mayor, the Honorable Kotlarchyk, advised the citizenry to welcome and cooperate with them, reasoning they would stay for only a short time. That same day local Communists, after capturing the municipal building promptly hoisted a red flag atop the building. A Polish army unit while retreating opened fire on them, killing two, one a Ukrainian, the other a Jew.

The next day we locked ourselves in our homes. Outside, chaos and lawlessness reigned. In the dark, we sat and prayed for someone, anyone, to restore order. We could hear shooting in the streets all during the day and evening. Later that night a family friend arrived with news. Peasant gangs had entered the city, taken to plundering government and army depots and setting fires. The local Communists had taken over the city jail and freed political prisoners and criminals. While peasants plundered in the name of "a free Ukraine," nationalist gangs were robbing in the name of Hitler, as Communists shot nationalists in the name of freedom. Caught in between were the many innocent victims. Meanwhile the local militia stood by, immobilized, unable to halt the deteriorating situation.

Later that night our friend returned, this time with news more encouraging. Earlier in the day Ukrainian gangs had attacked Jewish homes in Bohoroczany, but providentially, Russian tanks arrived and dispersed the attackers. Then the Russians in short order gained full control of the city. Better days, we hoped, were now in store for all of us.

Chapter 7

"Better days" of course was a relative term, considering what awaited us at the hands of the Germans. Still life under the Russians was difficult. Russian propaganda was especially obnoxious. Determined to control people's minds there existed little tolerance for independent thought. We heard much of freedom and equality, of the right of the people and justice for all, but these were all just words, empty promises. Under Russian occupation we experienced no freedom, no equality, no rights and no justice.

Shortly after they occupied Stanislawow, we had an occasion to find out to what degree the rulers of Russia had succeeded in brainwashing their own people. Some friends and I, coming home from the Gymnasium one day, met a group of Russian soldiers, male and female, waiting on a street corner. We struck up a conversation with them, making some small talk, also asking about their life in Russia.

"Do you have enough food in Russia?"

"Plenty."

"Can you get good clothes?"

"The best."

"Can you get all the *kadakhat*[1] you want?"

---

[1] A Hebrew word meaning "plenty of nothing" (also Malaria).

"All we want."

That the Russians meant business was clear from their expropriation of every house and every business in the city. Each branch of the Russian government assumed ownership of a section of the city, our section, for example, becoming the property of the railroad authority. Soon after an official came to inform us that from that day on our house belonged to the railroad authority. We would have to look for other quarters. Begging and pleading were to no avail; the man insisted that he had to follow orders. My mother began to cry; then Celia came in the room. When the man saw Celia, his face brightened.

"Who is she?" he asked my father.

"Our daughter, Celia," he replied.

"She is truly beautiful," he said, unable to conceal his admiration. Later on I learned that Russian men are mad about buxom women, which Celia certainly was.

"I'll tell you what I'll do," the man said. "I will put my name on the door of your apartment and report it as my official address, and you can go ahead and continue to live here as before."

It was a real stroke of good luck, but our troubles were far from over. Still maintaining everyone was equal the Russians now issued I.D. cards, which became the basis for discrimination and intimidation. Most fortunate were working class people. Their I.D. cards had no special notation, allowing them access to all work. The cards of middle class people carried special designations, stigmatizing them as "social parasites." As a result many of our friends and acquaintances lost their jobs and had to leave Stanislawow and apply for work in the smaller towns. Our own cards included a paragraph "11 (eleven)" stating ominously that we could be sent to Siberia at any time, day or night. Cards for Jews bore the word *YEVREY* (Jew). Given a choice between a Jew and non-Jew, the non-Jew always got the job. The Communists rejected emphatically the right of Jews to a national homeland and so the Russians showed special contempt for Zionists. The leaders of the Zionist movement in Stanislawow, many of them close friends of my father, were promptly jailed.

We lived in constant fear. "Don't talk too much in school," "never speak to strangers"—such were the warnings from my parents. Suspicion and distrust reigned supreme. NKWD, the Russian Secret Police, were, we imagined, everywhere. Just how active they were became clear when people kept disappearing from their homes. At the same time from the Russian news agency came forth stories about outrages committed by the Germans in occupied Poland, particularly atrocities against Jews. These stories we discounted, accustomed as we were to dismissing anything the Russians offered as truth. The Germans we knew were mortal enemies of the Communists; sooner or later the two would be at each other's throats. My parents were actually prepared to have the Germans in Stanislawow—they said so on numerous occasions. Nothing for them could be worse than living under Communism.

I drew close to Celia in those days. I remember sitting with her on the balcony of our apartment, overlooking the main avenue, my arm around her shoulder, assuring her that the war would soon be over and the world would once again be a beautiful place to live in. Why, Celia inquired, was so much hatred in the world? Wasn't love better than hate? Wasn't good more rewarding than evil? What could I say; I had no answers.

"I wonder what Pepka is doing right now," Celia said to me one afternoon as we sat on the balcony watching a beautiful sunset.

"Probably sleeping. It's night now in Eretz Yisrael."
"Oh how I wish we were there."
"Some day we'll be there."
"You really think so?"
"You've got to believe."
"Yes . . . I guess you're right.
During the early days of the occupation I had a chance to escape to Rumania, where I might have been able to board a ship for Palestine. The offer came from my boyfriend, Alek Lamensdorf, whom I had known for a few years. Very gentle and mature for his age, he was tall, blond and aristocratic looking. His father was a high official in the railroad authority and he had a *drezyna* (a private railroad car) at his disposal. Since the Rumanian border was only 60 miles away, chances were good we could cross it into freedom. I was seventeen at the time, Alek was eighteen. I was too young, I told him; it would never work.

Two years later in the last days of the Russian occupation a second chance appeared. With the Germans about to attack in the region of Stanislawow Russian authorities announced that Jews were free to go east into Russia since it would not be safe for them to stay. Many went, particularly professional people and intellectuals, leftists and active Communists. Poor Jews and riffraff, who had nothing to lose, also left. Mostly the middle class stayed. Alek, who worked as an accountant for the Russians, again wanted to leave, this time with his younger sister, Cesia. He offered to take me and Celia along. This time I decided to go.

I would, however, not go without my father's permission. His reaction was more violent than I anticipated. Seldom had I seen him so livid. "Go to Russia?" he shouted. "What, have I raised a Communist in this house? If you go to Russia the door will close; you will never be allowed in this house again!" Discussion closed. I gave up and dropped the matter.

On June 22, 1941 Germany attacked Russia. The Russians immediately evacuated Stanislawow. For one whole week chaos once more held sway. By week's end a new occupation army arrived, the Hungarians, allies of the Germans.

Chapter 8

For one month we lived under the Hungarians. In many ways it was a repeat performance of the Russian occupation. Again our apartment was requisitioned; once more my parents thanked God for giving them daughters who for a second time were instrumental in getting the requisition canceled. Instead of a Russian official fancying Celia, this time a Hungarian Count, a Dr. Emil Sigmund Ultchitz Amade it was, who owned an estate at Komarom Medye and a residence in Budapest, who took a liking to me. He was tall and had matted, curly blond hair and green eyes. Extremely good natured and generous, he took our family under his wing, advising us to hide the fact that we were Jews. Our apartment soon became the meeting place of Hungarian nobility and important officials. The Count showered us with attention; most importantly he supplied us food ration cards, which gave us access to his staff kitchen, this at a time when food was becoming ever more scarce.

The war now raged all over Europe. Stories of German atrocities against Jews circulated widely, but many Jews, my parents included, dismissed them as exaggerations. Such behavior would after all have been totally out of character. Germany had always been considered the most cultured, the most civilized country in Europe. Before the war, prior to our moving into our apartment, we had lived in a suburb of Stanislawow called Niemiecka Kolonia, or German Colony. Always my parents held up the cleanliness, good manners, self-discipline and respect for learning which they observed in our German neighbors as examples for all of us. So what explained the German violence against the Jews? Some strange quirk of fate, we reasoned, had placed Germany under the rule of a ruthless dictator who hated the Jews. It would not last, we thought. Once Germany triumphed in Europe, order would return and the Jews would then be left alone.

Two weeks after the Hungarians had arrived, an event occurred which gave us a foretaste of what was to come. A trainload of Hungarian Jews arrived in Stanislawow. Eyewitnesses reported a horrible scene at the train station. Starving and frightfully weak, these people could barely stand on their feet. Still they were pushed out of cattle cars by guards who cursed at them and prodded them with their rifle butts. They were then marched to the flour mill (Rudolf's Mühle) in Halitzka Street, a huge unfinished red brick building which now became their prison. Forced onto the upper floors of the mill they were given no food or medicine. Members of the Jewish community made many attempts to help them but were rebuffed each time. When finally allowed to visit they discovered many of them dead.

One evening the Hungarian Count came to our apartment. It was while standing before a large mirror in our dining room that he asked me to marry him.

"Look in the mirror," I said jokingly. "You are so tall, (he was about 6'7") and I am so short next to you."

He took a ring from his little finger and held it out to me.

"Let's be serious," I said. "You are a Catholic, a nobleman; I am Jewish."

"I'll speak with your parents," he said, and walked out of the room.

Later, at the dinner table, he informed my father the Hungarians would be leaving Stanislawow in a few days. "The Germans will be taking over the administration of the city. Now I don't know if your people are aware of it, but the Germans are determined to kill all the Jews. I wish I could save you, but I don't know how I can."

No one said a word. What was there to say? The count turned his head and looked at me.

"Let me at least try to save her. I am going back to Hungary now. Because of my rank I know I will not be searched at the border. I can hide Manya in my trunk when we reach the border. She will lack nothing in Hungary. As the first born son I am heir to a very large estate. The only thing she will need to do is to convert to Catholicism."

My father did not take long to reply. "Believe me, Your Highness," he said, trying to keep calm, "when I tell you how deeply I appreciate your kind and noble offer. But we are a close-knit family, and we have decided to stay together during these difficult times. Whatever fate befalls one of us, will befall all of us."

"What a world," he said, "what a truly senseless world. And what a strange fate God has picked for His chosen people."

Chapter 9

On July 26, 1941, Stanislawow came under direct German rule. The city was now the domain of the Gestapo, the Kripo (Kriminal Polizei), and the SS. Gestapo headquarters were established at the stately courthouse on Bilinski Street, and a new kind of justice, particularly for Jews, came to Stanislawow.

Having established themselves in the city—it was, I think, on the third day—the Germans ordered all Jews over the age of twelve to wear white armbands with a blue six-pointed Star of David. From that day the fate of all the Jews in the city was bound together. No longer was it a question of poor or rich, pious or non-observant, educated or ignorant. The special rules applied to all; ignoring them could mean death. How well I came to understand that.

Walking down the street during the first days of the German occupation a Pole came by and, seeing my armband, cursed me, then began to pull at my purse. I screamed for him to let go. I appealed to passersby— Poles as well as Germans—for help but they all ignored me. Later I found that the Germans had declared open season on Jews that day, and all over the city Jews were assaulted by Gentiles. My assailant made off with my purse. I was stunned. I stood in the middle of the street, unable to comprehend how in Stanislawow, my home town, in plain daylight, a young girl could be robbed in front of people, and no one, not one person even bothered to turn and look. I ran home in a state of shock and once in the house fell into my mother's arms and cried bitterly until complete exhaustion set in. That night, unable to fall asleep I thought of the words of the Hungarian Count: "The Germans are determined to kill all of you Jews." Those words sounded altogether unreal. Such a thing was not possible. And yet after what happened today. . . . The world seemed to have been turned upside down. What I had seen was only the beginning. Clearly the Germans had set about to undermine our spirit and break our will. Then we could become easy, unresisting instruments of their evil. This we could not allow; we needed to remain strong, determined. The little lecture I gave myself that night proved effective. Not that I was able to drive away my fear. On the contrary, I realized I would have to live with fear probably for a long time. But I was determined to deal with it, to endure a great deal if necessary. I would not be shocked so easily anymore. I would be strong.

My trials and those of the entire Jewish community of Stanislawow began in earnest as the Germans reorganized our lives to fit their purposes. All Jews were ordered to report to the *Kultus Gemeinde*, the Jewish community center for work assignments. Given pails and scrub brushes, I, my sister Celia, my best friend, Dziunia Lorber, and many others were assigned as cleaning girls to Gestapo headquarters. For food we depended on Ukrainian farmers, who in time learned to exploit our hunger by charging exorbitant prices.

So petrified with fear was I that first day reporting to work at Gestapo headquarters that it more than blotted out the keen humiliation I felt having to wash floors and clean toilets for the Germans. Only two days before, a former classmate who lived near the courthouse had told me about hearing the groans and screams emanating from that building all night long. Later on I found out that the Germans had rounded up the Jewish intelligentsia of the city—doctors, lawyers, dentists, engineers—brought them to Gestapo headquarters, then beaten and tortured them. Later they were taken away, and never seen again. The Germans for a time assured their families nothing had happened to them, that they were alive in a prison camp near Lvov. All had, however, been taken to a forest right outside Stanislawow where mass graves awaited. They were shot and quickly buried.

The thought of going to Gestapo headquarters, a place where tortures were committed daily, was absolutely horrifying. I went there in a daze. Over the building flew a red flag with a black crooked cross; it flapped in the wind like an evil omen. A whole group of girls like myself, pail and scrub brush in their hands and fear in their eyes, were waiting outside. A young Gestapo man came out and sized us up with a contemptuous stare. After ordering us into a line, he yelled out, "Do you know before whom you are standing? You are standing before a member of the master race. And do you know who you are? You are dirty, filthy Jews, the scum of the earth. You are now given the great honor of working for the master race, and you will show your gratitude by being humble, obedient and hard working. Remember now, you are to do exactly what you are told to do, or else you will be taken out into the back yard and shot on the spot."

We were marched into the building and divided into small groups. Each group was assigned to a different Gestapo man. Mine, Josef Daust by name, came to personify for me all the horror that went under the name of Nazism. How such a person could actually exist in the world I have never been able to understand, and never will.

That first day, however, nothing unusual happened. The man had to leave right after I met him, and I was able to work without interruption. About a week later after arriving at the Gestapo building I got into line and marched with the rest of the girls into the headquarters. Someone was yelling orders, but I did not even bother to see who it was, I simply followed the girl ahead of me. Suddenly I felt something striking my back, and when I turned to look I saw my boss, Josef Daust, his bulldog face a flaming red.

"Du sau Jude, heraus!" he barked. "You Jew pig, get out!"

I stepped out of the line. Another girl had already been ordered to step out; her name was Vita Schickler, a refugee from Berlin.

"Leave them alone," I heard a woman's voice say in German. I looked sideways and saw Frau Z., who was in charge of the Jewish cleaning girls. Daust turned to the woman and slapped her across the face, not realizing that she was a German, the aunt of two Gestapo men, two brothers named Maurer. Daust then ordered us back in line, and left the room. Frau Z. signaled to me to join her at some distance away from the rest of the girls. "You better not come to work tomorrow," she whispered, "Herr Daust is not a forgiving man."

I took her advice and did not report for work the next day. I was taking a risk staying at home, but I decided it would be more dangerous to report for work. I was not sure what Daust planned to do with me and that other girl, but considering that one of his favorite games was to single one or two Jews out of a group and shoot them in front of the rest—I saw such an incident later with my own eyes—I decided to stay home.

The *Judenrat,* or Jewish Community Council, organized by the Germans, was responsible for supplying girls to the Gestapo. With the Gestapo personnel about to move into private apartments near headquarters, they needed help with cleaning and setting up these apartments. I received a notice to report to work, so the next day I was back with my pail and scrub brush.

Celia was assigned to clean the main Gestapo headquarters and with a group of girls was sent to the private apartments of the individual Gestapo members. We were marching toward the main entrance of an apartment building reserved for Gestapo men, when we heard someone shouting at us from a window. We all stopped and looked up. It was Daust. He pointed at me and told me to come up. With the resignation of a condemned person I walked up to his door. He let me in and stood facing me in the middle of the room.

"You didn't report for work the other day, yes? Do you know that you get shot for disobeying a German officer?" I did not reply.

"What is your name?"

"Manya Petranker."

"Your age."

"Eighteen."

"What is your occupation?"

"Student."

"What kind of student?"

"College."

"Is that so? So you are a real Fraulein, is that it? All of you Jews, you all have to go to college, don't you? Now remember, from this day on you're no longer a

Fraulein. You are to report here on the first floor to work every day, and you'd better do a good job if your life is dear to you. You can go now."

I heaved a deep sigh of relief once on the other side of the door. My end I was sure had come; my life, so it seemed, had been given back to me. I worked hard all day on the apartments. Later that afternoon a group of Jewish prisoners came in carrying chairs, tables, consoles, carpets, and crates full of china and silver. One of them told me that the Gestapo had raided Jewish homes and carried away everything. Each Gestapo man had put in a request to Krueger, the chief, to have his apartment furnished in a certain style. Krueger made the Judenrat responsible for procuring the exact articles which his men, in giving free rein to their fantasies, had requested.

That evening my sister, my parents, and I were having our austere meal of soup and bread, and we girls were telling our parents about our day's experience.

"I met this German woman there, Frau Z., whom we used to know when we lived at Niemiecka Kolonia," Celia was saying. "I said hello to her, but she turned away. I think she was ashamed to look me in the face."

My father, who spoke very little in those days, looked up from his plate. "Frau Z.," he said, trying to remember. "Oh yes, I remember her, she was a fine lady. What would she be doing at Gestapo headquarters?"

"She is a German, isn't she?" my mother said. All Germans are the same." My father made no reply. He had long ago stopped getting into any discussions.

"They have all the Hungarian Jews locked up in the next building," Celia went on to say. "I think they are starving them to death."

"Don't brood about those things," my mother said. "You can't worry about the whole world. Just think of yourself and remember that your first duty is to survive."

But the next day Celia chose not just to think of herself. Whether what she did was a spontaneous act brought on by the wailing and crying of the Hungarian Jews locked up in the courtyard of the Gestapo headquarters or whether it was something she planned to do I cannot say. We had not talked about it. And when it happened I wasn't there, having been sent off to clean private quarters in another part of the building. What Celia did was take the bread and cheese she had brought with her to work in a brown bag and toss it to the Jewish prisoners below. There's no mistaking why she did it, so distraught was she over their distressed state. Unfortunately her bold act of defiance did not go unnoticed. She was observed by a Gestapo officer and taken away.

I learned this when a Ukrainian policeman arrived where I was working. Celia, he said, needed my help.

What could I do? I was so frightened. I ran out of the room and to the entrance of the building, where a guard was stationed. I blurted out that my sister had been taken, that she was guilty of nothing, that I must obtain her release. Nothing I said moved him in any way. I was ordered back to work.

The agony of that day was excruciating. I was stunned, overwhelmed, devastated about the effect it would have on my mother when I came home that evening. I said simply that Celia had been detained, but that she did nothing and I would see to it that she was released.

I was crushed. I realized that night that if there was anyone in the world for whom I would lay down my life it was my sister Celia. Were she not to return what reason would I have to go on living?

The next day I dressed and went to work like a robot, devoid of thoughts and feelings, unaware of anything around me. I could find out nothing about Celia. At home my poor mother grieved day after day. So shocked was she by the disappearance of Celia that her hair turned completely gray in a month. I too was overwhelmed by sorrow. We spent hours talking or simply holding each other, saying nothing at all. Again and again I assured my mother that the war would soon be over and our Celia would return; then we could resume our former life. Hope was all we had left even if we had to invent it.

Daust had brought with him his fiancee after his new quarters had been prepared. She was a beautiful, docile German girl from Katowice, in southern Poland. She looked up to him as if he were a god, and spent most of her time taking care of the apartment. One day she stopped me in the midst of cleaning the windows and asked me, "Why do you look so sad all the time?" It was the first time a German had spoken to me as one human being to another. I hesitated, not knowing if I should reveal anything.

"Is something bothering you?" she insisted.

"I really don't wish to burden you with my troubles . . ."

"It's all right, you can tell me. If there is anything I can do to help I'll be more than happy to."

"It's about my sister," I said, suddenly starting to cry.

"Here," she said, handing me a handkerchief. I took the handkerchief, but did not use it. I swallowed hard.

"My sister, Celia, who is seventeen, was taken away while cleaning in the main Gestapo building a few days ago and never came back. That same day about a hundred girls disappeared after having been picked off the streets. I am very close to my sister, and I can't stop thinking about her for a moment. My mother also is heartbroken over it, and I am very worried about her, too. If only someone could tell me what happened to her."

"I will speak to my fiance about it this evening. I am sure he will be able to find out what happened to her."

For a few days she kept avoiding me, and I did not dare ask her if she had spoken to Daust. Then one day she brought it up. She told me that the girls had been sent to a farm outside Lvov, where they were helping with the harvest; when the harvest was over I could expect my sister back.

My poor mother clung to this bit of information as if it were the absolute truth. But I couldn't. Why would they take the prettiest girls to help with the harvest? Daust's fiancee may have made a sincere effort to help, but the truth might have been more than she could bring herself to tell me.

Losing myself in work became one way of maintaining my spirit. Daust and the other two Gestapo men whose apartments I cleaned were quite satisfied. Daust began to treat me with more consideration. He was without doubt a heartless murderer, but what choice did I have other than to try to stay on his good side? That way I would not constantly fear for my life. Each Gestapo man in the building, I discovered, treated the girl who worked for him quite decently; all the others he persecuted. We were in one respect fortunate: we did not fear being sexually molested. At first we had been afraid we'd be forced to serve not only as cleaning girls but also as concubines. But we learned that the Nazi high officials had given strict orders on the subject—Germans were not to have sexual relations with Jewish girls. Some undoubtedly ignored this edict, but I had no problem with Daust or any other German. Other torments awaited.

The apartment above Daust's was occupied by a Gestapo man named Willie Maurer, one of the two Maurer brothers, who were among the most sadistic members of the local Gestapo. Willie Maurer would look out of his window each morning, and when he saw me coming into the building would knock on the window pane with his riding crop. My blood curdled when I heard the knocking. Then he would laugh so loudly I felt as though someone were twisting a knife inside me. This went on until one day after work, the girl who worked for him mentioned to me that Maurer had been bragging about his feets, telling her how much he enjoyed seeing the fear in my eyes each time he did it. "Try to overcome your fear," she suggested. "He is not going to hurt you; he is only trying to scare you." The next day when Maurer repeated his performance I played along with him and pretended to look scared; but he no longer was able to frighten me.

Later that afternoon, when I had completed my work, something made me think of Celia. Before I knew it I was crying and sobbing, more than I had done since the day that I was assaulted and left alone on the street. I cried for a long time but then quickly wiped my face and straightened my hair, when I saw Daust coming in from the street.

"You have been crying," Daust said. "Is anything the matter?"

"No, nothing."

"Go ahead, you can tell me."

"I would like to know what's happened to my sister. There has been no word . . ."

"I'll tell you what you could do," Daust said. "Go over now to the Gestapo headquarters, and tell them that your sister disappeared on such and such a date, that she is a person of good moral character, and you would like to know how she is doing. Go quickly before they close."

I thanked him and rushed out. I ran all the way there; when I reached the desk in the main office I was so out of breath I could hardly speak. A Gestapo man named Brandt looked questioningly at me.

"I would like to fill out a form about my sister."

"What about her?"

"She has been missing for many days . . ."

"Why has she been missing?"

"I think she was taken away. She disappeared the day all the other girls were taken away."

"Then your sister was Jewish, and you are Jewish, too?"

"Yes, sir."

Brandt's face turned purple. Pounding on the counter, he screamed, "If you are Jewish why aren't you wearing your armband?!"

I looked at my arm. I had forgotten all about putting it on. Just the day before Daust had told me that I could take the armband off while I was in the apartment, and put it back on only when I was ready to go outside. In my rush it had completely slipped my mind.

"I'm sorry, sir. I forgot to put it on."

"You forgot to put it on? You'd better get out of here this minute before I shoot you. Don't you ever let me see you without your armband on!"

I left quickly, knowing in my heart that whatever hopes I had entertained about my sister were false ones. Still I couldn't grieve; my father and mother needed all the support I could provide them.

Walking back without my armband, I allowed myself the luxury of proceeding along the sidewalk. The Gestapo had decreed that Jews were forbidden to walk on the sidewalks: the few Jews who ventured outside were obliged to walk in the middle of the street. I saw an old Jew ahead, walking in the street, carrying a heavy sack on his back; from behind me a Gestapo car raced down the street towards him. The driver, spotting the old man, swerved, forcing him to jump back on the sidewalk. The car slowed down to a stop. Then a hand with a revolver appeared and riddled the old man with bullets. He let go of his sack, his arms waving frantically in the air, then without uttering a sound reeled off the curb and collapsed. The car sped off. When I passed him by, the old man was lying along the curb, motionless.

As the Jewish high holy days approached there was considerable commotion in the city, as if some great event was about to take place. It was not the activity of Jews preparing for the season of prayer, fasting and repentance; but of their enemies preparing for some large scale undertaking. What was planned no one, of course, knew; but rumors were everywhere. Finally the Germans officially announced that in two weeks all Jews were expected to move into one area of Stanislawow, not yet clearly defined, but which corresponded roughly to the section already most heavily Jewish and which was soon to be known as the ghetto. My parents quickly found an apartment in this section and moved most of our furnishings there, leaving behind only some bedding and cooking utensils in the old rooms, hoping that at the last moment things might change and we could stay put. A friend of my father, who played in a Jewish band which was often requisitioned by Krueger, the Gestapo Chief, told us that for a whole week the band had been dispatched to the Jewish cemetery to entertain Krueger and his men, who were overseeing the digging of large trenches on the cemetery grounds. The most likely explanation one heard was that the Germans, retreating from the Russian front, were preparing new defense lines. If true this was good news, for it meant the Germans were losing the war and that our liberation was at hand. Did we really believe it? I can't say for sure. Certainly we chose to believe it; the other possibility was unthinkable.

Chapter 10

On Sunday, October 12, 1941, the unthinkable happened. The day of Hoshanah Rabba[1] became the blackest day in the history of the Jews of Stanislawow.

We were still living in our old apartment, now empty except for some mattresses and utensils. It was dark outside when I was awakened by my mother sitting next to me, crying bitterly. "What happened?" I asked her. She was saying goodbye to me, she answered. She did not know if she would ever see me again. It must have been a bad dream; it comforted her and we both went back to sleep.

Early in the morning we were all aroused from our sleep by sounds and noises which seemed to come from another world, a world of demons and evil spirits. We threw on some clothes and went out on the balcony overlooking the main street. A gloomy, cloudy morning; it had just started to drizzle. The streets were choked with German and Ukrainian police. A large number of vehicles, mostly canvas-covered trucks, were going up and down the main street and turning off at the corners—truly an ominous scene. But what could we do?

We expected the Germans would at some point do to us what they had done to the Hungarian Jews. They

---

[1] The seventh day of the holiday, Succoth.

had brought trainloads of them, all men, to Stanislawow, and kept them as slave laborers. By doing so they
left their families back in Hungary without bread-
winners, and unlikely to survive. Now our turn, it
seemed, had come. The Germans, we concluded, were
going to round us up and move everyone to some
point outside of the city, separate the men and take
them away to an unknown destination. What needed
to be done, we decided, was to hide my father.

As is common in European cities, the houses on our
block were joined together, through an intricate system
of interconnected attics and cellars. Each apartment
had its own individual attic and cellar, access to which
was difficult unless one were familiar with the building.
After some deliberation, we decided that my father
should hide in the attic. He took along a book and
some food and climbed the stairs with my mother and
me behind him. We kissed goodbye and locked the
door. My mother put the key in her housecoat pocket,
and we returned to the apartment.

Outside, the noise and commotion intensified. We
could hear shouts, screams, clanging and screeching,
bursts of rifle and machine gun fire, the wailing of
sirens. We were petrified. My mother kept wringing
her hands and mumbling to herself. There was a knock
on the door; I heard someone calling my name. It was
a Jewish neighbor from across the hall, a boy of about
fourteen. I opened the door and let him in.

"Aren't you going to hide?" he practically shouted
at us as he came in. His eyes were staring wildly, and
he was breathing heavily. "I just got back from the
street. The Germans are pulling all the Jews from their
homes and loading them on trucks! They are going
from house to house, yelling *'Juden heraus! Juden zu
Arbeit!'* (Jews get out! Jews to work!) Everybody in the

building is going to hide in the cellar. Aren't you coming?"

While we were speaking, we saw several Jewish neighbors in the hall, huddling together. We went out and joined them. They all decided to hide in the cellar of our building.

"I don't think it's a good idea to hide in the cellar," I suddenly announced, surprised at myself for speaking up so boldly. They all looked at me.

"Why not?" someone asked.

"If the Germans come into the buildings they will search the cellars first. The best thing is to hide in some back room in our apartments where they wouldn't expect anyone to be."

My mother looked apologetically at the rest of the group. "She is upset," my mother explained. "Come," she said to me, "We are all going into the cellar."

"No!" I objected, "I am going to stay in the apartment!"

"She is right," an old woman said, "I am going to stay with her."

I don't know what made me disobey my mother. It wasn't like me.

"Come," someone said to my mother, "let's go down, it's getting late." They all went to the cellar to hide, while the old woman and I went into our apartment, which was a maze of rooms, and locked ourselves in the last room.

We sat there all morning. The commotion did not let up. Around noontime we heard footsteps in the apartment, and someone called my name. It was the same boy who had knocked on our door that morning. He came with a message from my mother, who wanted to know if I had changed my mind about joining her in the cellar. I was staying where I was, I told him to tell my mother.

As evening approached the old woman and I became tired of being locked up. We decided to venture out. When we went to the staircase a Polish couple who lived in our building came rushing at us. *"Boze drogi,"* the woman exclaimed, "Dear God, you are still here? The Gestapo men came into the building around three o'clock and took all the people out of the cellar and loaded them on trucks and took them to the cemetery."

I froze when I heard "cemetery." It could only mean something terrible. What about my father; was he still in the attic?

I ran up to the attic and called out my father's name. He answered, and asked to be let out. But my mother had taken the key; I had no way of opening the door. I went for help. Our neighbor agreed to force the attic door with a crowbar, breaking the lock. I fell into my father's arms. Feeling the warmth of his body and his love helped calm me down.

"Mother was taken away," I told him.

"Come," he said, "Let's go down."

We went back into the apartment. Later that evening one of our Jewish neighbors came in, a woman about my mother's age. She was shaking and frantic with fear, her face twisted with pain. With great difficulty she finally managed to speak, though every few minutes she broke down and cried. From what she said, we pieced together the fact that she had been taken to the cemetery with the other Jews. There by the thousands they were machine gunned where they stood. She was one of the few survivors. My mother, she said, while still on the truck continually agonized about not having listened to her daughter, Manya. At the ceme-tery she stood with her in the back of the crowd when the killing started. She, too, might have survived, but unable to endure standing there waiting her turn to be shot, she ran up to the front and never came back.

"She might still be alive," my father said after the woman left. "We'd better go over there and find out."

"Now, in the middle of the night?"

"I guess not. It wouldn't do any good to go now, would it?"

"I'll go to the *Schutzpolizei*[2] headquarters first thing in the morning to try for permission to go to the cemetery."

Later that night, unable to sleep, my father said, "They tried to kill all of us, the entire Jewish com-munity of Stanislawow, in a single day. It was more than they could handle. Sooner or later they will try to get the rest of us." He spoke with a calm voice, numb, almost without emotion.

"They won't get away with it," I said. "They can't go on killing people like this. They are sick, crazy people; they'll lose the war."

"Manya . . ."

"Yes, Papa."

"I should have let you and Celia go to Russia that time."

"Oh, Papa, don't start blaming yourself now. You were trying to keep the family together because you loved us."

"Yes, I loved you, and always will. But what good did it do you?"

"It's not your fault, Papa, that people have turned into beasts. You are a kind man, and you always had

---

[2] The municipal police.

great faith in everyone. I'd rather be here with you than by myself, even if that would make me safe and secure."

My father was crying. I got out of bed, went over to him and put my arms around his neck, hugging and rocking him. His crying frightened me. I was overwhelmed and devastated at the loss of my mother. I was afraid I might go to pieces in front of my father, who was already on the verge of collapse. I couldn't let that happen, I kept telling myself as I continued to rock my father in my arms. I was young, still I had to be strong. "I never want to leave you, Papa," I said, stroking my father's hair.

"Yes, Manya, we will stay together. Whatever happens to one will happen to us both."

The next day I went to the *Schutzpolizei* to ask permission to go to the cemetery. It was not safe to go there, I was told. The area was guarded by Ukrainian militia; the Germans could not be responsible for my safety. If my mother were alive, they argued, she would be back, or I would find out about it somehow. The day before they executed thousands of Jews at the cemetery; now, pretending a concern for my welfare, they warned it would not be safe for me to go there! What bizarre and twisted ways these Germans had.

Over the next few days we heard from neighbors, friends and relatives who had survived the massacre just what happened on that black Sunday of Hoshanah Rabba. Over and over in my mind I visualized the stories they told me. Still a part of me insisted this was all a product of my fevered imagination, a nightmare of horrific images pieced together from the last few years. Logically such a thing could not happen. Not in 20th century Europe. Certainly not in the world I grew up in and came to know. But it did happen. Each person who came back from the cemetery that night provided living proof. Taken together their stories recreated the events of that day.

The Aktion began early Sunday morning. The German police, headed by the Gestapo, had been mobilized, assisted by hundreds of Ukrainian police and militia. Scores of German army trucks lined up at the marketplace in the center of the city. Police detachments went from house to house forcing Jews into the streets. Those who resisted were shot on the spot. During the day the Germans rounded up some 30,000 Jews—nearly the entire Jewish population of Stanislawow—and marched them to the marketplace. There they were loaded on trucks, squeezed together so tightly that some suffocated on the way. Many pushed their way onto the trucks, fearing that if left behind they would be shot. When the trucks had been filled, those remaining were forced to make their way to the cemetery on foot under guard.

The entire operation was overseen by Krueger, chief of the Gestapo, a tall blond German in his mid-thirties, with a face devoid of human feelings. Krueger was in high spirits that day, certainly not his usual mood. When the first truck arrived, he had just been laughing at a joke one of his underlings had told as he stood outside the main gate of the cemetery. As the trucks rolled past him, Dr. Teitelbaum, the man who served as liaison between the Gestapo and the Judenrat, approached Krueger.

"What are you going to do with them?" Dr. Teitelbaum asked.

"Take a guess," Krueger said, which made his men roar with laughter.

"I am joining them," Dr. Teitelbaum said. "I am going to die with my brothers."

"You are, are you?"

"Yes, I am. And I can tell you that the Hitler gang will not win this war. Your day will come."

Krueger took out his gun and shot Dr. Teitelbaum in the head. "Throw him in the pit," he ordered two of his men.

The cemetery was completely surrounded by Ukrainian militia, who stood guns drawn inside and outside the walls. Gestapo and other German units were posted with machine guns at several locations. On the fortress-like, square building inside the cemetery, several Gestapo men manning machine guns were stationed as guards and observers. One operated a movie camera. A row of machine guns stood at one end of the cemetery, on one side of a row of several long deep pits, with mounds of earth piled alongside. In front of the pits were boards, forming a crude platform.

Truck after truck unloaded its human cargo. As they came off the trucks, the Jews were ordered to put their hands behind their heads and march to the back of the cemetery. Those not complying immediately were beaten. In time the cemetery was filled with rows of Jews lined up like rows of gravestones.

Krueger was now pacing in front of the battery of machine guns. He had sent a group of young Jewish girls to collect all the valuables from the lines of people in the cemetery. The girls returned again and again with baskets filled with watches, jewelry, gold coins, and various personal objects. While the collecting of valuables went on, German and Ukrainian guards prodded the people in the first row, using their rifle butts, forcing them to line up on the boards in front of the first pit. They were then made to take off their clothes, which were piled up to one side.

A hush fell upon the cemetery. Even the babies

stopped screaming and now whimpered softly. All about people mumbled prayers. Then a shot was heard. It was Krueger. He shot the Jew standing directly in front of him. That was the signal. The machine guns began to rattle. The blood bath had begun.

The machine gunning went on for several hours. The gunners did not stop even to eat—food was brought to them; they ate and continued shooting.

The girls kept bringing valuables in their baskets. Finally there were very few items left to retrieve. Should they continue to look for valuables, they asked the Gestapo man in charge.

"Go bring some more," he said.

As they turned he shot all of them in the back with his machine gun.

Row after row of Jews fell into the pits; more were brought over to take their places. Many who fell in the pits were not dead. Some lay for hours before they died. A few managed to extricate themselves and escape. There was a great deal of pushing and shoving in the crowd; some were trampled underfoot and killed before they reached the pit.

While the massacre was in progress, Krueger was entertaining his friends. He picked out a single beautiful girl and had his friends rape her in front of the crowd. Krueger himself was more interested in killing than in raping. He shot some people at such close range that his uniform was spattered with blood.

It was getting dark. The drizzle had turned to rain mixed with snow. Krueger gave the order to stop firing. A voice was heard shouting, *"Wer lebt gruesst mit dem Ruf 'Heil Hitler!'"*—whoever is alive yell "Heil Hitler!" Then a moment later, *"Wer lebt kann gehen."*—whoever is alive can go.

A wild stampede ensued. In their rush to escape,

people fell upon each other. Many were trampled.
Twelve thousand Jews perished in the cemetery. My
mother, many relatives, and entire families who had
lived in Stanislawow for generations, their lives all
were snuffed out in that one day.

This, Naftali, was the beginning of the end. Shortly
after the massacre we moved into the Ghetto. I will
describe for you life in the ghetto, and how I managed
to escape. But first tell me about yourself, your family,
and your town.

Part Three

KOLBUSZOWA DOOMED

Chapter 11

My town, Manya, was no different from thousands of little towns and villages all over Poland and eastern Europe, where Jews had lived for centuries. It was a typical *shtetl*; Sholom Aleichem[1] might have had us in mind instead of Kasrilivka or Anatevka when he told his stories. All the characters in his books: the rabbis, cantors, beadles, butchers, water carriers, village idiots, saints and sinners, scholars and ignoramuses, rich and poor—we had in good supply.

All these towns are now gone. Those thousands of communities where Jews lived their Judaism, often intensely, passionately, the homes of our greatest scholars and leaders where the Hassidim[2] spoke to God as to an intimate friend, where young Jews began organizing to fulfill the dream of returning to the land of Israel after 2,000 years, are no more. Centuries of Jewish piety, learning, love of life, folk wisdom, obliterated, gone up in smoke as if it never existed. Martyred communities, all of them including my own.

When I speak of Kolbuszowa, my home town, I speak of it with fear and reverence as one does that which is

---

[1] A Polish Jewish writer, best known for descriptions of Jewish life in the shtetl or small village. Author of "Fiddler on the Roof."

[2] Members of a sect of Jewish mystics which originated in Poland in the 18th century.

holy. We were of course mere mortals, and Kolbuszowa was by no means paradise—on the contrary, it was full of squalor and misery. Young Jewish boys and girls for the most part saw little future there, and either singly or in groups planned to leave, to move to a big city or to America or to settle as pioneers in the land of Israel. Even if Kolbuszowa was still there chances are I would have joined this exodus. Yet its grip on me is for life. My heart always will be tied to its people and traditions, its sounds and sights. The kind of life I knew there in my childhood and youth is one which my children, if I have any, will never know.

I was the ninth child of Reb Yitzhak and his wife, Esther, may they rest in peace, and may God avenge their blood. My father was a devout Hasid, who kept all the minutiae of Jewish law. He had a full, long beard and long earlocks. To him, every moment and every act, no matter how trivial, was for the sake of heaven. True joy was the joy of *mitzvah*, of fulfilling God's many requirements. A marvelous storyteller, his conversations always were sprinkled with proverbs and parables. For every situation he had a story. When pressed for an explanation his inevitable response was, "Let me tell you a story." Once completed, there was no longer a need for explanations. The owner of a large wholesale general store, he was well respected in Jewish circles, and accepted also as a community leader by the Poles. It was rare for a Hasidic Jew with a long, gray beard to speak Polish so fluently, without a trace of Jewish accent. Because he did, it was natural that he became active in both the Polish and Jewish institutions of the town.

My mother was everything expected of the wife of a Hasid. Her whole life focused on her children and their families. She ran the household and helped my father in the business. On Friday nights, after the festive Sabbath eve meal, and especially during the long winter evenings, she sat with us and recited from memory long passages from the Bible and the Talmud. A big heart she had, the biggest of anyone I have ever known. There was love in her for all her children, grandchildren, enough even for the stranger and way-farer, and even then more remained.

My childhood was in many respects typical for a Hasidic family of that day. At the age of three I was sent to *Cheder,* a one-room Hebrew school. Afterwards I attended a Polish public school and a *Talmud Torah*[3] simultaneously. My hair was clipped short atop my head, my earlocks allowed to grow down to my shoul-ders (though I always tucked them in behind my ears). I wore the traditional black Hasidic long coat. In public school my Polish classmates regarded me and other Jewish boys as strange, even alien beings. For the most part, though, I got along with them, even be-friended several, but it was not always smooth sailing.

It happened in second grade with a new teacher named Wisniewski. That he objected to the way the Jewish boys looked was an understatement. To his mind their appearance was an affront. Accordingly he devised his own remedy. One day without warning he gathered all the Hasidic boys in the first four grades into one room, then announced he was going to cut off their earlocks. He instructed us all to stand up and remove our skullcaps. Putting a glove on his left hand so, as he explained, he could avoid touching "those slimy Jews," he brandished a pair of clippers in his other hand. He posted a lady teacher at the door to

---

[3] A Hebrew religious school attended in the afternoon after public school was over.

make sure no one would run out. Then from bench to
bench he went, clipping off one earlock from each
child. Many of the boys started crying. Behind me
stood Moishele, a boy whose father was a "dayan," a
member of the Rabbinical Court in our town. He was
quite proud of the fact that he had the longest earlocks
of us all, so when Wisniewski drew closer he began to
wail and scream. It came as a shock to me to see
Moishele lose an earlock. But Wisniewski never got to
me. As he approached I turned and fled, skipping
over the desks and knocking down the teacher at the
door, then dashing home, screaming all the way—
"Tateh, m'chnaht payes—Tateh, m'chnaht payes." ("Daddy,
Daddy, they are cutting off earlocks!")

My father, hearing the commotion, came running
out of his store and, joined by Mr. Greenstein, the
director of the Jewish bank, hurried over to the school.
There they found some fifty wailing Jewish children,
each one missing an earlock. Immediately my father
summoned the principal and later the police and the
photographer. He would not let the matter rest. Word
traveled quickly. Over the next few days the pictures
of the crying children with the missing earlocks appeared on the front pages of newspapers all over
Poland. Wisniewski was suspended and the matter
taken to court. My father's friends, however, persuaded
him to withdraw the charges, fearing they would
arouse the enmity of our Gentile neighbors. In the
end the whole matter was dropped.

From early on I was a rebel, the rigidities of our
religion no doubt sparking my resistance. My future
had been all worked out in advance by my father. I
was to go to a Yeshiva at age seven, excel in my studies
of Talmud and all the other holy books, be given a
bride of my father's choosing at age eighteen, and live

exactly the way my forefathers had for generations. Until I was sixteen, I lacked the courage to stand up to my father to tell him of my determination to be a modern man, to go where I wished and make my own decisions. When I was twelve I fell in love with Rozia Susskind but I wouldn't risk telling my parents nor would I even dare speak to her for several years thereafter. Instead I would watch her come home from school every single day, then dream every night of Rozia, with her bluish green eyes and blonde braids. I wanted to be with her always, but of course never could because Hasidic boys and girls were strictly segregated. My fantasies no one could deny me, but there was much more that I wanted.

When I graduated from public school I cried for weeks because it marked the end of my secular studies, although I enrolled in an evening vocational business program. Ahead was the cloistered life of a Hasid. When I was fifteen my father sent me to Tarnow where I attended the Yeshiva of the Dzikiver Rebe for two semesters, which interested me not at all. To run away to a large town and enroll in a gymnasium was the answer, but I lacked the courage. Instead I chose the path of moderation, modified my appearance, cutting my earlocks shorter and shorter, and wearing more modern clothes (though sticking to the most conservative fashions). I went into my father's wholesale grocery business and became a buyer and salesman. In 1938 I became a member of *Hanoar Hazioni*, a local Zionist youth group, something I had long been eager to do. Rozia was also a member, and so I now had a reason to be near her. You can well imagine how much I welcomed that. But Zionism was for me a serious matter indeed; I along with my friend Yankel Schifman hoped to be smuggled into Palestine and had completed making arrangements for such a trip when the coming of war dashed our hopes. The day before the war broke out found me heading toward Rzeszow, the largest city in our area, in order to buy merchandise for our store. But when I arrived there the shelves had already been emptied; everything had been bought up. There was nothing to do but return home and prepare as best as possible for the expected crisis.

Chapter 12

On Friday evening, September 1st, 1939, the day the war broke out, I was home with my family, enjoying our traditional Sabbath eve meal. It was our custom to have the whole family—my brothers, sisters and their children—together at my parents' home to welcome the Sabbath. Always it was a happy occasion. My mother would produce a lavish feast, and during dinner we would sing *zemirot* (traditional Sabbath hymns). The Sabbath was God's day, a joyous interlude, a time to put aside all troubles and cares, and welcome the angels of joy and peace.

This particular Friday evening the angels of joy and peace were not expected. The Germans would be arriving, having unleashed the demons of war and destruction. The Polish army, with its antiquated weapons and anachronistic cavalry, was no match for German tanks and planes. The moment the Germans set foot in Kolbuszowa we Jews knew to expect the worst.

That night the singing did not last long. It was important to discuss the immediate future. The response of the women was to cry. All looked at me, for I was of military age and could be drafted. Unknown to them I had gone already to the recruiting center and tried to enlist. As a Polish patriot I felt obligated to defend it from enemies. The recruiting officer simply laughed.

"We don't have uniforms for our regular army, where are we going to find one for you?"

The Polish army was on the run. During the days that followed we saw Polish soldiers, first in trucks, in wagons, on horseback, then on foot, coming through our town retreating from the front. Some of them stayed long enough to loot the stores. The reason: "It is the duty of every patriotic Pole to clean out Jewish stores," a Polish officer declared, "so that merchandise does not fall into the hands of the enemy."

Each day more refugees, mostly Jews, passed through Kolbuszowa. They came from the west, fleeing the Germans, most from Cracow, Tarnow, and the surrounding area. Some of them had walked over 100 miles, their feet badly swollen and bleeding. Would it be advisable to escape to the east, we asked them. Their advice was to remain. They had fled because the Germans had bombed their towns. With the Polish surrender imminent, they argued, it would soon make no difference where one was. Had we not listened to their advice and gone east to Russia many, many of us would today still be alive.

Poland was falling apart, food was scarce, and disease beginning to spread. The Germans were attacking everywhere, flying low over towns and villages, bombing and strafing at will. The end was in sight.

The war was just one week old when the first German tank, accompanied by a motorcycle, appeared in Kolbuszowa. Polish soldiers opened fire, killing the motorcyclist, and forcing the tank to retreat. The following day the Germans returned in force. As we hid in our cellars, we listened with growing apprehension to the crack of bullets and the muffled explosions. Two hours later it was all over. We could hear voices shouting in German, "Vorwärts, achtung," and other commands. I climbed out of the cellar and peeked out in the direction of the marketplace. There at the four corners of the market were tanks, crosses painted on their turrets. German soldiers emerged from the tanks to join the infantrymen, all wearing helmets and holding rifles with bayonets fixed. They were entering my house, firing into the air while shouting, *"Alle heraus!"* (Everyone outside)!

Quickly we left the cellar and headed for the street, rapidly filling up with people, many thousands of them refugees who had jammed into Kolbuszowa. The order came forth to raise our hands and keep them over our heads. I had my first good look at the German soldier who stood guard over us. He was about my age and height. I tried to imagine myself in his uniform, holding his rifle, and he wearing my clothes, his hands over his head.

We were frisked, all our valuables taken. Some entered nearby houses and emerged with loot which they then piled on the sidewalks. We were all taken to the edge of town, perhaps 10,000 of us, a sea of upraised hands moving to an unknown fate. Scattered about the streets were dead soldiers and civilians, Polish, German, Jewish, also many dead horses. "Halt." The march came to a stop, whereupon a German officer announced that because Jews had offered resistance, had caused the death of some sixty Germans, all those assembled would be burned alive.

A gasp went through the crowd. Women and children began to cry, some men started reciting prayers. Looking back at the town I saw flames rising at many points, heading in our direction—the Germans had set homes on fire. Seeing the fires who could doubt the German threat? All around the murmuring and crying intensified. Husbands and wives kissed each other and their children goodbye. At this point time stood still; each minute seemed an eternity.

I stood there unable to think, transfixed by fear, by the prospect of being burned alive. I was enveloped by a feeling of total helplessness and resignation. Next to me an old Jew was intoning the *Vidui*, the confessional prayer of the dying. He was saying it, I sensed, not only for himself but for me as well.

Still no blood had been shed. Instead a child behind me asked his mother for water, and wailed when told there was none. I, too, longed for water, also for life. I wanted to run, but how? Where? One move and I expected I'd be shot.

I looked around. The German guards in front of me were getting tired and started to mill around and talk to each other. Slowly I edged my way to the back of the crowd. Soon I was standing next to the fence of the last house at this end of the town, when I noticed a man crawling behind the fence in an attempt to sneak into the house. There was a breach in the fence. I bent down, crawled through, and followed behind him. He stopped when he heard me and looked back, shaking with fear. Realizing I was not a German, he stopped quivering and continued crawling toward a side door around the corner of a house. We got there at the same time and let ourselves in; for the moment we were both safe.

"What do we do now?" I whispered.

"We'll jump out of a back window and run away," he replied.

There was no one in the house. We went to the back and opened a window.

"Let me go first," I told him. "I'll be quick."

"No, no," he refused, "I'll go first."

As he spoke, he had already taken hold of the window frame, put one leg over the sill and then the other. I heard him land outside and was about to follow when a burst of machine gun fire made me change my mind. I saw the man fall and roll on the ground holding his side with both hands. Without wasting a moment I dashed through the house back to the side door. So much for escape. After I was sure that no German guards were on that side, I crawled back to the assembly of the doomed.

All afternoon we stayed there. Toward evening the German officer spoke to us again. The order had been revoked, he said. Obviously the Germans had wanted only to scare us. Still we were not allowed to go home, and for good reason. The Germans were now busy ransacking Jewish businesses and homes; having us out of the way simplified their work.

Family members gradually found each other, then huddled together. The children, many of whom were hungry, started to cry. Next to me in the field stood the Stitshiner Rabbi, Yitzchak Horowitz, who with his family, had come as refugees from Tarnow just the day before. As it grew dark, he began to recite the *Havdale*, the ceremony marking the end of the Sabbath. The ceremony requires a braided candle with wicks. When he came to the blessing over the candle he turned and looked toward the burning shtetl; the houses going up in flames would that evening serve as the candles.

That night no one slept. We were kept in the fields until late the next day. Just before noon I was surprised to see Rozia and her mother. They had come to where we were, bringing food and water. They had not been rounded up with the rest of the Jews because their house was on the very outskirts of town. The Germans did not stop them now probably because both were blonde and did not look Jewish. Having learned the Germans were keeping us in the fields without food or water, they decided to risk helping us. Everything they brought I gave out to my sister's small children.

At last we were told we could go home except for two refugees, both Jews, who were detained and hanged two days later on a tree in the town's main street. To make sure no acts of sabotage were directed against the occupying army, five additional Jews remained on as hostages. With great effort, and a large sum of money, they were eventually released a few months later.

This was how we began to live under German occupation.

Chapter 13

I was nineteen when the war started. I had by that time decided to get away, head off into the larger world. I had begun to see my childhood sweetheart, Rozia, and together we had become active Zionists. To get to Palestine and establish myself there, then send for Rozia—that was my dream. But war is no time for dreamers.

Strangely the new life under the German occupation provided me with a sort of independence. No longer was I tied to my father's business, which had almost come to a standstill. Beyond that, traditional Jewish restrictions had necessarily to be relaxed. Still I faced a harsh taskmaster. In the first days of the occupation I was drafted, along with other able-bodied young men, all Jews, to do hard labor for the German army which included the burying of countless dead horses, the cleanup of debris and the collection of unexploded shells from all over the area. The work was severe, sorely taxed even the strongest. In addition, we were constantly beaten even while we worked. I remember the first beating from a German. He was a member of the S.A., or Brownshirts, about my height, perhaps a little younger than I. He was standing by in his riding boots, a brown uniform, a leather strap across his chest with a large pistol in its leather holster at its lower end. He was wearing a small round Nazi hat. He stood with his legs parted; his acne-covered face flushed, his nostrils dilated. He kept shouting in a shrill voice, shaking his riding crop most menacingly, *"Schneller, Jude, schneller, du Schweine!*—Faster, Jew, faster you pig!"

The crates we were carrying on our backs weighed over 200 pounds; some of the young men could hardly move them. One of them, named Samson Schochet, who was despite his name quite frail, collapsed under his burden. His face hit the ground and his mouth and nose began to bleed. The young Brownshirt, assisted by two older guards, struck him repeatedly with his whip and did not stop the flogging until he somehow got back on his feet and started to walk.

Next it was my turn. I was walking past the Brownshirt when without the least warning he started to beat me. I stopped, balancing the crate on my shoulders, and asked him why he was beating me. Was I not doing what I was supposed to do? He looked at me as if trying to decide whether he need bother with an explanation.

"I don't like the way you're dressed," he finally said.

"What's wrong with it?"

"You don't come to work dressed up," he answered. "You should be wearing old clothes to work."

I clenched my teeth and walked on. When I came back I saw the Brownshirt beating my old schoolmate and best friend, Noah Hutner. I walked over and asked him why he was doing this.

"I don't like the way he is dressed," he replied with a smile.

"But he is wearing old clothes."

"He should be wearing better clothes for work."

My blood boiled, but what point was there questioning the German's behavior or explanations.

Every day was the same; backbreaking work, no food all day, constant beatings and widespread abuse (most shameful that committed by a German soldier named Eckhard who each day would harness Jews to his wagon and force them to pull him through the streets of town).

Among the unsavory characters in my town, there was one Jewish fellow who had a long record of shady deals and dubious behavior. And when the Germans came to Kolbuszowa he immediately turned informer against his fellow Jews. Soon he was collecting handsome sums by blackmailing Jews afraid he might tell incriminating stories about them to the Germans. Better to pay him off and buy his silence. My father fell victim to this contemptible scoundrel, who came to our store every day asking for coffee beans. (During the war coffee beans were worth their weight in gold.) Each day my father gave him a little, but his appetite was not easily appeased.

"Itche," he said to my father one day, "you are being very stingy with your coffee."

"And where do you expect me to get all that coffee from, now that no new shipments can get in?"

"That is your problem, Itche, not mine."

Shortly thereafter I followed him to the corner and tapped him on the back. "You'd better stop harassing my father if you know what's good for you," I told him. Instead of heeding my warning he advised the Germans that my father had hidden away coffee beans and other items. The German response was to enter our store and confiscate most of our merchandise.

Next, word got to me that this informer had told the Germans that I was once a member of the Communist

Party and that I had pledged to carry out acts of violence and sabotage against them. An order was issued for my arrest.

I stayed at Rozia's house that night. My father came to see me. I told him I was leaving in the morning for the eastern border, where I would try to escape to the Russian side. To my surprise he did not object. He embraced me, and wished me luck.

A group of my friends had been planning to run away to Russia at the same time. That night I got in touch with them and urged them to join me, since the longer they waited the more difficult escape would be. They agreed. The next day five of us moved on to Rzeszow, then headed for the San River, which served as the new border between the German and Russian zones of occupation. We had no difficulty getting through the German checkpoint—at the time they were encouraging Jews to cross over to Russia. But once on the Russian side we were arrested. Fortunately the Russians were having their hands full with refugees. Accordingly they had converted a schoolhouse near the border into a temporary jail. But only one guard was posted there. In the middle of the night we decided to escape. We broke a window and simply climbed out. The next day we arrived in Lvov, where I found some distant relatives and moved in with them. I was to spend three months in Lvov. I enrolled in a gymnasium and also joined a Jewish theater group. For a brief time the war receded into the background, although it was with a small black market business that I supported myself.

It appeared I might sit out the war in Lvov when, toward the end of December, I received a message from Rozia. Her father, brother and sister had escaped to Lvov, but she remained with an ailing mother, afflicted with cancer. Both knew death was not far off but they kept this knowledge from her father, fearing he might then return. I decided, however, to go back the next day.

This time the border was sealed off. The only way to get through was to steal across the frozen San River at night. I was referred to a Jewish horse dealer, Sachar Furman, who knew the area, traveling back and forth as he did several times a week. Along with a group of about fifteen young men we approached the border. Our guide had given each of us a white sheet for camouflage in the snow. We had come within a mile of the border when a Russian border patrol spotted us and took us to the station house. There we had to empty our pockets and lay everything on a table. I had a picture of my father which attracted the attention of one of the guards. He wanted to know who the man with the long beard was.

"My father," I explained. He looked at me incredulously. "He is a very religious Jew," I added. He still did not understand.

"*Yevreski pop,*" another guard explained to him, "a Jewish priest." This he understood.

We would be taken back to Lvov, we were told. That we knew meant jail and then off to Siberia. One Russian guard escorted us to the train station. It was late at night; the station was completely deserted. After about an hour the guard began to doze off. Our guide, the horse dealer, motioned us to prepare to get away. He stole up behind the guard and snatched his gun. We then tied him up with pieces of clothing, gagged him, and stowed him neatly under a bench. Now we could cross the border to the German side.

After walking for a time through the snow we came upon a secluded house. In the house, the horse dealer informed us, were several girls, good friends who would help us get on the train back to Kolbuszowa. Why, I wondered, would a group of girls be living in such a secluded area? Why was there such gaiety and sauciness among them such as I had never before encountered? Then to my total astonishment the horse dealer announced he'd be spending the night in the same bedroom with two of the girls. Unless they were married, who had ever heard of a man and a woman sleeping together?

I chose not to ask any questions. I went to sleep in the kitchen. In the morning we all got dressed, and one by one the girls took each of us to the train station, bought a ticket and came back. Reunited on the train, the trip back to Kolbuszowa proved uneventful.

It was noon when I reached my father's store. He had just finished his lunch, and was sitting in the kitchen in back of the store, poring over an old Hebrew book.

"Shalom aleichem, Papa. Hello."

"Naftali!" my father said without looking up. He slowly closed the book and rose to greet me. His eyes were happy and sad at the same time. "Naftali, my son, I am happy to see you, but," he said shaking his head, "I must tell you that you have made a terrible mistake coming back."

Chapter 14

It's true, Manya; it was a terrible mistake. I might have continued my studies and worked in the Jewish theater in Lvov. I could have joined the Russian army and fought against Hitler. In Kolbuszowa all I could do was suffer and be persecuted like all of the Jews in town. I could not help anyone.

Rozia's mother died four days after I returned. Her uncle would now care for her. Rozia quite naturally was glad to see me, but like my father, considered my return to be a mistake. Now we were trapped together as the Germans progressively tightened the noose around us all through a calculated policy of assault and intimidation.

Upholding the "law" was a local police force clothed in blue uniforms we nicknamed the "Blue Police." Mostly young *Volksdeutschen,* these Germans from eastern Europe were notorious for their hatred of Jews. They were quartered in Bezalel Orgel's house in the marketplace, from which they had a good view of the Jewish neighborhood, over which they ruled with an iron fist. Any Jew, they decreed, who passed a policeman had to take off his hat and greet him. But whenever an old Jew would do so, the policeman would spit in his face, grab him by his coat lapels, slap his face, and shout at him, *"Du Verfluchte Jude,"* (You cursed

Jew) "why do you greet me? Am I your friend?" Then
if the same Jew would later see another policeman and
this time refrain from greeting him and taking off his
hat, he received the same treatment, then a scolding.
"How long does it take for you to learn that when you
meet a policeman you must take off your hat and greet
him?" Soon, whenever a Jew went out into the street,
he would look all around; if he spied a policeman he
would quickly hurry off in a different direction.

That was only the beginning. Before long the Blue
Police imposed a strict curfew on the Jewish community: individuals were allowed on the streets only
between ten in the morning and noon, and between
four and six in the afternoon. The curfew was ri-
gorously enforced. Any Jew caught a minute before or
after curfew was dragged into the police station and
forced to pay a fine. Life was severely crippled as a
result.

In an emergency we could not leave to summon a
doctor. When visiting we risked being unable to get
back to our own quarters. During the hours when they
were permitted outside, Jews constantly scurried
about, fearing time would run out before they attended
to all their tasks.

The curfew imposed a terrible hardship. After two
months' time it became obvious to the Germans that it
did not serve their interests, and it was revoked. They
now dedicated their energies to recruiting forced labor
from the able-bodied Jews in town, ages twelve to sixty.
We Jews now became, as in the Bible, the "choppers of
wood and drawers of water," doing the menial labor
which neither the Germans nor the Poles cared to do.
They set a daily quota of 200 workers, out of a total of
about 1,000 people capable of any kind of work at all.
Each day they entered Jewish homes and took the first

200 workers they could find. Many people hid, and so the hunt for workers continued sometimes until late at night. We lived in constant fear of being dragged out for forced labor. One never knew when he would be taken away.

The people rounded up for work would be lined up in the street, given pails and brooms, ordered to shoulder their brooms like rifles, and head off to the place of work. Men and women, graybeards and children, marched together. Often they were ordered to sing Jewish songs. I remember marching one day and singing the hymn, *Vetaher Libenu,*

> Purify our heart,
> That we may serve you in truth . . .

Why, I needed to know, was I being punished by God? Was it for some grave sin? Was I suffering for having turned from my father's orthodox ways? But if true, what of my friend Moishele, now marching behind me? He was a devout Hasid, who kept every aspect of Jewish law. And what about the Jews of our town who spent their lives in prayer, in caring for the poor and hungry? What were their sins? Was this how God treasured those who loved him? Or did God have nothing to do with what was happening to us? Perhaps God had left us to our own devices; maybe it was up to us to remedy such an intolerable existence. But what could we do? Surrounded by a mighty foe, escape seemed impossible. Just managing to stay alive was a miracle. Still we kept praying for the greatest miracle of all, deliverance from German occupation.

One ray of light during those dark and somber days was Dr. Leon Anderman, a physician who practiced in Kolbuszowa before the war (and was our family doctor).

He was an assimilated Jew, who had never set foot in a synagogue, had never been associated with any of the Jewish institutions in the town. He was a Polish patriot who had served with distinction in the Polish army, and for that reason was highly regarded by the leaders of the Polish community. If there was any Jew whom one might have singled out as a saint, it was Dr. Anderman.

Tall, broad-shouldered, dark, with strong features and an open, honest face, Dr. Anderman belonged to that unusual breed of human being who, like the prophets of Israel, proclaimed then pursued high moral principles, and subordinated personal interests to what they knew to be the just and right cause. About a year before the war broke out Dr. Anderman somehow sensed that terrible times were in store for the Jews. More and more he became concerned about their fate. He could easily have run away, but he chose to stay in Kolbuszowa and cast his lot with his fellow Jews. In 1938, when German Jews were forced across the border into Poland, Jewish communities throughout Poland organized relief committees to help the refugees. Dr. Anderman joined the committee in Kolbuszowa. In this connection he made his first appearance ever in our synagogue. There I heard him deliver an impassioned appeal for funds for the hapless refugees. I admired him the moment I saw him. Years later whenever his name was mentioned I always felt the deepest reverence for his memory.

In every Jewish community large or small in Poland the Germans appointed a Jewish council or Judenrat shortly after they arrived. The council was a puppet government which enabled the Germans to get what they wanted from the Jewish community with minimum effort, and in the end to facilitate the extermination of the Jewish population. More often than not, the Germans chose certain disreputable elements of the Jewish community for the council, weak, cowardly men on whose collaboration they could depend. In 1940 the Germans looked about for people in Kolbuszowa whom they could use for the local Judenrat. The Polish mayor of our town, Januszewski, had prepared a list of questionable characters for the council, and the Germans prepared to make these appointments. Jews throughout Kolbuszowa understood the consequences, and made strong efforts to have the composition of the council changed. The Germans reconsidered, recognizing that the new candidates submitted carred more weight in the community than those selected by the mayor.

After some discussion, community leaders decided that the most suitable person for the office of the president of the Jewish Council was Dr. Anderman. A delegation called upon him with the offer, but he at first refused; he would not become a stooge of the Germans. But once it became clear it was either Anderman or the mayor's unwelcome choices, he accepted. Anderman selected twelve council members, taking care to choose upstanding individuals but also younger men, men without beards and so less likely to antagonize the Germans. Among the council members was my brother, Leibush, and my brother-in-law, Shaya David Lische.

Dr. Anderman's administration brought a measure of stability and confidence to the Jewish community. The task of providing workers was put in his hands; no longer were we the victims of random kidnappings at odd hours. The council organized a system whereby each Jew took turns working for the Germans. My brother Leibush was amazed at how the doctor dealt

with the enemy. Where other Jews stood in awe and
trembling, he was cool and composed. One time the
Germans asked him for 100 workers to chop down
trees. There was no way, however, to provide the many
axes necessary for the job. The Germans made it clear,
however, that if he did not comply the whole community would suffer the consequence. The next Wednesday, when the S.S. officer in charge came to Kolbuszowa, Dr. Anderman presented him with 100 men,
mostly teenage boys.

"Here are your men," the doctor reported in his
typically unperturbed manner, "but I'm afraid they
cannot do the work."

"Why not?" the German snapped.

"Because they have no axes, and without axes you
can't chop down trees."

"Is that so?" the German replied in mock surprise.
"Let me remind you, Herr Doktor, that in the German
Reich, under Hitler, everything is possible."

"I am sorry," Dr. Anderman rejoined, "you are
asking me to do something I can't do."

The German *Landsrat* was furious. "And what would
you do," he shouted, "if I ordered all these Jews to be
hanged?"

"Nothing, I suppose. Your hangman is the one who
will have a great deal to do."

The German walked away in a huff without saying a
word. Later he ordered the group to disperse, and he
left town. For twenty-four hours the community lived
in fear and dread. The doctor, it was felt, had gone too
far this time; we would all have to pay a high price.
The following day a German truck came roaring into
the marketplace. Dr. Anderman was immediately
summoned by the police. When he arrived, he was
told that the *Landsrat* had sent him a supply of axes for

his workers. That evening, in all the Jewish homes in Kolbuszowa, and even in the surrounding villages, a toast was raised in honor of our brave doctor. In our home we uttered a prayer that Dr. Anderman would remain our leader until we would once again be free.

When the Germans issued the order forbidding the Jews to use the sidewalks, Dr. Anderman promptly went out, on the day the order was issued, and walked in the street, a message to the Jews to obey the order strictly. He did the same when we were forced to wear an armband with the Star of David. He walked with his head lifted, making a point of showing that he was proud to wear the emblem of the Jewish people. The Germans referred to the armband as *die Schande Bande*, the sign of shame, intended to single out the Jew and degrade him. Instead Dr. Anderman taught us to wear it with pride.

One time four Gestapo men came to Kolbuszowa, and demanded from Dr. Anderman a list of the richest Jews in the town. The doctor informed them, "There are no rich Jews in this town." Nevertheless he was pressed to give a few names. He then wrote something on a piece of paper and handed it to the Gestapo men. "Yes, there is one rich Jew in Kolbuszowa, and here is his name." When the officer in charge unfolded the paper, he found Dr. Anderman's name on it. Without saying a word, the four men got into their car and drove off.

On another occasion, a truck with S.S. officers came to the Judenrat and asked Dr. Anderman to point out some Jewish homes from which they could conscript good furniture for their headquarters. He took them to the poorest Jewish homes, where they could find only the most dilapidated broken pieces. This was the best he could do, he told them, since Kilbuszowa had always been a poor Jewish community. Next he took them to his own house, to prove he was the only Jew in the town with money enough to buy new furniture. They went away empty handed.

It was springtime, the first under German occupation. The Germans, it was now obvious, were not about to disappear. They had invaded and occupied Denmark and Norway. They had overrun Holland and Belgium, had broken into France and cut off the British, who were being evacuated from Dunkirk. France had been brought to her knees, and England's turn seemed next. But in our part of Europe things were relatively quiet. Dr. Anderman had organized an ambulatorium, a free clinic in my sister Malcia's house, where poor Jews were given medical care. He prevailed upon the community to pay a voluntary tax, each according to his means, for various charitable works undertaken by the Judenrat. And when Passover approached, he got permission from the German authorities to bake matzos.[1] When we sat down to the Seder[2] table and recited, "This year we are slaves, next year we shall be free," who could ignore the significance of these ancient words? And when we got to the phrase, "Pour down your wrath on the nations who know you not," we recited the words with special fervor. Jews had been frequently enslaved over the ages; always they had outlived their oppressors. There was, we felt, a force operating in the world far more powerful than the pharaohs and the Hitlers.

---

[1] Unleavened bread used during Passover.
[2] The Passover service conducted at home.

Chapter 15

Northeast of Kolbuszowa, in a wide basin where the Vistula and San rivers meet and run north to Warsaw, lay a huge area of wild, virgin forest, known as Puszcza Sandomierska. Once a desolate, uninhabited area, it attracted either hardy hunters or fugitives from the law. Not many people outside of Poland have ever heard of the place, yet what the Germans did there changed our life on this earth irrevocably. They chose that secluded place to test the V-1 and V-2 rockets which, at the close of the war, would usher in an age of rockets and missiles—a new era in warfare and a new dawn in scientific research. In the village of Pustkow, at the southern edge of the forest, the Germans established a slave labor camp for Poles and Jews, who unknowingly were performing work relating to these rockets. Later this camp was converted to a concentration camp and an *Industriehof*, in which thousands perished.

In the fall of 1940 I became an inmate of that camp. For a few weeks, until I escaped, I became witness to even worse bestiality than had taken place in Kolbuszowa. It was, however, only a foretaste of things to come.

All the people in our town from age twelve to sixty were now registered with the German authorities, and each received a labor card. Periodically they conducted a *Kontrolle,* or checkup, of the labor force. Each Kontrolle resulted in a number of ablebodied young people being taken away for some project in the district requiring hard labor. Many young men escaped from those places of backbreaking work and returned to town.[1] The Germans kept replacing them with others.

One such Kontrolle was run by an S.S. officer named Schmidt, one of the commandants of the labor camp at Pustkow. It was a dreary day when we assembled at the municipal building for the checkup. Then we waited hours before the inspectors arrived. Finally a group of S.S. men, headed by Schmidt, stormed into the building, and immediately shut the doors and windows. Amid curses and blows from their whips we were ordered to line up and await our turn to be inspected in an adjoining room. When mine came, I was shoved in the back with a rifle butt, and sent flying across the room. Everything went black. When I regained consciousness I was lifted to my feet, held up by two S.S. men, while a third slapped my face, urging me to wake up. Freeing one hand I wiped my eyes. They had been covered with blood from a cut on my forehead. I wiped them again, and then saw Schmidt sitting behind a desk.

"Is anything wrong?" Schmidt asked.

"I am bleeding," I answered, immediately wondering whether I had said the wrong thing.

"So I see, so I see," he said in a pleasant voice.

---

[1] It had for example occurred previously when the Germans had sent many young men, myself included, to a prison camp at Lipie, a village in the Carpathian mountains, near the town of Nowy-Sacz, a place distant from Kolbuszowa. There we did nothing but break up rocks and then move the debris from place to place. Fortunately the Judenrat in Kolbuszowa sent packages to its counterpart in Nowy-Sacz and these were distributed to us weekly. In time all of us escaped and made our way back to Kolbuszowa.

Taking out a clean handkerchief and handing it to me, he said, "Here, use this. Go ahead, don't be afraid."

I took the handkerchief and dabbed my forehead with it. Schmidt got up and walked around the desk in front of me. "Get down on your knees," he ordered. Three S.S. men were flanking me, watching my moves. I did as I was told.

"Now, shine my boots with this," he said, pointing to the blood-soaked handkerchief. Over and over I had to wipe my wound and apply my blood to his boots.

"That will do," he said at last. Turning to his men, he added, "Put him on the list."

The list was of the names of the men who were to be taken that day to Pustkow. I found myself on a truck, sitting next to my friend Noah. It was a terrible trip, the driver deliberately steering the open truck past low branches which struck some of the occupants. Two of our group lost eyes on the way to Pustkow. We arrived at the camp in the evening. Early the next day we were awakened and taken into an empty barracks where our heads were shaven. From there we were brought outside to a central square and told to line up in four rows. In the center of the square was a gallows with a new rope hanging from the upper beam, a wide noose at its end. There we stood in absolute silence wondering what would happen next.

Schmidt finally appeared and had his assistant take the roll. Next Schmidt pointed to a man at the end of the second row and had him step out. He ordered a second man to do the same. That individual was then told to put the noose around the neck of the first. The man obeyed. "Proceed with the hanging," he then told him.

An air of grim unreality attended the entire procedure. A random, wanton murder was being performed before our very eyes. Worse, we felt helpless to do a thing about it. No one, not even the man being hanged, uttered a sound or even made a gesture as they played out the macabre script. We were like robots. Surrounded by a heavy guard with machine guns we simply stood there and watched. The rope jerked, there was a gurgling sound, and soon a limp body dangled in mid-air. All day long, as we worked in the forest felling trees, I saw that body in front of my eyes.

When we returned from work the terrible scene was repeated. This time the man picked to do the hanging refused to do it. He was a young man from Tarnow, with dark, defiant eyes. He stood next to the gallows and refused to budge. Schmidt's face was contorted with rage.

"Get moving, you dirty pig!," he bellowed, the veins in his neck bulging. The man remained glued to the spot.

"Take him away," Schmidt ordered his assistants.

Two SS men took him by the arms and dragged him away. As they went past Schmidt he called upon them to stop. With a sudden jerk he pulled out a knife and plunged it into the man's neck, then quickly drew it out. The two S.S. men then resumed dragging the victim, leaving a trail of blood along the way.

The next day I was ordered, with two other inmates, to go to the barracks where the dead Jews were kept temporarily. We were to take the bodies, place them on handcarts, and bring them to the edge of the camp, where they would be buried. I had never handled dead bodies before; I felt ill before I was even close to the barracks. Still I entered the barracks, where several bodies were piled in a corner.

"All right," one of my companions prompted me, "get that one by the arms and I'll grab him by his legs." Turning aside, so as not to look the dead person in the face, I did what he said. About to take hold of his legs, I heard a groan.

"Good God," my companion exclaimed, "he's still alive!"

I mustered my courage to look into the man's face. It was the young man from Tarnow who had refused to hang his fellow inmate the day before and was knifed by Schmidt. His dark eyes were wide open, and he was moaning softly. We stood there a long time, wondering what to do, when our S.S. escort came in. What was taking so long, he inquired. We didn't answer but he soon sized up the situation and decided to check with Schmidt.

Schmidt came back, accompanied by his entourage, some carrying cameras as if prepared for a show. He ordered us to stand the man on his feet. We obeyed. He was barely able to keep his balance.

"Dance!" Schmidt yelled in his ear. The man's eyes were blank, devoid of comprehension.

"Dance!" Schmidt repeated. The man still did not budge. Then his lips began to move. He was trying to speak.

"What is it?" Schmidt asked.

"Water," the word finally came out.

Schmidt motioned to one of his men to bring him a canteen of water. He held it out in front of the dying man.

"Here is water. Would you like some?" The man nodded. "Then dance!"

The man's feet began to sway. "Good, good," Schmidt exclaimed, clapping his hands. "There, go on, go on, dance."

Amid the cheers and jeers of the S.S. audience the man swayed back and forth, cameras clicking. Moments later he collapsed to the floor like a sack of potatoes, lying on his side, breathing heavily.

Schmidt ordered someone to bring him some wire. The wire was tightened around the man's neck. He was taken to the middle of the camp; the other end of the wire was attached to a branch of a tall tree; he remained hanging there for several days.

And so it went each day at the Pustkow concentration camp. Each morning and evening the same hanging ritual, each day random killings by Schmidt, who would often shoot haphazardly into a work party as they left for work in the morning. He once boasted with pride that he could not sit down to breakfast in the morning unless he had first killed at least one Jew.

We were all, it became obvious, condemned men; sooner or later our turn would come; the only uncertainty, the method of our execution. A week later the first man from our Kolbuszowa group escaped. While we were working in the woods he disappeared, and was never found. Taking heart from this, many of us planned our own escapes. The next day, while marching to work, Schmidt as usual fired his pistol into our ranks. This time a bullet hit my right hand; it went through the flesh, luckily without touching a bone. I tied the wound with a rag to stem the bleeding, and went on to work. During the day my fellow inmates did their best to help me out, sparing me from the most strenuous work. I realized I would not be able to hold an axe in my hand for some time, and sooner or later the S.S. men watching over us would realize that I was wounded and finish me off. With the help of a man from Tarnow named Kleinhandler, a cousin of Rozia, who had a position of some authority in the camp, I was able to transfer to another labor detail. Each morning we left the camp by truck to install telephone poles alongside the roads in the direction of Tarnow. It was hard work, but because there was no close supervision, I was able to avoid using my right hand. I was also able to exhcnage valuables for food with peasants we encountered while performing our work. Truckloads of new prisoners were arriving daily in the camp, and the Germans were, for the moment at least, somewhat lax in guarding the Jewish laborers. Accordingly more and more of the contingent from Kolbuszowa were managing to escape. Just when I was making my own final plans I suffered an injury. Lifting a telephone pole, something snapped in my back. I collapsed and couldn't get up. With the help of friends I managed to get to the truck and return to camp. One of the inmates, a Jewish physician, diagnosed it as a slipped disc. It would, he told me, take a long time to heal. Meanwhile I would need a support for my back. "You must run away," he insisted. With "lame" workers Germans had little patience.

The next day, assisted by friends but with great difficulty, I was back at work, hopefully for the last time. With the help of a man from Dembica, who was also determined to escape, we both set out for his town, and hid there. After a few days, still barely able to straighten up, I made it back to Kolbuszowa, where I kept out of sight in Rozia's attic for a week.

Chapter 16

During the entire week following my escape from Pustkow I awakened each night in a cold sweat, breathing heavily and moaning. Each time I was tormented by the same dream. There I was hanging from a tree, wires attached to my hands and feet. S.S. men held the ends of the wires and kept pulling on them. Demented laughter rang in my ears—it was Schmidt. He stood on a ladder leaning against the tree, a long knife in one hand, a gun in the other, repeatedly shooting and stabbing me. My entire body ached when I woke up; the pain lingered for hours.

My friend Noah came to visit me at Rozia's house; he wore no hat.

"Don't tell me you are no longer an observant Jew," I said.

Noah sighed. "When the war is over and I am still alive I will become an observant Jew again. Right now I follow just one *mitzvah*—and thou shalt choose life."

"I see. But tell me, why are you so anxious to survive?"

"Because God wants me to, and the Germans don't want me to. Look, we are trapped by the Germans, we are in no position to fight, but we must resist them. The only way we can do this is to stay alive. And we have to help as many Jews as possible to stay alive."

"What do you suggest?" I asked.

"Dr. Anderman has organized a free clinic. Why don't we volunteer to help him?"

I liked the idea. That day we offered our services to Dr. Anderman, who was happy to have us. He agreed to teach us to wash and dress wounds, adminster medications, and perform other tasks normally done by a doctor's assistant. We learned quickly, and received many compliments from him. I was now sleeping soundly at night, my spirits restored.

There was no lack of work at the clinic, but one day, during a slack period, I found myself alone with Dr. Anderman. He was sitting in his office, looking out at the marketplace. It was the end of winter, the snow was melting, the old facades of the houses were shining in the morning sun, the sky was a perfect blue. An old water-carrier crossed the marketplace, two pails dangling at his sides.

"You seem to know a lot of the people who come here," Dr. Anderman said to me with a twinkling smile.

"I used to meet many of them in the synagogue and other public places," I explained.

"The old Jew who came in just before," the doctor said, "Reb Eli, he's going to need a hernia operation."

"I'm not surprised," I replied, suppressing my laughter.

"What do you mean?" he asked.

"His hernia is quite famous. Each Friday before the war, the religious Jews would go to the steam bath next to the large shul,[1] where we would sit in the hot steam and flail each other with branches. It was one of our favorite places, especially in winter time. I recall many times sitting there while all around me naked

---

[1] Synagogue.

Jews with long beards would sway and sing, *"Oy, oy, s'is a mekhayeh, oy, oy, s'is a mekhayeh"* (oh, oh, it's such a pleasure). There was one Jew who came regularly to the bathhouse, Reb Eliezer, who was partly blind. He would walk across the steam room, without his thick glasses naturally. As he passed he would touch each man, recognize him, and greet him. One time he passed Reb Eli, with the hernia. He touched him and recognizing him said, 'Is that you, Reb Eli'?' To which Reb Eli answered, 'Yes, that's me.' At that moment Reb Eliezer happened to touch Reb Eli's sizable hernia. 'And who is this?' he asked. Reb Eli replied, 'My grandson.' So Reb Eliezer said, 'God bless him. A big boy, already, he'll be celebrating his Bar Mitzvah[2] soon, eh?'"

Dr. Anderman shook with laughter. "You are quite a storyteller."

"Not really," I said, blushing. "But this town is full of characters."

"You know, Naftali, I don't know how I ever got caught in this web, of becoming the go-between between the Jews and the Germans. Before the war I had nothing to do with Jewish affairs. I happened to be born a Jew, but I considered myself a humanist, equally concerned with all people. But when the war broke out, I saw what was happening. I realized that no one could stand up for the Jews except the Jews themselves. Still, I don't know. What business do I have being president of the Judenrat? I am a physician, not a politician. When I was asked to take this position I had grave misgivings. But I realized I could stand up to the Germans, being an officer in the Austrian army in the first World War, while no other Jew in Kolbuszowa could. So far I've been lucky. I stood up to

---

[2] Confirmation ceremony at age 13.

them several times, and got away with it. But how long can my luck hold out?"

Dr. Anderman then revealed that the Germans were about to send a Gestapo chief to run our affairs and those of the surrounding area from here in Kolbuszowa, instead of from Rzeszow. This in itself was bad news; worse still was the fact that the man picked for this job was one of the most infamous Gestapo men in our district. His name was Twardon. While authorities in Rzeszow were debating whether to send him here or to nearby Strzyzow, Dr. Anderman remarked, with a bitter chuckle, he went to Rzeszow to bribe the German officials so they would send Twardon to Strzyzow. There he encountered an emissary from Strzyzow who had come bearing bribes so that he would be sent to Kolbuszowa. In the end the choice was left to Twardon who, as luck would have it, chose Kolbuszowa.

The following week Herr Landskommissar Twardon arrived in our town. He immediately summoned all the members of the Judenrat, as well as those of some neighboring small towns. From my brother Leibush, who attended the meeting, I learned what had been said. Twardon he described as evil personified. He was half German, half Polish, and combined the worst traits of both nationalities. He was in his mid-thirties, short and fat like a barrel on legs, with a bulldog face, two small piercing eyes, a shiny clean-shaven scalp, and a grating shrill voice. Unlike other Germans, he meant business—so he informed all assembled. Everything would have to click. Jewish life meant nothing to him, he announced most ominously.

Without wasting any time, he issued his first decree: all the Jews of Majdan had to evacuate the town within twenty-four hours, and move to Rzeszow, where some hovels had been prepared for them. That same day he dispatched a contingent of Sonderdienst to round them up. About 80% of Majdan was Jewish. It was not long before we saw a caraven of horse-drawn wagons going through the main thoroughfare of Kolbuszowa, on the way to Rzeszow. It was a ghastly picture: hundreds of Jews evicted without notice, heaped like garbage on the high wooden wagons, children screaming and crying, women fainting, men with eyes full of despair, old men mumbling their prayers.

I was home with my mother when the caravan came through the marketplace, in sight of our house. The wagons had halted to regroup. My mother and I went outside and stared at the woeful scene. Her eyes filled with tears, and I heard her murmur to herself, "Those poor souls, they have no food and no clothes. They will die of hunger and cold in a few days. We must do something to help."

She went back to the house and returned with a basket of bread. Every time one of my sisters married, my mother would bake huge loaves of bread the week before the wedding for distribution to the poor. Feeding the poor, she insisted, was the greatest mitzvah one could perform. I offered to carry the basket for her, but she insisted on doing it herself. I followed behind her as she walked over to the wagons. Just then a Sonderdienst man with a riding crop approached, demanding to know what she was doing. She pointed to the bread and then to the wagons. The Sonderdienst's face crimsoned. He lashed at the basket with his whip, striking my mother's knuckles and forcing her to drop the basket. My mother drew back and looked over her shoulder in anguish at me. I clenched my fists and prepared to pounce on the man, when my mother placed herself between us and, clutching my arm, whispered to me not to do anything foolish. At that moment it took more courage to do nothing than to do something; my mother, of course, was right.

What befell the Jews of Majdan would in time happen to us. Most everyone accepted that as fact. A larger pattern was becoming clear. Jews from small towns like Majdan were being sent to larger towns like Rzeszow, then concentrated in one area with little or no means of subsistence. All of these expelled Jews of Majdan soon died of hunger and cold. Those few who had gone into hiding were turned in by local peasants and shot. Majdan thus became one of the first localities in Poland to become largely *Judenrein*, empty of Jews. Twardon received a citation from Hitler himself, and received favorable notice in German newspapers. Twardon's action, we later understood, was part of the master plan to confine Jews in ghettos from where it would be easy to ship large numbers of them to the death camps.

Twardon had promised Dr. Anderman that the Kolbuszowa Jews would not be sent away. We heard this with great relief; doom was forestalled, hope not yet lost. But this feeling lasted only two days. His promise was not 48 hours old when, in the middle of the day, two army trucks arrived in the marketplace. Some one hundred S.S. men jumped out, and rounded up the Jews who lived in the immediate area. Everyone had to turn over his house keys. Twardon, who personally supervised the operation, declared all Jewish homes around the market now the property of the German government. Our home was among them. My entire family was taken to the marketplace along with the other Jews who lived in the area. At the last moment, as the Germans were coming into our house, I ran out through the back door, jumped on my bicycle, and hid at Rozia's house. Later in the afternoon I found out from a Polish neighbor that the evicted Jews had been loaded on wagons and sent off to Rzeszow. The road to Rzeszow ran by Rozia's house. We waited in the house for the caravan to pass by. An hour later the wagons appeared, escorted by armed S.S. men. We could make out the people in the wagons, the unmistakable pain and fear in their eyes. Respectable Jewish citizens were suddenly transformed into destitute prisoners, being driven to an unknown fate. On the last wagon I saw my entire family, huddled together, silent and forlorn. Even the little ones were quiet. I had every intention of jumping out of my hiding place to join them, but Rozia held me back. "Don't be a fool, Naftali. You can't do any good by joining them." Instead Rozia went outside and signaled, letting them know that I was safe in her house.

As the wagons disappeared behind the hill I began to cry. I seldom cried, but this time there was no holding back. I lay on the floor, face down, and cried and cried until my bones ached. After I was too tired to go on crying I got up and trudged back to town in the dark. I reached our house and let myself in through a door in the roof. I knew it would be the last time I would be able to enter my house, so I proceeded to pack up all the valuables I could carry away with me, and gathered all the money and jewelry which my father had put away in several hiding places throughout the house. All this the Germans would not get.

I spent the night in Rozia's house, where I hid the money and jewelry. The next day my friend Noah and I were recruited by the police, along with a large number of young Jews, to remove the contents of the evacuated houses now the property of the German government. The clearing operation lasted a whole week. Nothing was left.

Twardon, it was clear, had planned to establish a ghetto in Kolbuszowa from the beginning. After all, the Warsaw Ghetto had been in existence almost a year and all over Poland Jews were being herded into such restricted zones. The evacuation of the Jews from the market area was part of the same plan. It had been an area in which 700 Jews and about 90 Poles had lived under extremely cramped conditions. The Germans now planned to jam some 1100 more Jews into the area (the Polish residents were removed). When Twardon made this plan known to the Judenrat, Dr. Anderman responded that as a physician, he could not allow replacement of 90 Poles with 1100 Jews, considering the extreme hazard of epidemics; besides which the whole idea was not feasible. Twardon realized Dr. Anderman was right, still he devised a way to make things fit. Without any forewarning he proceeded to round up several hundred Jews in the market area and had them sent away. Now the ghetto plan was feasible!

Dr. Anderman himself lived in a spacious house which was completed one year before the outbreak of the war. It had electricity, running water, and other comforts not ordinarily available in the small towns of Poland. Since the doctor and his family had to move into the ghetto with the rest of the Jews, Twardon expropriated the house for himself. He informed the Judenrat that he needed 10,000 zlotys to refurbish the house according to his specifications. Dr. Anderman refused to allocate the money. "If I could live in that house, you certainly can. And besides, you will not live there long. The war will soon end, and I will be occupying my house once again."

The order was given for all Jews to move into the ghetto within 48 hours. The area consisted of a few meandering alleys, densely populated with Jews of little means, and containing the old synagogue, the house of study, the public bathhouse, and a few other Jewish institutions. Now an additional seven or eight hundred Jews were forced to crowd into these cramped quarters.

Just moving to the ghetto was a struggle. It was considered crucial to get in quickly otherwise one might be without a place to live. No means of transportation were available. And Jews were not allowed to enlist the aid of Polish peasants, so old and young alike were forced to carry their possessions on their backs. The alleyways leading to and inside the ghetto became so choked with people that it took hours to go back and forth. Everywhere men and women were seen carrying old beds, cupboards, trunks full of clothes, blankets and pillows wrapped in bedsheets. All about, goose feathers poured out of torn pillows and featherbeds and filled the air like snow.

Belongings which had taken generations to acquire were transferred in such haste that the scene contained both tragic and comic overtones. The poverty of most Jews was inescapably evident. Everything that could be carried was brought into the ghetto. There was the old school teacher lugging his school bench, the only tool of his trade left to him; Basheh the lady baker was dragging boards for making bagels; Naftali Nessel and his sons lugged a heavy stand for splitting logs. People were seen carrying pails for drawing water, crates full of coal, broken mirrors, rusty ovens, old wagon wheels. Everything imaginable was brought in; few calculated where all those things were going to be kept. In reality most items had to be left in the street, where they cluttered the way, fell apart and, what was combustible, finally put to use as fuel.

By Saturday night all the Jews were packed within the ghetto walls. In every house in the ghetto, including the synagogue and the house of study, Jewish families were thrown together. Altercations and squabbles were inevitable. Dr. Anderman and the councilmen went to work trying their best to settle these disputes and establish some order. But clearly Dr. Anderman was discouraged, realizing Twardon would probably not stop here.

"We are in trouble," he told my brother Leibush, "because Twardon lied to us twice, once when he sent the people to Rzeszow, and the second time when he ordered us into the ghetto. If someone lies to me twice I won't believe him the third time. Now I have to deal not only with a murderer and a sadist but a liar as well."

Twardon himself entered the ghetto the next day to check on the progress made. He saw Dr. Anderman and the councilmen scurrying around, attempting to put a roof over everyone's head, even exchanging quarters when people were dissatisfied. Twardon stopped Dr. Anderman and inquired if he had yet picked an apartment for himself since, as president, he rated the best place. Dr. Anderman replied that he would only when all the others had a place to live. Twardon walked away without a word.

Later the same day Twardon returned with some of his henchmen and arrested twenty-six Jews, including most of the councilmen. Everyone looked to Dr. Anderman to arrange for them to be freed, but the following day he himself was arrested, a severe blow to us all. The community mourned deeply the loss of their leader, a man who had been like a father to them, who had fought so bravely in their behalf. They were left frightened and helpless. A delegation from the Polish community even went to Twardon requesting his release, testifying about how honest and trustworthy a person he was, respected by Jews and Poles alike. "This is precisely why I had him arrested," Twardon replied. "He is too honest for my liking."

Dr. Anderman was later sent to Auschwitz. He never returned.

Part Four

THE GHETTO—STANISLAWOW

Chapter 17

Listening to you, Naftali, it strikes me that one of our greatest sources of strength as Jews, namely our family ties, became our greatest source of weakness during those horrible years. You ran back to Kolbuszowa, back to slave labor, because of your sense of family loyalty, not only to Rozia, but to your family and community. I had many opportunities to escape Stanislawow, but always I held back because of family ties. How many thousands of Jews would have survived the war if it had not been for family loyalty? We will, of course, never know.

When the Germans took my mother, with 30,000 other Jews, to the cemetery that Hoshana Rabba, and slaughtered nearly half of them, it was not a sudden arbitrary act. It was all part of a satanic scheme of extermination worked out in advance. In your town they expelled part of the Jewish population and put the rest into the ghetto. In mine, they went one better: First they killed as many as they could during that Black Sunday, then they created a ghetto and drove the survivors into it.

I lived in that ghetto for about a year before I escaped. It's not easy for me to recreate life there. I can scarcely believe I made it through that experience, or that I am sitting here now, able to tell you about it.

What kept us going? Hope? We clung to straws. My father firmly believed that soon the Americans would enter the war, the Germans would be defeated, and we would be liberated. Our consuming desire was therefore to live one more day, then another, then another, until we would be set free.

My parents, you may remember, had anticipated the move into the ghetto, and had secured an apartment there. As it turned out, the apartment was not included in the ghetto area, and we had to look for other quarters. Luckily my mother's stepsister, my Aunt Clara, lived in what was now designated the official ghetto, and she invited my father and me to move in with her.

I don't have to tell you what it was like living in the crowded conditions of the ghetto. In Stanislawow the Germans assigned ten Jews to a room, a regulation enforced by regular inspections. Use was made of every square inch of living space because shipments of Jews from the surrounding towns and villages continued. At one point the population in the ghetto reached almost 100,000. Privacy became impossible. Food grew scarce, and cash savings vanished, as did gold and other items, such as clothes, which could be bartered for food. It was not long before most everyone was reduced to the level of a starved animal obsessed with self-preservation.

But there was no shortage of self-sacrifice—that of parents toward children, and children toward parents, of individuals toward strangers and in behalf of the community. Take the case of my Aunt Clara. She lived in a two-room apartment with her husband and four grown children. Not only did she agree to take us in, but she looked after me as if I were her own child. I slept with my cousins, while my father slept on the kitchen floor with Aunt Clara and Uncle David. Each of us had his own labor card, and thus a measure of independence, but Aunt Clara at the center of things saw to it that we became a close-knit family.

My father began to regain some of his old self-confidence. Taking advantage of his many contacts with the Polish and Ukrainian population which dated back before the war, when he had served as assistant director of the Polish forestry agency, he began exchanging money and valuables for food, and helped support all of us. His activities restored some sense of self-esteem, and lifted his spirits.

I, myself, had been dismissed from my job with the Gestapo before moving into the ghetto, and I was idle much of the time. Most all the young people were restive and frustrated, often torn between our desire to escape and the reluctance to leave our families. What was the point of staying in the ghetto? Wasn't it obvious we would all be killed? Each time the same answer came back: Now the Germans would leave us alone. Each Aktion was the final one, so spoke our Judenrat. When we pointed out it was an all too familiar story, we were assured that this time, beyond the shadow of a doubt, it was true. In such a way did faith obliterate the facts.

My father and I were lucky, in a way, because both of us had class A labor cards, which meant that we were fit for work. Those with class B or C cards were unfit for work, and their fate was sealed—sooner or later they would be taken away, never to return. Those categories included children, the old, the sick, the handicapped. But soon the class A card no longer made any difference. The Gestapo's sole concern became

killing Jews to fill their quotas. At first we were not
aware of this change in policy, and when word reached
us that the Germans were coming into the ghetto to
round up Jews for summary execution, we did not
bother to go into hiding, as many with class B and C
cards did. We were sitting at home one noontime, my
aunt and uncle and my father and I, trying to keep
warm as we fed the fire sparingly in the large baking
oven in the kitchen, when we heard knocking on the
door and the familiar words, *Alles heraus!* To my astonishment in came Willy Maurer, that young Gestapo
officer who used to enjoy frightening me. His brother
Hans, also in the Gestapo, was with him, along with
two Jewish policemen. The two brothers were overseeing the operation, looking at us in their usual contemptuous manner, thoroughly enjoying the situation.

"All right, everybody out," Willy snapped. He and
his brother started pushing everyone into the yard. So
this is the end, I said to myself. It had to happen
sooner or later. But another voice inside me said No,
not yet. I turned to face the elder Maurer. He looked
at me in surprise, opened his mouth to speak, checked
himself, then pushed me into a room. "Stay here," he
hissed. "Stay here in this room and don't come out!"

As he kept pushing me I kept looking over my
shoulder at my father; he was standing all by himself,
bidding me farewell with his melancholy eyes.

"Wait, don't take him away, he's my father!" I
pleaded.

Willy Maurer stopped and looked back. "Don't try
to trick me," he said angrily, "he's too young to be
your father."

"He *is*, I swear he is!"

"What do you think?" Willy asked his brother Hans.

Willy's brother smiled slyly. "We'll soon find out," he said. He pulled out his rubber club, and looking at me from the corner of his eye began beating my father on his arm and head. I stretched out my arms, trying to shield him, but Willy held me back.

Hans kept beating my father a few more minutes, then stopped, out of breath. "What do you think," Willy asked him.

"It's her father," Hans said.

"All right," Willy said, "let him go."

My father put his arms around my aunt and walked with her in my direction.

"Your mother?" Willy asked.

"Yes, and he is her brother," I said, pointing to my uncle.

"All right," Willy said, "let them go."

After the Maurer brothers left we went inside and watched them through a window overlooking the street. We were still recovering from the shock of what had just happened when we saw Hans Maurer draw his gun and shoot a woman who was walking away from him. At first she tried to crawl away, but then two more shots were heard, and she lay still. We recognized her—she had been our neighbor when we lived on Ulica Sapiezynska. Her name was J. Richter. We stood as though turned to stone, our eyes riveted on the dying woman.

Good fortune had smiled on us this time, but luck was becoming a commodity most scarce in the ghetto. My aunt's oldest daughter, Elona, disappeared one day and, just like my sister Celia, was never again heard from. Elona's brother Jacob was deported to Janovska, a concentration camp near Lvov, where he died of typhus. Uncle David became ill with dysentery.

Since no medical treatment was available, he grew steadily worse, and like so many of the ghetto residents, succumbed.

Hunger and disease stalked the ghetto. Human shadows roamed the streets, begging for food, asking God for mercy, wandering aimlessly, sitting on street corners staring into space, lying down in gutters and dying without making a sound. Each time I recognized one of those walking skeletons I was transfixed by the sight, unwilling and unable to believe my eyes.

Some of my friends from before the war were still with me, though it brought tears when we contrasted our former carefree days together with our present wretched condition. We gave to each other as best we could. Dziunia Lorber, for example, after my mother's death offered to have me take meals with her though I knew she and her family could not have had enough even for themselves. But little as people had, still many were willing to sacrifice for others. Genia, the sister of one of my best friends, Betka Pipper, contracted tuberculosis then refused to eat any food, insisting that she would not recover and that her portion go to others. I spent countless hours with Rivka Rechtschaffen, who after her sister Dushka was taken by the Germans, lapsed into a deep depression, then lost her mind. I was one of the few persons she yet recognized. Holding her hand I tried comforting her, urging her to stay alive. But how much comfort could we provide one another? What could we say to lift our spirits?

The havoc starvation played with human appearances was more than I could bear. Yet there was no way to avoid seeing it; its victims were all around. Puffed eyes and cheeks, blackened skin, boils on the skin which hardened, cracked, and oozed, disfigured faces, bones showing through the skin—and worst of all the expression in people's eyes. They spoke of suffering and fear, of an agony that haunted my waking hours.

The Germans kept raiding the ghetto, entering the houses, deporting hundreds or thousands at a time, loading them onto cattle cars and shipping them off to the death camps. Not on Sundays, however. That day the Germans came with their families to visit the ghetto, as if on an outing to the zoo. They stared at the human shadows and laughed derisively, all the time snapping pictures.

I lived in the ghetto less than a year, unquestionably the longest year of my life. My father was occupied with arranging deals between hungry Jews and Poles with food to sell. Aunt Clara's two surviving children worked in a factory, which left Aunt Clara and myself together much of the time. The days dragged on forever; the nights were endless. I heard stories of suicides; indeed, it was said, poison was fast becoming scarce because of this. My father fortunately was doing well wheeling and dealing, and we had more food than most. Our talk therefore was about staying together, of surviving, not dying.

The chances for survival increased beyond the ghetto but still this outside world was savagely hostile, almost everyone there on the lookout for us. Few Gentiles were willing to hide Jews, and usually only for large sums of money. Real hope came when one obtained false identity papers, and could pass for a Gentile. But few Jews could do this. Physically most were easily distinguishable from the Poles and Ukrainians, whose Slavic features were quite different. Only those resembling Slavs could even begin to think about a change in identity. Further, most Jews did not speak fluent Polish or Ukrainian, which eliminated many

with suitable appearances. My father and I spoke
perfect Polish. While we did not look typically Jewish,
we were not unmistakably Gentile looking either. But
at least we had a chance.

My boyfriend Alek Lamensdorf was now living in
the ghetto, and occasionally he would visit. His father,
Stefan Lamensdorf, had at first been a member of the
Judenrat, but resigned after concluding it simply fur-
thered German plans for our extermination. Others
might have retained the position since it meant more
food and privileges, but Alek's father would not allow
himself to benefit at the expense of his fellow Jews.
Eventually he died of starvation. Alek's mother was
ill, and Alek himself looked far from healthy.

One evening Alek came to visit me. I was shocked at
his changed appearance—all skin and bones. I offered
him some soup left over from supper. He refused,
unwilling to deprive us of our meager supplies, but I
insisted. After he had gulped it down, we went into the
hall, where we could be alone, and sat down next to
each other. We did not talk much—what could we talk
about other than suffering? The less we spoke the
better.

"How is your mother, Alek?" I finally said.

"Not too well."

"Have you decided whether you are going to stay,
or try and get away?"

"I can't get away now, I have to look after my mother.
Besides, I would have to put some flesh on my bones.
The way I look one could easily guess where I came
from."

"I would like to escape with my father."

"Easier said than done," Alek said, shrugging his
shoulders. "Incidentally, someone gave me the I.D.

paper of a Ukrainian girl, about your age. Would you like to have it?"

"Why don't you sell it? You could get a lot of money for it."

"I would like you to have it."

"And what about my father?"

"We'll have to work something out for him."

"I don't think it will work. I speak very little Ukrainian."

"Well, it's a thought."

"Alek?"

"Yes?"

"What are you thinking about?"

"Nothing."

"Tell me."

"I am wondering whether I wish to go on living."

"You wouldn't take your life, would you?"

"My life is mine, Manya. If I decide to do away with it, I will."

He spoke calmly, as if talking about the weather. He didn't really care if he were alive or dead. He was sick—the worst sickness of all—the weakening of the will to live. Or was it I who was sick, determined as I was to go on living?

When he got up to leave, I walked with him to the door and put my arms around his neck and held him close. I wanted to cry, but tears would not come.

Chapter 18

We had developed an elaborate system in the ghetto for uncovering German plans. To survive one had to keep a step ahead of them. The most important bit of information was the date of the next Aktion, the periodic police raid to round up and execute Jews for the death camps. We found out about these plans through the Jewish police or through Ukrainian or Polish police who had been bribed. Whenever an Aktion was to take place, everyone promptly hid. This might work once or twice, but the Germans were as ingenious finding people as the hunted were discovering new places; sooner or later one's luck ran out.

At home with Aunt Clara one day we heard a raid was about to take place in our neighborhood. My aunt's son and daughter were at the factory, and my father was also away at work. It was much safer to be working during a raid than to be at home or on the street. My aunt was very agitated. "We must do something," she kept saying, wringing her hands, "we can't stay here another moment. To stay is certain death."

"Where can we go?" I asked.

"Anywhere, anywhere is safer than here."

"I have an idea. Why don't we hide inside the baking oven? We can pile up wood in the opening and hide behind it. The Germans will never suspect there would be someone there."

"My aunt did not like the idea. Instead, she suggested we go to her daughter's factory and stay there until the raid was over.

"How can we stay there?" I asked. "We don't work there; the foreman will turn us in.

"We can bribe him," she insisted.

"It's still not safe."

"There was no point in arguing with her. She had made up her mind, and prepared to leave. Living in the shadow of death made all of us superstitious. We lived by hunches and omens; when we got a strong feeling nothing could talk us out of it. For Aunt Clara safety lay in the factory; for me it was the oven. She wrapped a shawl around her shoulders and gave me one last pleading look.

"You go ahead," I said. "I'll stay here."

I walked to the door with her; we embraced each other. As she drew back, she held my arms and looked into my eyes, shaking her head. I looked at her, and suddenly saw my mother, holding my arms that terrible Sunday and begging me to come to the basement with her. "Manya, my sweet little girl," she said, "I am never going to see you again." She embraced me again, covering my face with kisses, letting out a cry of pain like a wounded animal. "Oh Manya, why, why? What did we do to deserve this?"

My heart was numb. I held her face in my hands. "Please Aunt Clara, stay here."

No, Manya, you come with me."

"I wish I could believe that you are doing the right thing. But I can't."

"Well, so this is it. Goodbye, my dear. Good luck."

As soon as my aunt left I began to remove the neatly piled pieces of wood from beneath the oven, until I had an opening big enough to crawl through. I eased myself into the opening, feet first, and began putting the wood back in its place. It was hard work, and I was soon bathed in perspiration. I had to stop from time to time to catch my breath. I was putting the last pieces in place when I heard shouts and commotion—the raid was on. I held my breath and listened. The noise outside intensified, grew closer.

My hiding place was hot and suffocating. As I lay there curled up tightly I suddenly felt a sharp pain in my back. The pain was so intense (probably a torn muscle, I thought) that I had to bite my lip to keep from screaming. Then there was a knock on the door. Another knock, then the sound of someone kicking it in. A crash, then footsteps. They were searching the apartment.

"*Los, niemand ist hier*, let's go, no one is here," one of the Germans was telling his companion.

The other grunted in agreement, and they left. It was quiet again in the house, but outside the commotion continued. How long I lay there I couldn't tell, but when I crawled out it was growing dark. My body ached all over; but what matter—I was still alive!

I was lying in bed when my father and my cousin came back from work. My father rushed over to embrace me, so relieved that I had not been taken away. Then I told him that Aunt Clara, not feeling safe in the house, had gone to the factory. When she failed to return we decided to check with a neighbor whose daughter worked in the same factory. When we arrived and saw others there as well, all speaking in hushed voices, we knew at once the news was bad. The Germans had raided the entire ghetto, and also the places of work, including the factory where my aunt went to hide. Jews had been rounded up by the thousands. Someone remarked on how senseless it was to deport workers contributing to the German war effort along

with those who were old and sick—but clearly the
Germans were intent on our extermination, no matter
what the cost to their war effort. There was now no safe
place for any Jew.

And so, as she had predicted, this was the last I saw
of Aunt Clara, who had been like a mother to me, and
of my cousin, whom I loved as a sister. Local Jews had
been rounded up, along with those who had been sent
to Stanislawow from Hungary. All were now on their
way to the death camps.

Chapter 19

It was summertime now. Life in the ghetto was even more unbearable. Dead bodies were lying in the streets; it took days before they were taken away for burial: the stench of death was everywhere. My father and I were constantly talking about plans for escape, waiting for the right moment, the opportune time. These right moments never seemed to come; but then something happened which forced us into action.

It started this way. A young Jew named Yuzek was beaten by a Ukrainian policeman for some reason that was never made clear. Yuzek resisted, wrestled the rifle away from the policeman and beat him into unconsciousness. Then he ran away and went into hiding. The Germans, worried this might be the beginning of a general uprising, decided to move quickly. They summoned Mordecai Goldstein, the president of the Judenrat, and ordered him to apprehend Yuzek within twenty-four hours. But after twenty-four hours there was no sign of Yuzek. It was a hot August day, when Krueger, still Gestapo chief, rode into the ghetto on his white horse, surrounded by a heavy guard. He immediately summoned Goldstein, all the other Councilmen, and the entire Jewish police force. Krueger dismounted and walked over to Goldstein.

"Where is he?" he demanded.

"I don't know," Goldstein replied.

Krueger struck him across the face with his riding crop. "You are lying!" he shouted.

Goldstein did not move.

"I'll give you another chance," Krueger said. "I assume your life is dear to you, so here is what you will do. You will make up a list of 100 Jews, and you and your Jewish police will be responsible for rounding them up and delivering them to me personally right on this spot by tomorrow at this time. Is that clear?"

"Whom shall I put on the list?" Goldstein asked.

"I leave that up to you."

"I am sorry, I am not God, and I am not going to make such decisions of life and death. If you want to do it, then that's your business."

Krueger looked at the council president in disbelief. His face hardened with fury; he turned to the second in command. "Put the entire council and all the Jewish police under arrest!" His assistant clicked his heels. The Ukrainian police who were with him seized the councilmen, awaiting further orders from Krueger.

"I need some rope," Krueger said, pointing to Goldstein. "Get me fifty yards of rope." Goldstein was led away. An hour or so later he was back with the rope. In the meantime the Gestapo had singled out every tenth Jewish policeman and put them aside in one group. The rope was cut into sections; the lamp posts in the street were rigged into gallows. Goldstein and the councilmen, their hands tied behind their backs, were led to the gallows and hanged. Goldstein was the first to be hanged—his rope snapped, he fell to the ground, and was immediately shot in the head. Later more rope was obtained, and the group of Jewish policemen were hanged. One of the policemen had luck with him; the rope tore, he fell to the ground and was able to run away. (He managed to find refuge in a nearby village, and survived the war.) But as a result another policeman was taken and put in his place. The hangings went on into the next day. About 100 Jews were hanged, their bodies left there dangling for a week.

The shock of the hangings was indescribable. I remember walking down the street and recognizing one of the victims. He had been a friend, a young dentist, who had been drafted into the Jewish police. As a policeman he could have taken bribes and obtained food, but he refused to exploit his position, and he went hungry. His frail body swayed at the end of the rope, his lips swollen and blue, flies buzzing in his open eyes. I thought I would faint. Again and again I would recognize someone. Most of the victims were young, people like myself. I was unable to eat. I sat in the house for hours, motionless. I had to run away.

So it was during that week that my father and I decided we could not delay our escape. We knew that we had to plan carefully. We had to be sure of a place to stay outside the ghetto for a long period of time. Yet we did not have time to secure such a place. We had to take a chance.

My father knew a Ukrainian peasant family in a small village outside of Stanislawow who, for a substantial sum, would keep us for a month. We would, we thought, use that time to find yet another place to hide. The first problem was to get through the inspection point at the ghetto gate, but this could be accomplished with a small bribe. Then we had to sew paper money and coins into our clothes. My father dressed himself in as many clothes as he could without looking conspicuous, and we left the house for the main gate.

The gate was heavily guarded, which was a bad sign; presumably the police were expecting people to try to escape after the hangings. There were German, Ukrainian, and Jewish police standing at the gate. My father gave me an anxious look.

"You stay here. I'll go to the checkpoint and take care of them, then you will join me."

I waited. I waited a long time. I didn't know whether I should go away or stay, but I decided to wait. My father finally came back. He was white.

"What's the matter?" I asked.

"Come, let's hurry back." He walked quickly back towards our house. I was hardly able to keep up with him.

"They took everything away," he said after we were back in the house. "Everything, all the extra clothes and all the money, about two thousand dollars."

"How did they know we were running away?"

"I don't know. They suspected something, and they started to search me. They told me to give them everything, or they would turn me in. I'm lucky I was able to get away alive."

"Don't despair, Papa, it's only money. I still have some. We can try again."

"I have an idea. We can both get jobs at the railroad. The work isn't pleasant, cleaning railroad cars and toilets, but we'll come in contact with Gentiles and we may be able to find a place where we can stay for a long period of time. We would be working outside the ghetto, in a place where many people come and go. I think it's our best bet."

Three days later, after bribing a member of the new Judenrat, we started to work at the railroad. We were now part of the slave labor force of men and women who were lined up each morning and marched to the main railroad station under the watchful eyes of Ukrainian policemen. There we were given a pail and scrub brush, and made to spend hours on our knees cleaning the station floor and the railroad cars. Soon, as my father had predicted, we had made contact with a number of Poles and Ukrainians, and had several offers of hiding places. Of course these all had to be checked out, no easy matter. Most wished to hide me alone. All these we refused. We needed to find a way of getting on the train—strictly off limits to Jews—and once aboard, avoiding discovery. In the meantime we had to elude future roundups, such as we had narrowly escaped a short time before. We planned that if one of us were caught and sent away, he or she would try to escape and send some sign to the other. If three weeks passed without a sign, then the other would set off on his own.

We had been working for the railroad about a month when I took ill one day and could not go to work. A high fever made me weak and listless. Since no medical help was available, my father decided to lock me in the house and go to work by himself. It was the first day of Rosh Hashana,[1] but public services were out of the question. I was lying in bed when I heard a sudden noise and commotion. The din grew progressively louder. I thought at first I was becoming delirious, but soon I could distinguish shouts, curses, cries, gunshots, explosions. Another raid was underway. My immediate response was to hide under the oven again. I began to remove the wood from the opening, but I was weaker than I had realized; it would not budge. Somehow I summoned the strength and was able to remove enough of the wood to crawl inside the oven, and then replace it to conceal me. I lay there, exhausted mentally and physically. Again the police knocked, forced the door

---

[1] A Jewish holiday, the first day of the Jewish year.

open, and stormed into the apartment. I waited until they left, gave myself plenty of time before attempting to crawl out. As I was about to I heard someone outside shout, "You can come out already, the raid is over." I suspected a trick, and sure enough I found out later, it was a German policeman, trying to lure Jews out of hiding.

My father did not come home that night, which did not upset me, because workers who returned to the ghetto after dark were not admitted through the gates and had to wait outside until the following morning. But that night pandemonium prevailed in the ghetto. The raid had been the most brutal to date. The streets were strewn with corpses and rubble. The Germans, I was told, had fired indiscriminately in all directions, had hurled gas grenades into halls and doorways, had beaten people to death, thrown babies out of windows, shot children in front of their parents, slashed open pregnant women's bellies and pulled out their unborn babies. The entire ghetto was one aching, bleeding, mutilated body, writhing in agony.

At daybreak I got dressed and prepared to search out my father. My fever had subsided during the night, and I felt better. I rushed to the gate and was let out, but I could not find the railroad workers. I comforted myself with the notion that they must have been taken to work already, but my anxiety was mounting. An old Polish woman, whom I had often seen scavenging outside the ghetto gate, gave me a searching look. I asked her if she had seen the railroad workers. No, she said, she hadn't seen them; but she had overheard a Ukrainian policeman tell his friend last night that after they came back from work they had been picked up at the gate and put on the train with the other Jews who had been rounded up. "Why do you look so worried?" she asked.

"My father was among them," I said.

"Don't worry, they sent them off to a labor camp, Maidanek, I think. They'll be better off there than in the ghetto, that's for sure."

She kept on talking, but I was no longer listening. These so-called "labor camps" were in fact extermination centers, from which no victim left alive. My father and I had agreed that if we should be put on one of these trains, we would do our utmost to escape. But what was the likelihood of escaping from locked and guarded boxcars? The awful reality was that my father was gone. Here I was all alone in the world, a young girl, living among condemned people, facing a relentless enemy and God knows what unspeakable trials before the ultimate outcome: death. My thoughts drifted back to the time the Germans had first come to Stanislawow, when a Pole had snatched my pocketbook in the middle of a crowd which turned away, did not help. I had then determined to be strong, to remain steadfast. But now again I felt so alone, so frightened, so vulnerable. I summoned my strength and reported to work at the railroad.

I would stay on the job for three weeks, and wait for a sign from my father. If none came, I would try to escape.

Chapter 20

Winter was about to set in. The first snow came early, and it turned bitter cold. Many people in the ghetto, weakened by starvation and disease, and with firewood exhausted, simply froze to death. I was no longer seeing much of Alek. His father had died of starvation; his mother was extremely ill. His sister was being sheltered by a peasant family, but Alek refused to leave his mother. When I saw him for the last time he was like a skeleton. Even if he wanted to escape, it was no longer possible.[1]

On the day it snowed, I was searching for wood for the kitchen oven, but could find none in the apartment. Then I remembered an old table we had brought with us when we had first moved in with Aunt Clara. It was left in a shed in the back yard. I had never chopped wood before, but now had no choice. With a small hatchet I swung at one of the table legs, but missed. Instead I hit my own leg, producing a deep wound in my calf. With medical treatment out of the question I

---

[1] Only one relative of mine still survived, Aunt Clara's oldest son. He was being hidden by a German cobbler for whom he had once worked. This old man had taught my cousin how to make arches for shoes, and he had done such excellent work that the man had taken a genuine liking to him, and had offered to harbor him in his house.

tore up my blouse, tied the wound best I could, and limped back into the house. I ignited some wooden utensils, made a small fire, and tried to keep warm.

The next day I went to work, but was terrified that my wound would get infected, dashing any hope. Utterly dejected, I felt the end was near. A lucky break was the last thing I expected.

That very day I met the man who would turn out to be my savior. His name was Edmund Abrahamovitch, but everyone called him Mundek. He came from a tiny sect of Jews, the Karaites. This sect had broken away from the mainstream of Rabbinic Judaism in the eighth century. Followers refused to accept the authority of the Talmud or of any oral tradition, adhering only to a strict interpretation of the Bible, the written law. Only two towns in Poland had a Karaite community: Troki, near Wilno in northern Poland, and Halitz in southern Poland, not far from Stanislawow. In Halitz, the German authorities decided that the Karaites were, in reality, Turks, not Jews, and left them alone. Mundek lived in Halitz with his mother. He was a mechanic and a carpenter, and came every day to Stanislawow, where he was in charge of repairing railroad cars. Since his labor card did not have "Jew" stamped on it, he could come and go as he pleased.

I had been working all morning sweeping floors; but gradually my leg became more and more numb; in time I could not move it at all. I limped toward the door, using my broom as a crutch, and went outside. Jews were not permitted to sit on the bench, so I leaned against the wall, and closed my eyes in response to the throbbing pain in my leg.

"What's wrong?" I heard a pleasant, soothing voice next to me. Opening my eyes, I saw a short, sturdy, brown-haired young man, looking at me through large good-natured green eyes. He was wearing work clothes, and had a toolbox in one hand.

"My leg, it's killing me." I didn't realize how literal a figure of speech had become. I sensed the wound in my leg would be my undoing.

"What's wrong with your leg?"

"I cut it, trying to chop wood."

"Can you walk?"

"Not too well."

He looked at my leg, scratching his head. "I'll tell you what," he said, looking around, "I'm doing some work inside that box car over there. I can tell your supervisor I need you to help me. Once you're inside you can sit down and rest."

"I really don't know if I should," I said.

"You're not afraid of me, are you?" He gave me a disarming smile.

"I guess not." I followed him into the railroad car. He helped me up the short ladder, and had me sit on a bench in the corner, propping up my wounded leg.

"How do you feel, er . . ."

"Manya Petranker."

"Edmund Abrahamovitch, at your service."

"Abrahamovitch?"

"Yes, I know it's a Jewish name; I'm not exactly Jewish, I'm a Karaite."

I remembered reading about the Karaites in Hebrew School and how once excommunicated by the rabbinic courts they had become a separate, isolated sect, clinging to its beliefs against great odds.

"You must be from Halitz."

"Yes, I am," he confirmed.

"Thank you for helping me out. I feel much better."

I saw Mundek every day at the station, and we became quite friendly. Sometimes, when no one was looking, he would slip me a radish or a piece of bread or a hardboiled egg. Then one day he told me he wanted to help me escape from the ghetto.

"Why do you want to help me? I don't have any money, and you would be risking your life doing it."

"I like you very much," he said, "and I don't want you to die. You could come to Halitz and stay with my mother. I'll get papers for you, and you can pass as a Pole. Once the war is over, and if both of us are alive, perhaps you would become my wife."

I thanked him, but told him I would have to think about it.

"Some Jews here know me. I can give you some names and you can inquire about me."

He gave me the name of a man who had been my father's friend. I went to him that very night and inquired about Mundek. He knew him quite well, he said, and he was an honest man. I should, he advised me, accept his offer. Mundek, he added, had already helped several Jewish girls escape from the ghetto, had obtained false papers for them and had relocated them in Lvov where they were masquerading as Catholics.

That night I lay in bed and for several hours thought only about this. Might I be raising Mundek's hopes too high? I doubted I would want to marry him. But how could I repay him? He was a very nice person, but should I wait for another chance?

I couldn't make up my mind. I kept putting Mundek off, until he told me a few days later that the Germans were planning another raid and that my life was in grave danger. He urged me to stay at the station that night and take the train with him to Halitz the next day. I could no longer postpone my decision. I told Mundek I would do as he said.

Mundek then bribed the stationmaster, so that he could work overtime that night, and I could remain at the station. He had, I found out, persuaded the station-master that he wanted to make love to me, an explana-tion the stationmaster found perfectly reasonable. Mundek bought me a ticket for the train leaving at 5 o'clock in the afternoon. I was, he reminded me, to dispose of my armband before getting on the train. Surprisingly the time passed quickly that night and the following day. At ten minutes to five I heard the train entering the station. I asked Mundek not to sit next to me. If I got caught I did not want him im-plicated. I went outside, took off my armband, and threw it on the track. It was, I later realized, a foolish and careless act. What if someone had seen me do it and notified the police? I boarded the train and took the first seat I found. Others were getting on, bundled in winter coats and shawls. Among them were some workers I recognized, and who recognized me, nodding their heads. I tried smiling at them but my lips would not move. With their hands they signaled me not to worry; they would say nothing.

Once the train started up, the ticket inspector ar-rived to punch tickets. He was halfway down the aisle when two policemen, one Ukrainian and the other German, suddenly appeared and began checking papers. But I had no documents! My heart began pounding. What was I to do? Should I tell them my fiance had my papers, and have them take me to Mundek in the next car? No, it wasn't fair to put him in jeopardy. If I got caught, I would deal with it alone.

The German train policeman did the checking, while the Ukrainian followed behind him. He ap-parently knew a lot of the passengers and waved at them not to bother taking out their papers. When he reached me I pretended to fumble in my pocket as though looking for mine. The German sat down next to me; my heart sank.

"Where are you heading?" he asked in a jovial voice.

"Halitz."

"Business or pleasure?"

What was he up to? "Family business," I said, expecting the worst.

"Have a nice evening," he said, and got up and moved on. Had Mundek bribed him, or was I plain lucky? I never found out.

I arrived in Halitz with no further problems, followed Mundek through the sleepy streets to his home, and met his mother at the door. She was a tall, stern looking woman, with suspicious eyes and drooping lines at the corners of her mouth. I greeted her as I came in, but instead of responding, she turned to her son and said in a gruff voice, "Who did you bring me this time, Mundek?"

"This is Manya Petranker. Manya, meet my mother."

"I am pleased to know you, Mrs. Abrahamovitch," I said. "How long is she staying?" she asked her son, completely ignoring me.

"I don't know, Mother. Till I get her some papers, I guess. She could no longer stay in Stanislawow."

"So what concern is it of mine?"

"Mrs. Abrahamovitch," I said, trying to get her attention, "I'll go back to Stanislawow on the first train tomorrow."

"You'll do no such thing," Mundek said emphatically. Turning to his mother he said, "She won't be staying here any longer than is necessary, Mother. But if she goes back now the Germans will kill her, and her blood will be on our heads. Doesn't the Torah say, 'Thou shall not stand indly by thy neighbor's blood'?"

His mother made no reply. She went into the kitchen to prepare supper for her son.

I stayed at Mundek's house, knowing I was not a welcome guest to his mother, but telling myself I could not afford to be proud. Mundek was right—I was lucky to be out of the ghetto, and my one concern was to survive.

Mundek would go to work each day, and I had to stay home with his mother, who hardly spoke to me. I tried to be of help around the house, but she always rebuffed me. She never offered me any food, and when Mundek became aware of this he decided I would have my meals with him. Food was scarce, and few people ate more than one meal a day. I would wait for Mundek every day until he came home from work, and we would eat together.

Eventually Mundek realized that my staying at his home was not the best arrangement. He then placed me with a Ukrainian peasant woman who lived with her daughter outside Halitz. She agreed to take me for a certain amount of money, which Mundek paid out of his own pocket, since I had left Stanislawow penniless. I stayed with her a week, but it was a living nightmare. The woman's daughter had two boyfriends, both in the Ukrainian militia. Each time one of them came to visit I had to run up into the attic and hide in the hay until he left. At night the attic was freezing. Mundek came to visit me each evening. I told him finally that I would like to obtain false papers, come out of hiding, and try to pass as a Pole.

Mundek spoke to a Polish friend whom he knew well and who could obtain false papers. He had contacts with a scrap metal company, and he would see to it that I got papers certifying that I worked for that company. After three weeks Mundek gave me the good news that it was all arranged, except for my name. I would have to invent one; also a date of birth, place of birth, and a few other details. Since I had a little difficulty pronouncing the Polish letter "R" like a native Pole, I chose a name without an "R" in it. For my first name I chose Felicia, which means "good luck" in Latin; and for my last, Milaszewska, the name of my favorite Polish female author. I kept my own birth date, which meant one less fact to confuse. The next day Mundek presented me with my new document, and I became Felicia Milaszewska, a Gentile, Polish girl, ready to begin a new life.

One night soon after, Mundek came to see me. "Sit down," he said. "I've found out what happened to your father. I've been waiting for the right time to tell you."

From his manner it was plain the news was bad. He told me he had met a girl who had related to him her escape from the train headed for the death camp at Belzec. They were all—men, women, children—packed into a cattle car, with hardly room to breathe. She told him how my father, with the help of a few other men, without tools, with his bare hands had been able to remove two boards from the floor of the car and had let himself out through this gap, landing between the wheels of the moving train. The only other person who dared follow him was this girl. My father had bruised both knees rather badly, but the two of them were able to limp, under cover of darkness, to the house of a peasant woman who lived on the outskirts of Halitz. The woman's husband was away in the Russian army, and she needed extra hands, and so was glad to have my father stay. He stayed for three weeks, always trying to find a way to contact me, unaware of course that I too was in Halitz. After the three weeks he decided to try to get back to Stanislawow, and boarded the train. But he was recognized by a Pole, an architect from Stanislawow, a friend of my father before the war, who called for the train police. My father was arrested, taken to Rudolf's Mill in Stanislawow, and executed there.

After Mundek finished relating this to me, I sat quietly, blankly, my heart nearly bursting. Such a ghastly trick of fate—my father free, within walking distance from where I was staying, and neither of us dreaming that the other might be so close.

My father lost his life trying to save mine. I lay on the bed, totally drained, empty; no tears, no feelings, only emptiness.

Part Five

THE GHETTO—KOLBUSZOWA

Chapter 21

Yes, Manya, I understand. They took away every-thing. They even took away our tears and sorrow. They stripped us of every human feeling, but not our will to live.

We had become a doomed people. Against such overwhelming power, what could one do? Great coun-tries with large armies were powerless to stop them. We, unarmed, unorganized, what could we do?

The only thing that we could do was escape, get away, hide, and try to stay alive. That is what my brother Leibush and I eventually did. We obtained false papers and, disguised as Poles, we did survive. If I had an advantage it was my Slavic appearance and fluent Polish. As for Leibush, his Polish was far from perfect, but he had other assets, not the least of which was his great physical stamina.

Leibush was much older than I. When the war started he was in his mid-thirties, married, the father of three children. Leibush was the kind of older brother every boy would want. No one would dare start up with him; his physical prowess was known in all the surrounding towns and villages. His name became synonymous with unusual strength, and stories circulated about his exploits. In reality, Leibush was a quiet, unassuming man, who led a simple and sedate life. He had grown up during the first World War, and had missed out on most of the formal education he would have otherwise acquired. This was a pity, because he had a prodigious memory, and could have become an exceptional scholar. Instead, assisted by my father, he entered the business world, and became a hard-working storekeeper. Each Sabbath he would join the rest of the family at our parents' table, and after the meal would take his wife and children for a stroll through the park. This and work was the fixed pattern of his life before the war; he hardly ever deviated from it. Needless to say, when the Germans came, everything changed.

When the Germans organized the first Judenrat, Dr. Anderman, its President, sought out councilmen who would serve the community honestly and effectively. Among those chosen was my brother Leibush and, as I have told you, my brother-in-law Shaya David. When Twardon came to rule our town, he abolished the Judenrat and threw all its members in jail. The rest of my family including Shaya David was deported to Rzeszow. To help free my brother and to bring my family back to Kolbuszowa became uppermost in my mind.

Along with Chancia, his wife, and his three children I visited Leibush every evening. We would stand outside the cellar window of the jail and wait for him to show up. When he saw us he would put his hands through the bars and kiss his wife's hands, then ask for news of the children and of the ghetto.

"Tell me the latest trick of the little one," he urged his wife regarding his three-and-a-half-year-old nephew.

Chancia sighed. "Henoch was playing with his friend, the one who lived next to the police station. His friend was pretending to be a German policeman. *'Ich bin Hafen-*

bier,' (Hafenbier was a German policeman known for his cruelty) he said, pointing a pretend-gun at him. *'Du bist Jude?*— You're a Jew?' Henoch said *'Ja.'* So his friend went 'Poof, poof, *So wie du bist Jude bist du todt*— since you are a Jew you are dead.'"

"The children know what is going on," said Leibush, "you can't fool them. Speaking about policemen, this man Schmucker owes me a favor. Why don't you speak to him, maybe he'll be able to get me out."

When the German police first came to our town, one of their sergeants, a man named Schmucker, immediately began terrorizing the town. Tall and powerfully built, he walked the streets accompanied by a German Shepherd dog, and at night would knock randomly on any door and beat up the first Jew he encountered. Then he would help himself to whatever in the house struck his fancy. Schmucker did these things without authority from his superiors, but no one dared to complain.

One night Schmucker came into Leibush's apartment, and told Leibush to take him to the basement, where his store was located. "It's too dark here, light some candles," he ordered. Leibush lit some candles. The German looked at him, sizing him up.

"I am told that you are the strongest man in Kolbuszowa. Is that true?"

"I am sure that there are others stronger than I."

"You're modest, aren't you?" Leibush knew he was up to no good, and made no reply. "You see that work table over there; how much would you say it weighs?"

"I don't know," Leibush answered, "but it must be quite heavy."

"Can you lift it up by yourself?"

"I never tried."

"Try."

The table was a huge slab of oak on four huge legs. Leibush rolled up his sleeves and lifted up the table as though it were hollow. He put it down and waited to see what Schmucker would do next.

"You can't be all that strong," Schmucker said. "You must have used some trickery; you Jews are a bunch of weaklings and cowards, all of you."

With that, he grabbed a long pole, about three inches in diameter, and started to beat Leibush. He beat him all over his body until he collapsed on the floor. Schmucker then poured a bucket of water on his head to revive him, and beat him some more, until he was too tired to lift the pole. Three days later he stopped again at Leibush's store and was surprised to see him waiting on customers. "Come over here," he ordered my brother, pointing with his thumb to a corner of the store. Leibush was afraid he was going to be beaten again, but it was senseless to refuse, so he obeyed.

"I thought I had put you out of commission for at least a month," the German said with a grin.

"I can't afford not to work."

"Listen, I like your kind of Jew. Tell me, have you any coffee?"

Coffee beans were worth their weight in gold; the Germans were addicted to fresh brewed coffee.

"I think I can get some."

"Good. You get me some coffee beans every week, and if you happen to be in trouble, you let me know and I'll help you out."

Now, a year later, we hoped Schmucker would make good his promise. My sister-in-law did get to him, and he agreed to intervene.

Two weeks went by; Leibush was not released. But in the meantime, many Jews who had been sent to Rzeszow returned, including my family, thanks to substantial bribes. It was a tremendous relief to have them back, especially once we found living quarters (in Leibush's house) in the ghetto. All our attention now focused on freeing Leibush, as well as Dr. Anderman and the other councilmen. But to no avail. Ominous rumors circulated that they would be sent away. Chancia again spoke to Schmucker, who promised once more to help, though we no longer believed him.

Then one day without warning, Schmucker arrived at the jail with a list of three prisoners who were to be set free, by order of Twardon. The three were Herzl Landau, Moishe Landau, and Leibush. Herzl Landau was a local Jew who had moved to Germany for a time, but had returned when Hitler came into power. He had brought back with him the most beautiful furniture. Schmucker, on one of his night visits, had taken a liking to the furniture, and had it transferred to his apartment. As happened with Leibush, he promised Herzl that he would help if he ever got into trouble. Moishe Landau was also on the list simply because Schmucker couldn't remember which "Landau" had owned the furniture, and so in his confusion had requested release for both.

The three men, having run to see their families, wasted no time, but headed over to the police station to thank Schmucker, and to beg for the release of the others. But it was not to be. The next day all were transferred to the jail at Rzeszow. Afterwards they were sent to a place familiar to hardly anyone then, though later all the world would know of Auschwitz. All the families of the prisoners in the next several weeks received telegrams notifying them of the death of their loved one in prison. Each telegram listed a different cause of death—cancer, tuberculosis, a heart attack. Each widow was required to sign a statement for the

Gestapo, affirming that her husband had indeed suffered from the disease stated in the telegram. Why the
Germans went through this fiendish formality I could
never figure out. One further indignity: Each family
had to bear the cost of cremation.

Chapter 22

We were all joyfully united now; my parents back from Rzeszow, Leibush out of jail. We lived close by each other. My unmarried sisters, Rachel and Matil, and I lived with our parents, in Leibush's house, and three married sisters and their families crowded into a three-room ramshackle apartment down the block. We prayed for better days but no one could say from where help could come.

It was now two years since the outbreak of the war. Once again, as we had done on that fateful Friday, we all (including Rozia) gathered around my parents' table for the traditional Sabbath meal. But now the meals were austere, the festivity of former times gone. Yet the very fact that we were together, young and old, lifted our spirits, and we sang the Sabbath songs with a fervor long absent. My mother, as she had often done, remarked on just how lucky she was to have given birth to nine children and to have had all of them survive and remain healthy. How many other women, she noted sadly, had been so fortunate?

Our guest this particular Friday was one of the most respected scholars of our town, a cousin and close friend of my father, whom we knew as Rabbi Saul Saleschütz. He was a man of great learning, and had he not been so modest a person could easily have served as a rabbi.

He was the dean of our Talmud Torah,[1] and was commonly addressed as Rabbi Saul. Sitting at opposite ends of the table the two of them, with their long gray and white beards, their deep-set eyes and bushy eyebrows, resembled Biblical patriarchs presiding over their households. Taking turns they led us in the traditional chants and songs. In this way we managed for a brief period to forget our fears and become once again the grateful people, children of our Heavenly Father.

After the meal, Rabbi Saul offered prayerful thanks to God for the release of Leibush and for the family's safe return from Rzeszow. He prayed that we might all remain united after Hitler, may he burn in Hell, was defeated.

"Many thanks, Saul," said my father, in response to his prayer. He paused and started to breathe heavily; I could tell that something was bothering my father. There was anguish in his eyes.

"Tell me, Saul," my father went on, "I consider you a learned and truly righteous man, a real Tsadik.[2] Granted, we cannot question the Almighty; his ways are kept from us. But we still have to ask ourselves, what is going to become of us, what is going to become of our people? The sword has been unsheathed, yes, and many will die. But if the Germans kill all of us, and none remain alive, what will become of the holy Torah, the holy Sabbath, and all the commandments—will they die too; is that possible?"

All our eyes were riveted on our father. We looked at him in amazement—we had never heard him question the ways of the Almighty, even by inference. Nor

---

[1] A school for Hebrew and Jewish studies.
[2] A holy man.

could we imagine what Rabbi Saul's reaction would be. Rabbi Saul cleared his throat to speak. His eyes looked sadly at my father, who looked away from him—I think he was sorry that he had spoken those words.

"You are right to ask these questions, Itche," Rabbi Saul began. "Without the Torah the world cannot exist. The Torah can exist without the world, but the world cannot exist without the Torah. Now the Holy One, Blessed be He, wants the world to exist, as he told Noah, and he will not permit the destruction of his people Israel, as he promised Jacob. 'A thousand may fall on your right, and ten thousand on your left, but you will not be harmed.' Unfortunately, Evil is powerful, and many of us will fall. But in the end Evil will lose. The Germans, may they burn in hell, are already spread too thin. They will lose this war; the only question is how soon. In the meantime they will kill many of us, but they will not be able to kill the Torah no matter how hard they try. The Torah is the word of God and is stronger than any human power. Now the real question is not whether we will survive as a people; we will. The real question is how will the Gentiles be able to expiate their guilt for what they are doing, not only the Germans, but the Poles, the Ukrainians, and all the other nations which stood idly by our bleeding. And how will those of us who survive be able to live in the same world with people so full of guilt. For as long as the guilt weighs on them, we will suffer, too. And so it will go on for a long time after we are gone."

At the time I didn't understand much of what he said, but what impressed me was his unconditional faith in God and vision of the future. Even I, the skeptic, was uplifted by his words. It was, I believe, the last Sabbath that the whole family would be together, as in the days before the war.

There was no relief from the endless burden of decrees, restrictions, harassments and deprivations. Still, I was luckier than most. First, I was young and strong. Second, I knew most of the Poles in town and in the surrounding areas. Third, I was able to come and go in and out of the ghetto at almost any time. I had Dr. Anderman to thank for that privilege. He knew of my experience traveling and buying for my father's business, and he respected my ability. While he was still President of the Judenrat he had arranged with the Germans for me to go to Rzeszow and other towns to buy supplies, mostly flour and potatoes, for the ghetto. (The Judenrat supervised the baking and distribution of bread. In addition, it organized a soup kitchen, which served for many as their only source of nourishment.) After the Judenrat had been deported, Twardon established a second one, with Pashek Rapaport as President. He reinstated me in my old job of shuttling between Kolbuszowa and Rzeszow, on a horse-drawn wagon loaded with flour, potatoes, beets and whatever else was available. I should also add that after Dr. Anderman's deportation I inherited his instruments, bandages, ointments and other medications. With these items I performed just such services as I could to the Jews in the ghetto. I received an official title and an identification pass as a Health Official (*"Gesundheitdienst"*). Soon I started an illegal business to supplement our meager rations. After buying the allotted quantity of flour, I would also buy additional flour on the black market, as well as other forbidden provisions, such as sugar, salt and sometimes meat. These I would sell in the ghetto. I was, I knew, risking my life doing this, but it also meant relieving hunger in the ghetto and providing additional food for my family.

Removing my armband and taking advantage of my Slavic appearance, I would often leave the ghetto after curfew hours and head off to neighboring villages to buy food and supplies from the peasants. These were the same peasants I might need if I ran away. Building friendships with them was possible, though risky. It was becoming painfully obvious that despite some exceptions the Jews could count on no one other than themselves. Few Gentiles cared whether we lived or died; most were eager to be rid of us. Our homes, our clothes, our possessions would then be theirs.

I remember going to Rzeszow during that time and stopping to see a certain Mrs. Kirschner, whom I had visited many months earier. Her husband, Oscar, had left for America shortly before the war; she and her two young children were trapped in Rzeszow. My oldest brother, who lived in America, had sent us a letter in which he wrote of Mr. Kirschner's desire to give his wife fifty kisses. This was a code which meant that he had given my brother fifty dollars, and wanted us to give his wife the equivalent in zlotys. My father charged me with delivering the money on one of my trips to Rzeszow. After attending to my official business, I went to see Mrs. Kirschner. She was a beautiful, proud looking woman, who lived in a stately house with two adorable children dressed like little princes. How, I wondered, would she be able to manage by herself during the war? Some time later we received another letter from my brother in America, (via a friend in Switzerland) again asking us to give Mrs. Kirschner "fifty kisses."

By now all the Jews in Rzeszow had been moved into the ghetto there, and I had difficulty finding her. I will never forget the scene which greeted me when finally I discovered her living now in a cellar. This once beautiful and proud woman had become a skeleton. On her hung a velvet dress which at one time must have been the height of fashion, but which now draped loosely like a rag on a scarecrow. Once my eyes got used to the darkness, I saw in a corner of the room her two children, lying on a heap of tatters, their bellies swollen, their eyes wide and shiny as if with the last flicker of light, like candles about to go out. In a pot on a makeshift stove I could see a few potato peels floating in bubbling water. She kept feeding this water with a long spoon to her children, who were too weak to sit up, and who craned their necks and opened their dark, parched mouths like hungry baby birds in a nest. So choked with emotion was I that I couldn't speak. I handed her the money and left. I never saw her again.

When I got back to Kolbuszowa, I asked to join my father at the daily minyan,[3] which met secretly in the basement at the home of Elimelech Wakspress, in defiance of the ban on public assembly or prayer. I had long stopped attending religious services, but that night I felt the need to be together with fellow Jews who refused to knuckle under, who continued to hold on to their faith. One by one they began to gather. I met one of my old friends, Noah, the Hasid who once before told me the only commandment now was to survive. I was glad to see him, and he greeted me warmly.

"What brings you here, Naftali?" he asked.

"I'm not sure. What about you?"

"I'm not sure either."

We still needed two men. We had to wait.

---

[3] A gathering of ten or more men for prayer.

"Have you heard what happened to Kalman Kern-weiss?" Noah asked me.

Kalman was one of my closest friends. I hadn't seen him in weeks. He was one of the most brilliant young men in Kolbuszowa, and also one of its most colorful characters. He came from a nearby village, from a poor and simple family. Yet at an early age he showed enormous talent, and he was accepted at the Lublin Yeshiva, one of the most prestigious in all Poland and perhaps in the world. But soon he began dabbling in secular studies—something strictly forbidden by the Yeshiva—and he was expelled. His great dream in life was to emigrate to America. He taught himself English, and mastered it in an incredibly short time. Just before the war, he wrote Eleanor Roosevelt, asking for her help so that he could come to live in America. To everyone's amazement, she answered him, promising to help. The letter was his prized possession; he carried it with him always as a good luck charm. Then the war broke out, and Kalman's dream, like those of the rest of us, evaporated. Kalman then came to live in Kolbuszowa, where he became known as "The English Tutor." I was one of his students, and soon we became good friends. He asked us to call him Charlie, the name he was going to use when he got to America.

"What happened to Charlie?" I asked Noah.

He chuckled. "You think you've heard everything? You haven't. Listen to this. Our friend Charlie was working in the police station yesterday, when the German commandant told him to go into a certain cell and clean it. In that cell they had locked up a woman whom they suspected of being Jewish, but who claimed she was a Catholic Pole. They couldn't disprove her claim, yet they were suspicious, and were holding her. So they decided to send a Jewish worker

into her cell while they eavesdropped through a small
opening, hoping to trap her. So Charlie went into the
cell, and who do you think the woman turned out to
be? His mother! Lucky for her, she never lost her
presence of mind, and she pretended she didn't know
him. They exchanged some pleasantries in Polish, and
Charlie came out of the cell. The commandant asked
him if he thought she might be Jewish, but he said he
was convinced she was a Pole, a peasant woman from
the area. In fact, he remembered seeing her more than
once on a wagon going to market. The Germans took
his word for it, and let her go."

As Noah finished his story, two more men arrived,
and the prayers began. An octogenarian, Avraham
Insel, led the prayers. He was a big, corpulent man
whose voice, unaffected by age, rang out loud and
crisp. Unlike Insel the rest of us were afraid to raise
our voices for fear of being overheard outside. After
the prayers the men, as a way of releasing some of
their rage, discussed how they would dispose of Hitler,
if they could but lay their hands on him. Elimelech
Wachspress would, each and every day, he said, cut
into his flesh with a dull saw. Avraham Insel preferred
inflicting a series of wounds with a knife, then pouring
salt on them. My father proposed building a cage on
wheels such as they have in the circus for lions and
bringing Hitler from town to town where the people
could look at and spit on him. Sadly, none of them
survived the war; Hitler got to them before they could
get him.

ISAK SALESCHUTZ'S Family, September 5, 1934. Bottom row from left, NAFTALI, SHULIM (LEIBUSH'S Son), RACHEL, SHEINDEL (GELA'S Daughter). Middle row from left, AVRUM (ALBERT OR AL), our Mother ESTHER, our Father ISAK, GELA, Her Husband RUBIN WEINSTEIN.
Top row from left, MATLA, SHAJA DAVID LISCHE, (MALCIA'S Husband), MALCIA, DAVID. (DAVID'S photo was inserted because he was in Palestine), CHANCIA, (LEIBUSH'S Wife), LEIBUSH, LIBA.

ISAK and ESTHER SALESCHUTZ, Kolbuszowa, September 5, 1934. (Naftali's Parents.)

NAFTALI'S First photo ever taken in 1925. From left,
RACHEL, DAVID, NAFTALI.

NAFTALI and GELA SALESCHUTZ.
My father's parents. He was called NAFTALI DIBISER.
He lived in a Village called "DUBAS", 5 Kilometers from
Kolbuszowa. I am named after him.

The PETRANKER Family in Stanislawow in 1937. From left AMALIE, FRYDA (Mother), MENASHE (Adopted Brother), CYLIA, DAVID (Father), PEPKA.

LEIBUSH

My youngest sister RACHEL in Ghetto with the Armband.

The PETRANKER Family when they lived on the NIEMIECKA KOLONIA, (German Colony). From left CYLIA, PEPKA, AMALIE, 2nd row — their father DAVID, Mother FRYDA. Picture taken 1930 in Stanislawow.

CYLIA — 1938.

BLIMCIA, my sister Malchia's daughter, HENOCH, my sister Liba's son. Both were killed in Belzec death camp, in July 1942. Both were 3½ years old. I took this picture in Kolbuszowa Ghetto on August 17, 1941.

Pepka, Amalie's sister, before she left for Palestine in 1939.

Dr. Bruce J. Dezube, Esther Cylia Salsitz Dezube, Dustin,
Aaron, and Michael. Picture taken 1990.

Naftali (Norman) Yeshiva Student. Naftali seated on right.

NAFTALI'S friends, who belonged to the same Zionist Organization, before the war (HANOAR HATZIONI). They took this picture with the arm bands with the Star of David which the Germans ordered them to wear. Photo was taken in 1940. NAFTALI is standing in the middle.

ROZIA SUSSKIND, 12 years old, 1934. ROZIA is 2nd from right.

NAFTALI and ROZIA, 1941 Kolbuszowa.

The DZIKIWER RABBI, ALTER HOROWITZ, to whose YESHIVA, NAFTALI attended in 1935. Rabbi with grey beard, 2nd from left.

STANISLAWOW, Jewish Gimnazjum in workshop class.
AMALIE is in first row, fourth from left. Above her is her sister
Pepka standing.

STANISLAWOW 1937 — sitting is PEPKA, standing from left
AMALIE, CIPORA JUDENFREUND, BETKA PIPPER.

AMALIE as FELICIA MILASZEWSKA, when she met
TADEUSZ ZALESKI (NAFTALI). January 19, 1945 in Cracow.

NAFTALI as TADEUSZ ZALESKI when he met FELICIA
MILASZEWSKA (AMALIE). January 19, 1945 in Cracow.

Cleaning the roads of snow outside KOLBUSZOWA, Picture was taken on March 9, 1940. NAFTALI with the shovel on his shoulder is to the right of the two German soldiers.

Same as above. NAFTALI is second from left.

Unloading trains filled with coal. NAFTALI fourth from left.

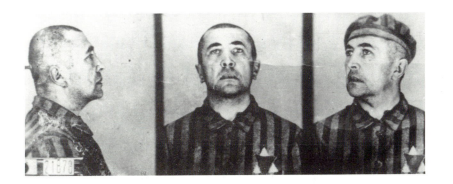

Dr. LEON ANDERMAN in Auchwitz, where he was killed, end of 1941. Mug shots Auchwitz — 1941. His prisoner's number 21878.

DR. LEON ANDERMAN, 1st Obman of the Judenrat in Kolbuszowa. When he built his new house in 1938.

PASHEK RAPPAPORT, 2nd Obman of the Judenrat in
Kolbuszowa, 1st row, 1st on left.
JOSEL RAPPAPORT (PASHEK'S Brother), the Commandant
of the Ordnungsdient in Kolbuszowa. Middle row, in the middle with the beret.

2 Jewish Hostages hanged in the first days of occupation,
early September 1939.

The Kolbuszower Rabbi, JECHIEL TEITELBAUM. Picture was taken in April 1942 in the Ghetto. The Germans forced him to put on Tallis and Tefilin. He had to pose while they photographed him. A week later the Gestapo came into the Ghetto and killed 22 Jews. My father was among them. The Rabbi was on the list but he hid. He was killed in the first akcja in the RZESZOW Ghetto UMSCHLAG PLAC, on July 7, 1942. (22 in the month of Tamuz, Hebrew Calendar). On this day, 12,000 Jews were transported to the Belzec Death Camp.

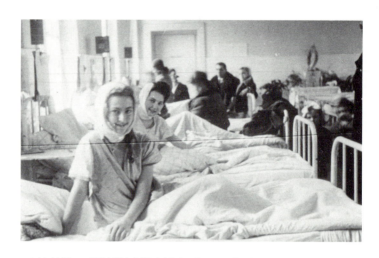

AMALIE as FELICIA MILASZEWSKA in Crakow Hospital,
December 1942. Next to her is KAZIA PILAT.

EDMUND ABRAHAMOWICZ "MUNDEK", who took AMALIE
out of the Ghetto.

ALEK LAMENSDORF, 1939 (AMALIE'S boyfriend).

FELICIA'S Picture in the dress with the red rose, which she
wore when she met DR. HANS FRANK the Governor
General of Poland.

LYBA LEIBOWICZ and JOZEK HODOR.

STASHKA HODOR.

BALTIC SEA

LITHUANIA

VILNA

GERMANY

DANZIG

POMORZE

POZNAN

Poznan•

GERMANY

NOWOGRODEK

•Rakow
•Wsielub •Mir
•Nowogrodek
•Nowopelnia
Zdzieciol•
Slonim•

UNION OF SOVIET
SOCIALIST
REPUBLICS

•Vilna

•Kaunas

•Suwalki

•Kolno

BIALYSTOK

•Grodno
Krynki•
•Bialystok
•Zabludow

•Piaski

Ciechanowiec•

POLESIE

•Luminiec
•Kozangrodek

•Pinsk

•Kamien Koszyrski

•Horodec
•Brzesc nad Bugiem

Pruzana• Malecz•

WOLYN

Dabrowica•

•Luck

•Dubno

•Wisniowiec Nowy

TARNOPOL
•Tarnopol
Chorostkow•

STANISLAWOW

RUMANIA

Goworowo•
Wegrow•

LUBLIN

Losice•
Miedzyrzec•
•Zelchow
Kurow•
•Lublin
Chelm•

Kowel•

Wlodzimierzec•

•Lwow

LWOW

Rozan•
Wyszkow•
Kaluszyn•

Warsaw•
Otwock•
Karczew•
Warka•

WARSAW

Nowy Dwor•
Kutno•
Zyrardow•

•Torun

Biezun•

•Kolo

•Lodz

LODZ

Piotrkow Trybunalski•
Wieruszow• Belchatow•
Zloczew•

Czestochowa•

Katowice•

SLASK

Kozienice•
Radom•
•Kielce
Ostrowiec•
Opatow•

KIELCE

Chmielnik•
Szydlow•
•Miechow

Belzin•

•Krakow
Oswiecim•
CRACOW

Tarnow•

Nowy Sacz•

Frampol•
Bilgoraj•
•Tarnogrod
•Lezajsk
Kolbuszowa•
Rzeszow•
Strzyzow•
Przemysl•
Sanok•

CZECHOSLOVAKIA

HUNGARY

POLAND (1921–1938)
•Provincial capitals

Map of Poland.

Ceiling of the Kolbuszower Synangogue. The first Synangogue was built in 1761. It burned down twice and was twice
rebuilt.

Kolbuszowa "Coat of Arms—Adopted 1785", A friendly
handshake between a Pole and a Jew. On the top a white
polish eagle, crusaders cross, star of David. Colors—White
and red for Poland, White and blue for the Jews. This hung
outside of the City Hall.

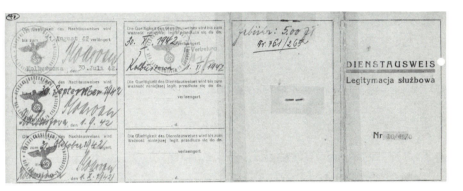

Traveling pass (Norman)

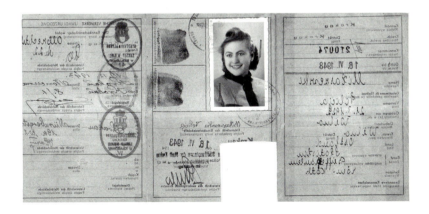

AMALIE'S KENNKARTE as FELICIA MILASZEWSKA, Roman Catholic.

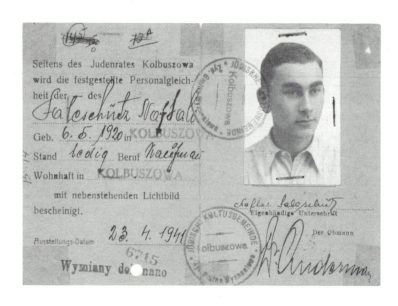

Labor karte (Norman)

Seitens des Judenrates Kolbuszowa
wird die festgestellte Personalgleich-
heit der — des

Falcschütz Naftali

Geb. 6. 5. 1920 in KOLBUSZOWA
Stand *ledig* Beruf *Naehmai*

Wohnhaft in KOLBUSZOWA

mit nebenstehenden Lichtbild
bescheinigt.

23. 4. 1941

Ausstellungs-Datum

6715

Wymiany do...nano

Eigenhändige Unterschrift

Der Obmann

Diecezja *Tarnow*
Kościół parafialny
PARAFIA RZYM.-KAT.
w *Werynia*
36-100 KOLBUSZOWA

ŚWIADECTWO CHRZTU

(Testimonium baptismi)

Dioecesis _____
Ecclesia paroecialis

św. *Maksymilian*
w *Werynia*   L. 26/87

s. _____
in _____

1. Rok i numer księgi chrztów   *1918 s. II Lp. 11*
   (Annus et numerus libri baptizatorum)

2. Imię i nazwisko   *Tadeusz Jan Jadach*
   (Nomen, cognomen)

3. Imię ojca   *Michał*   wyznanie *rzym.-kat.*
   (Nomen patris)   (religio)

4. Imię matki   *Janina* z domu *Kulawska*   wyznanie *rzym. kat.*
   (Nomen matris)   (nata)   (religio)

5. Miejsce i dzień urodzenia   *Werynia 4. IV. 1918 r.*
   (Locus nativitatis et dies nativitatis)

6. Data i miejsce chrztu   *22. IV. 1918 r. Kolbuszowa*
   (Dies et locus baptismi)

7. Uwagi w księdze chrztów — kan. 470 § 2, 1988 _____
   (Adnotationes in libro bapt.)

Zgodność z księgą chrztów stwierdzam
Concordat cum libro baptizatorum

Werynia dnia *12 czerwca* 19__
         (die)

PARAFIA RZYM.-KAT.
Werynia
(L. S.)

Ks. *Stanisław Wójcik*
(Proboszcz — Parochus)

D. P P-A. 36/77. 150.000. U-12/33

NAFTALI'S Birthday certificate as TADEUSZ JAN JADACH,
Roman Catholic. I received a copy on June 12, 1987.

NORMAN and AMALIE today.

Chapter 23

Winter was setting in again. Shortly before dawn as the first snow of the year fell, I was awakened by Leibush, who told me that Twardon had ordered the Jews in the ghetto to clear the snow from the roads around Kolbuszowa. A group of able-bodied men was assembled, half asleep, and marched out of the ghetto, to the accompaniment of Twardon's riding crop.

Twardon's clean-shaven scalp was glistening and red with perspiration. His beady eyes bulged as he grunted and bellowed. Surprisingly, he moved about with an agility that belied his rotund shape. I found out that the reason for his terrible mood was that his car had been stuck in the snow six kilometers from his home, and he had had to make his way home on foot.

Leibush picked me and three other men to rescue the car, a large sedan used by high-ranking German officials. Leibush directed the four of us to lift the front end of the car, while he went to the back, and by himself started to lift the back end.

Suddenly Twardon turned on Leibush and struck him in the head with his rifle. There was a cracking sound; the wooden gunstock split in two, and Leibush collapsed. We hurried to the back of the car to find out what happened. Leibush was sitting in the snow, rubbing his head. Twardon was standing next to him, turning his rifle in his hands, shaking his head.

"You broke my rifle," Twardon said to Leibush. "Your head must be made of steel. You're a lucky man, Saleschutz; I would shoot you now if my rifle weren't broken."

"What did I do?" Leibush asked. "I was only trying to get your car out of the snow."

"The way you were picking it up, you could have broken my bumper. Next time be more careful."

One night, having returned from Rzeszow, I suddenly felt weak and dizzy, and had to lie down. In the morning I passed blood, and had a high fever. A severe episode of dysentery was raging in Rzeszow at that time, and it was obvious I had caught the disease. My father and I were worried that I might be a carrier of this epidemic to Kolbuszowa. After brief deliberation, he decided to hide me in the attic and keep my illness a secret from the community. Medical attention was out of the question; there were no Jewish doctors, and a Polish physicians would report me to the Germans, who would probably shoot me. To minimize exposure and the possible spread of the disease, it was decided that my sister Rachel would be the only one who would take care of me. We also decided that Rozia was not permitted to visit me in the attic.

Rachel was at my side for three weeks. She nursed me like a mother, with utmost patience and devotion. Rachel was at my side for three weeks. She nursed me like a mother, with utmost patience and devotion. With such careful attention, I began to recover. Just as I was regaining my strength I awoke one morning with an excruciating pain in my ear, by far the worst I had ever experienced. Rachel applied warm oil to my ear, but the pain continued unabated. Each day my condition worsened. My suffering was too great to wait any longer (it had already been four weeks)—so my parents decided to put me on a sled and have me taken to a doctor in Rzeszow.

Two of my sisters, together with Leibush, took me to the ghetto in Rzeszow, where I was seen by a Dr. Heller. He examined me and decided that I had a middle ear infection. My condition, he said, was very serious. My ear was full of pus; the infection had already reached the lining of my brain. He recommended immediate surgery. Since there was no Jewish hospital in Rzeszow, my only hope was the Jewish Hospital in Cracow.

But to get to Cracow one had to take a train, and for that we needed a special permit, which Leibush fortunately was able to obtain, but only after traveling back to Kolbuszowa and returning incredibly that same night! (We also had to pay the Jewish police who in turn bribed the Polish and German police before we were able to leave the ghetto.) We took the first train to Cracow. No Jews traveled on trains in those days. The passengers were mostly peasants illegally bringing their produce to the city to take advantage of black market prices. Seeing the three of us get on the train, they moved away, afraid we might attract the attention of the German train police and that they might be caught. So we sat by ourselves until a young Pole passed, noticed our armbands, and gave us a hateful look. Moving on to the back of the coach, he began talking to a group of peasants huddled together. He had, I could hear him tell them, just returned from Germany.

"I was doing construction work there. You should see how everything there is so sparkling clean and beautiful. You know why? Because in Germany they've gotten rid of all the Jews. We should do the same thing here, and we should certainly not allow Jews to ride the trains."

Stirred up, the group approached us and insisted that we get off. My sister Rachel pleaded with them.

"How can we get off when the train is running?"

"Jump off."

"This boy is very sick; we're taking him to the hospital. He needs an urgent operation."

"Operation my foot. Get off the train, all of you, or we'll throw you off."

They started dragging us out of our seats, until one, who had remained quiet, now spoke up. "Leave them be, the train will soon stop, and we'll be rid of them." The others agreed to wait until the next stop.

A few minutes later the train did stop, and one of the Poles came into the coach with two German train policemen. They asked for our papers. Rachel showed them our travel permits, while we waited breathlessly as they inspected them.

"Where are you going?" one of them asked.

"To Cracow."

By now the train had started. "Let's go," he said to his companion. The Pole looked on incredulously. "Aren't you going to kick them off the train?" he asked in broken German. "In Germany Jews aren't allowed on trains."

"You're quite right," the policeman told him, "but they have proper papers, and we have to let them stay."

Returning at that moment were the Poles who had just harassed us, dragging another Jewish passenger.

"We demand that all these Jews be thrown off the train," one of the Poles said, pointing to us and their captive. I recognized this Jew as someone from Kolbuszowa, whom Twardon had allowed to travel to Tarnow.

The German policemen looked at each other. "You people are right," one of them said. "Jews have no business on our trains. You'll have to get off at the next stop."

But the Poles paid no attention. Rather than release the Jew they dragged him to the door and threw him off the moving train while the policemen looked on. Appeased by this violent act they then backed away, decided not to molest us further.

There was no going on. The next stop was Tarnow, a large town halfway between Kolbuszowa and Cracow. We were desperate. I could hardly stand on my feet. But luck was with us because we had a cousin living in Tarnow, actually not far from the railroad station. My sisters put my arms over their shoulders and dragged me to her house. Despite its large Jewish population (over 30,000) the Germans had not as yet established a ghetto in Tarnow. Jews lived in their own houses and were still free to move about. Better yet, Tarnow still had a Jewish hospital, and on its staff was Dr. David Rabinowicz (nicknamed "Golden Hands"), formerly Chief Surgeon of one of the largest hospitals in Lodz.

It was about two o'clock when I arrived at his office but then almost immediately I lost consciousness. Dr. Rabinowicz decided right then to operate, but as he informed my sisters, he was not hopeful. The membrane over the brain was already infected. Even if I survived the operation, I might, he warned, be blind, or deaf, or partly paralyzed, or even mentally dulled. "Recite Psalms," Rabinowicz said. "I'm going to need all the help I can get. This boy is 90 percent in the next world."

At four o'clock I was wheeled into the operating room, and didn't emerge until midnight—eight hours later. The next morning when I awoke and opened my eyes, my sisters were smiling. The worst was over, they said; I was going to live. My whole head was bandaged; I was still in great pain. But the thought that I had been so near death and had escaped with my life was exhilarating.

"You're a lucky boy," Dr. Rabinowicz told me several weeks later while I remained in Tarnow to recuperate. "You're regaining your hearing. You'll be as good as new."

I thanked him again. "Can I ask you a question, Doctor?" Is it safe for you in Tarnow?"

"Is it safe anywhere these days?"

"If for any reason you have to leave Tarnow, as I understood you left Lodz, please feel free to stay with us. I know a lot of Poles in Kolbuszowa, and we can always get food."

Dr. Rabinowicz's eyes moistened. He shook my hand and said he would be happy to do so if the need arose.

It never did. Sometime later we found out a certain Pole needed emergency surgery and was brought to him for the operation. But the Germans had decreed that a Jewish doctor could not operate on Gentiles. Rabinowicz knew this, but given the urgency of the situation he agreed to proceed. The Germans found out, informed by the brother-in-law of the Polish patient. Dragging him out of the hospital, they shot him in the yard outside.

Chapter 24

Early in April of 1942, I came back to Kolbuszowa but there was grim irony in my return. Here I had faced death in the operation, experienced a remarkable recovery, but now found myself back among the doomed.

The stench of death was everywhere. People were dying of starvation, others were being shot for seeking out a morsel of bread. The chief executioner in our town was Twardon, always on the lookout for someone he could himself kill. A week before Passover I witnessed him murder Itchele Trompeter, one of the best liked young men in our town. Itchele had married a girl from Rzeszow, and went to live there shortly before the war. He used to commute to Kolbuszowa to see his parents, who helped him out with food. That day he was going home with some food, when Twardon spotted him. He stopped the wagon to see if Itchele had smuggled anything forbidden. He found a pound of butter, shot Itchele on the spot, and ordered the wagon driver to take his body back to Kolbuszowa. That night the entire ghetto cried.

On Passover eve four Gestapo men came to the neighboring town of Glogow and dragged the four most distinguished leaders of the Jewish community from their homes. Among them was the Rabbi of

Glogow, Rabbi Elazar, a famous scholar and a grandson of the legendary Alter Rebbe of Kolbuszowa and
also Rabbi Mendele Rubin, the dayan of Kolbuszowa,
the head of the Rabbinical Court. All four were old
men with gray beards. The Germans tortured them all
day in public, making them crawl and lick their boots,
and humiliating them in countless grotesque ways.
One German set fire to the Rabbi's beard while another
took a picture of him lighting his cigarette from the
fire. Toward the evening they were ordered to climb
telephone poles. After struggling for a time they were
shot one by one.

Passover, the festival of freedom, was not celebrated
in Kolbuszowa. No matzos were baked, no one recited
the story of the Exodus of Jewish slaves from Egypt.
Hitler was approaching his fifty-third birthday, and
rumor had it that the Nazi party had promised him a
birthday present—a half million dead Jews. Each town
had to deliver its quota of victims. One German
policeman in our town, we called him Morris, (for
that's what he called every Jew) dedicated himself to
the task, cutting a notch in his rifle stock each time he
killed a Jew. His ambition was to have fifty-three
notches in time for Hitler's birthday. He did not fall
short. The rifle containing fifty-three notches he sent
directly to Hitler. In return he received a medal, and
a letter of commendation, praising him for his devotion to a noble cause.

Each day new demands were made, each more severe
than the day before. Furs, Persian carpets, jewelry and
gold had to be furnished on short notice. Pashek Rapaport, the new President of the Judenrat, was made
personally responsible by Twardon to see to it that
these demands were met. The townspeople would
groan and complain, but in their hearts they knew that

Pashek had no choice. If the demands were not met, Pashek and his councilmen would be shot, along with many other townspeople.

The day after Passover, Pashek summoned fifteen of the community leaders, my father included, to inform them that Twardon considered it a personal embarrassment to have so many Jews with long beards in the town; all beards must now be shaved off. To a pious Jew like my father, shaving was a violation of Biblical law. My father in his entire life had not cut off even one hair of his beard. When the barber came to our house, he sat at the table, mute and somber, his face pale and sagging. After the barber left, my father remained silent a long time. Then, as he got up from the table, he muttered, "Now I have felt the taste of death."

Chapter 25

There was something terribly prophetic about my father's words. I couldn't sleep that night. Something inside of me kept shouting, "No! I can't allow it to happen. I must see to it that it doesn't happen—not to my father." I got out of bed and sat at the table, propping my bandaged head in my hands, wondering what to do. Could I hide him at some peasant's house? Yes, but what about the rest of the family? He would never go into hiding and leave us behind. And to hide them all would be impossible.

"Is that you, Naftali?" I heard my mother's voice. "Is anything bothering you?" I hesitated. "Come here for a moment."

There was a light in the partitioned area which served as the bedroom for my mother and two sisters. My father joined us. I had never seen my father's face shaven; it looked naked and stripped of dignity. I found it difficult to look him in the eye. On the night table stood a yahrzeit glass in which he was collecting bits of paraffin from candle butts, from which he intended to fashion a memorial light for his father, the anniversary of whose death was two weeks off. It had taken him almost a year to fill the glass with paraffin sufficient to burn the required twenty-four hours.

"What's troubling you, son?" my mother asked,

smiling with closed lips to hide her toothless mouth, yet with eyes sparkling with love. I didn't have the courage to speak, but my father nodded to me to speak up.

"It's getting close to the end." I felt a bitter taste in my mouth. "How can we wait helplessly for the end? It's not me, it's you two that I'm worried about."

"We are old, Naftali," my mother said. "We have lived our lives. It's you who have to go on living. You have your life ahead of you."

My father brought out a small package from a hiding place, wrapped in a handkerchief, which he untied, revealing a gold lady's watch on a long chain and a gold cigarette box.

"See this watch? I gave it to your mother when we got married. And she gave me this cigarette box. Twardon has demanded five kilo of gold from Pashek, or else twenty leading Jews of this community will be executed. I would probably be among the twenty. So I am turning in these gold objects, and some gold coins, and we'll see to it that the quota is met. What more can we do?"

"That is the whole point!" I exclaimed. "They strip us of everything! They shear us like sheep. And when there's nothing left, they kill us. You don't really believe they will stop with the gold, do you?"

"I don't know, son. I have to believe, don't I? If I stop believing, then it's all over."

The five kilo quota of gold was met. Twardon did not hide his satisfaction. He informed Pashek that twenty lives had been spared because of the gold. For a few days everyone in the ghetto breathed more easily. But the Germans were not about to be bought off. It was our lives they were after. We decided for that reason to build an underground bunker in the house where my three sisters lived. In case of a raid the men of the family could hide there. It took us a week but we managed to complete it.

About three weeks after Passover, while our family was having lunch at Leibush's house (where we lived at that time) there was a sudden pounding on the door. We knew it was the Germans. We also knew they were after the men, so we quickly bolted the door on the inside, while the men ran out through the back door. There was an outhouse in the back yard, and Matil told my father to hide there; she would put a padlock on the outside, hoping to create the impression that no one was inside. Leibush and I went to a neighbor's house across the yard, and hid in the attic. From this hiding place we had a good view of the street and of the back yard. Two Gestapo men had been at the front door. When they were unable to force it open, one of them went around several houses, where he could enter the back yard through a gate.

By now we could hear shooting and screaming coming from other parts of the ghetto; we knew a raid was on. My sister Matil came into the back yard again. Apparently she thought that my father would be safer somewhere else, and she unlocked the outhouse. Just at this moment the Gestapo man who had come around the back saw them and told them to stop. He then asked my father his name, but he mumbled a different name. By this time the other Gestapo man had forced the door, and had come into the yard dragging a neighbor, Israel Hofert, by his sleeve. He asked Israel to identity my father, which he did. Then he released Israel—apparently his name was not on the list for that day—but both drew their guns and started to push my father into a shed that was used to keep firewood. My sister Matil screamed, and threw herself between my father and the Germans. Then Rachel came out of the house, pleading with them to spare his life. They made no reply.

So this is the moment, Naftali. They are going to kill your father. They are going to kill your father—are you going to sit here and do nothing?

I was paralyzed. I wanted to shout but nothing came out. I wanted to get up but I couldn't. I looked on, as if in a trance. I saw Rachel trying to wrest the gun out of the hand of one of the Germans; he struck her over the head and she fell, bleeding. Matil tried to seize the other man's gun; the first man struck her too. While this man was struggling with my sisters, the other was shoving my father into the shed, where he was no longer in view.

I heard two shots. They were the loudest sounds I had ever heard in my life. They resound in my ears even to this day.

After the shots I heard screaming and shouting, then my father's voice. The two bullets had wounded him, but he was still alive. "Pigs! Executioners!" he screamed. Then *Nekuma! Nekuma! Nemt Nekuma!*—revenge, revenge! Take revenge!" Then he called out the prayer of the Jew in his last moments: *Shema, yisrael, adonai elohenu, adonai echod*—Hear, O Israel, the Lord is our God, the Lord is One." It was in a voice I did not recognize, so loud, so unnatural, almost like the cry of a wild animal. Today, even after almost 50 years have passed, that voice continues to ring in my ears, those almost unearthly sounds haunting me still. The two Gestapo men left the shed after the first two shots but upon hearing the screams of my father returned. Five more shots rang out, then silence.

I had to go down, I told Leibush. He tried to dissuade me, but I insisted. When I got to the shed I saw my father, lying in a pool of blood. His right arm was almost severed from his body. The women and children in the family were there, caressing him and dripping their tears on his body. My little niece, Blimcia, with her curly blonde hair and blue eyes, was crying, not sure of what the commotion was about. I stood there consumed with shame for having been so helpless, for seeing my father murdered, unable to save him, for not even trying. One of the Gestapo men who shot my father, his name was Neuman. He was young, tall, blond and handsome.

Another Gestapo man, attracted by the wailing and crying, arrived, gun drawn. It suddenly occurred to me that with my bandaged head he might think I was on the list to be shot, and having only been wounded would now finish me off. Fortunately a Jewish policeman was with him to explain that my bandage was from a recent operation. The Gestapo man replaced his gun. "In that case," he said, "I want you two to collect the bodies and bury them in the Jewish cemetery."

The Jewish policeman, a sixteen-year old boy named Itchele Silber, told me to come along with him. I remained motionless.

"What's the matter, Naftali, come!"

"It's my father—they killed my father."

"They'll kill us too," he said in his boyish voice, "so let's go."

He was right; this was no time to mourn. We ran over to the house of Avrumche Polimer, who had a wagon and a pair of horses. On the way we heard constant wailing and screaming from the houses. Twenty-two Jews had been executed that afternoon.

Avrumche was not home. His wife told us he had gone over to Mechl Feingold's house with a wagonload of wood. We rushed over to Feingold's house and spotted the wagon full of wood standing in front. Inside we found Feingold lying in bed, dead. Near the door was another man, Naftali Nessel, also dead in a pool of blood. Nessel, who sustained himself by chopping wood, had seen Polimer taking over a load and followed him, hoping to make a zloty by lending a hand. He reached Feingold's house just as the Gestapo came looking for Feingold—he was a member of the Judenrat and on the list for that day—and when they shot Feingold they also shot Nessel.

My companion Itchele went to look for more men to help unload the wood, so we could use the wagon to haul bodies. In the meantime I went towards the house where Rozia lived with her two uncles, to learn if anyone there had been killed. As I crossed the street I saw someone lying a short distance from the boundary of the ghetto. I went to see who it was: it was Mordecai Freifeld, a seventy-year old man, a veteran of the Austrian army, a sturdy man, who worked as a postman; he was covered with blood. Freifeld was still alive. He recognized me, and begged me to save him. As I was trying to figure out what to do, two Gestapo men approached from the other direction. I told Freifeld to pretend to be dead until I was ready to haul him away in the wagon. A moment later the Germans came up and asked me what I was doing there. I told them I had been ordered to pick up the dead; they nodded and went on.

By now Itchele and his helpers had emptied the wagon of wood, and we started to load the corpses on the wagon bed. We hid Freifeld on the bottom and covered him carefully with corpses. Polimer then drove his horses to the cemetery.

I went to see Freifeld's son, who also owned a horse and wagon, and asked for his help. He harnessed his horses, and we rode around the ghetto picking up dead bodies. I left my father for last. My father had a cemetery plot next to his father's grave; I arranged with Leibush to be at the cemetery, so that when we drove past, we could remove our father's body from the wagon and bury him next to his father, instead of in a common grave. It was almost dark when our wagon arrived at the cemetery. When we got to my father's grave, we removed his body and hid it nearby. We then proceeded to dig the mass grave nearby where the victims of the 1919 pogrom had been buried, but exhausted as we were it was little more than a shallow depression. We planned to return the next day to bury the bodies properly.

I staggered home about four in the morning. No one had gone to bed. Everyone's eyes were red from crying, but no one wept any longer. They had cried themselves dry, and were sitting quietly. My mother was a statue of grief, having said not a word. When I put my arms around her, she held my hand with a grip so tight I could not believe her strength. I sat down, tired to the bone, but unable to sleep. At six o'clock I returned to the cemetery.

Before reaching the cemetery I stopped, hardly aware of what I was doing. I leaned against a tree and cried, shuddering and sobbing, pounding my fists against the tree. My father's screams reverberated in my ears: "Revenge! Revenge! Take Revenge!" Considerable time passed before I was calm enough to proceed to the cemetery.

The families of the victims arrived with shrouds and prayer shawls in which to bury their dead. We dressed each body in a shroud, wrapped the prayer shawl around their shoulders, and when the graves had been dug deeper, we lowered the bodies. Into the hand of each victim we placed a knife, an old custom of the region, probably stemming from a folk belief that the dead might need it to avenge their blood. In burying my father, we also placed in his grave the pieces of wood that were soaked with his blood, in accordance with the Biblical injunction to consider the blood as the soul.

As for Mordecai Freifeld, we had placed him the night before at the house of the cemetery caretaker. That very night he was seen by a Jewish doctor, a refugee from Germany who lived in Rzeszow and came to Kolbuszowa now and then to visit his family. He examined Freifeld's wounds, seven in all, dressed them, and left him at the caretaker's house.

The next day, as we were burying the dead, Twardon demanded a list of all the dead and wounded from Pashek. In this way he found that three of them were still alive, including Freifeld. He then sent a Polish doctor, Nickowski, an official of the Gestapo, to examine the wounded. This doctor found the other two, Moshe Landau and Liebele Zuckerbrodt, with head wounds, and ripped their bandages off. They both died later that day. I happened to be at the caretaker's house when Twardon's car came tearing into the driveway. The doctor came out, found Freifeld, and tore off all of his bandages, too. He never said a word. I told someone to bring Freifeld's son with his wagon. Freifeld lay there with his gaping wounds, looking at the ceiling, mumbling. His skin was smooth like a child's—not a wrinkle anywhere.

Suddenly Twardon's car was back in the driveway. But instead of the doctor, a Gestapo policeman stepped out and walked to the house. When he saw Freifeld, he announced he had orders to kill him and pulled out his gun. The wounded man raised his hand and pleaded with him.

"Please, I beg of you, don't shoot me. I served in the Austrian army during the First World War. I was in the cavalry, I saw action for four years, and I wasn't wounded once. Yesterday the Gestapo shot me seven times, and here I am, an old man, still alive. I'm old, but I still want to live. Spare me!"

The policeman did not answer. He took me to a corner of the room and said he would make it easier by killing him with one shot. I asked if we could first take him out into the cemetery. He consented. The caretaker and I carried Freifeld to the grave of the Alte Rebbe, for I felt sure it would be easier for him to die there, at the graveside of one of the most revered rabbis of this region. He was sobbing quietly when the German aimed his gun. I turned away.

I helped carry his warm body, smooth like a child's, to the mass grave. Just as we were about to lower him into the earth, his son, Chaim, came rushing up in his wagon. He got off and ran to have a last look at his father. "I knew it," he said through his tears. "I knew it. I saw a black crow when I left the house. I knew it would end this way."

All of us went back to the ghetto after we had finished our work at the cemetery. When I got home, I took the glass with the paraffin my father had been saving up as a memorial light for his father, whose *jahrzeit* was the next day, the 13th day of the Hebrew month of Yiar. I made a makeshift wick, and lit the candle for both.

Chapter 26

All night long I kept waking up in a sweat, startled, sometimes screaming, breathing heavily: a series of nightmares, one upon the other, kept repeating themselves. In my dreams my father appeared as a giant figure made of stone, brick and wood, wrapped in a gigantic prayer shawl all in tatters, scraps holding his severed right arm in place, and a black prayer book as big as a house on his monumental head. I couldn't tell whether or not he had his beard. His face radiated a blinding light which illuminated his chest and forehead, but his eyes were black and hollow with the darkness of death. He kept murmuring something but I couldn't understand.

At one point I said to him, *"Tateh, m'shnat payes—* Papa, they're cutting off our earlocks." But he just kept on mumbling. In the background were the shots that rang forth when he was murdered. Each one tore at my eardrums, pierced my heart, reverberated in my brain like a swarm of wasps. Each shot echoed inside his gigantic form with a deep muffled echo, like distant thunder from behind mountain peaks. Then the world began to crumble: the hills, mountains, rivers, sky, moon and sun—all melted away. But the radiant figure remained standing through it all, still murmuring something. Suddenly terrible laughter exploded and I awoke.

In another dream the whole world started to burn, an ocean of flames from one horizon to the other. The figure, however, was still standing there, unscorched, still murmuring. Now the fire was gone and the world had turned into a barren wasteland. The figure was now hovering in space, ascending upward like Elijah. Now I dreamt I was alone in the cemetery, surrounded by graves. I started to dig. I was digging a grave, but for whom? There was no body there to be buried. Then I realized I was digging the grave for myself. I kept digging until I woke up.

It was almost noon. My sister was in the kitchen stirring the soup. No one spoke. Outside the streets were deserted. Beyond tending to basic concerns no one seemed capable of movement.

Three days after the slaughter the same six Gestapo appeared in Kolbuszowa, prompting a renewed panic. But this time they came not for murder but on "business." They came with a list of special items to be provided, including furs, silk stockings, leather gloves, wool fabric, canaries, and other luxury items which could no more be found in the ghetto than at the North Pole. The Judenrat had to send emissaries to wealthy Poles to buy these items at high prices. They added to the list expenses incurred during the recent slaughter, including even the cost of the bullets! Before nightfall everything was paid for and delivered, and further bloodshed averted.

It was only a momentary respite. The Germans were playing with us as would a vengeful cat with a helpless mouse. We were like condemned men waiting in our cells for the inevitable but not knowing exactly when it will come. I wanted to live, for my father's sake, for my own sake, but mostly I wanted to be present when the tables turned, when the arrogant "all powerful" Germans would be defeated, humbled, brought themselves to ruin.

During the shiva, the week of mourning, Rabbi Saul came to our house to join the minyan for prayers. After the other guests had left, my mother made tea for us.

"Rabbi Saul," my mother said, "the Germans took away the crown of our family. I don't know how I'm going to go on living."

"Esther," he replied, "you should not let yourself succumb to your grief because of your husband's death. If there is another life in heaven, as we believe, then your husband is there with the other Tsadikim—the righteous ones. He is buried next to his father, my uncle Naftali, as I would like to be buried next to my father. Believe me, he is in a better world. On the other hand, if there is nothing there, then what are we? Animals, less than animals. Then, what is the difference if we die today or in ten years? It's better to be dead than to be part of all this."

Chapter 27

With seven days of mourning for my father at an end, each member of our family struggled to carry on. The Judenrat, fearing that all who remained might be deported at any time, attempted to avert what was in effect a death sentence. If people in the ghetto performed vital services for the Germans, it reasoned, they would be less likely to be deported to the concentration camps. So the whole ghetto was mobilized, and a cooperative workshop set up the synagogue. All the local trades were represented, including cobblery, bindery, tailoring, tinsmithing and a shop to make lingerie. Jancze Rapaport, a brother of the Judenrat president, was put in charge of the entire program. All available sewing machines were brought in, and anyone with the slightest knowledge was taught to work. And so men and women, young and old, pedaled or hammered away all day, making clothes and boots for the German soldiers and officials, with no promise of a better future, but with hope. At first it seemed to have the desired effect. A special committee came from the German district office in Rzeszow to inspect the workshops, and afterwards announced that the workers and their families could remain in Kolbuszowa. They even opened an employment office with a German director at the Town

Hall, and Rachel was selected by the Judenrat to be his secretary.

One day the director of the employment office sent Rachel with a message to the Judenrat: All Jews, male and female, from age 12 to 50, were to assemble in the marketplace "for registration." Then Pashek, the President, was told that he must select 200 people for the labor camp at Biesiadka, a village about ten miles away. Amid crying and wailing, 200 people were loaded onto trucks, as those remaining looked on in helpless despair. The trucks rolled away but, inexplicably, returned a short time later to unload their human cargo. No one could understand what happened, but no one dared to question—if it was a miracle, better not to inquire.

It turned out to be not so much a miracle as a last ditch maneuver by my sister Rachel. She offered the director two gold watches to spare these people. He consented, one of the few Germans I encountered who still retained a recognizable streak of humanity.

It was springtime again, the most beautiful time of the year in this part of Poland, the wide fields running to the farthest limits of the horizon, the virgin forests on the other side of the river bursting with new life. I stole out of the ghetto one Sunday with Rozia, taking a back way through the fields, among the peasants I knew and who were friendly to me. We sat next to a brook. I ran my fingers through Rozia's hair; she giggled.

"Why do you laugh?" I asked.

"Oh, nothing."

"Still, you must be thinking of something."

"I'm just happy to be with you, Naftali."

"'Happy'—the word sounds so strange, doesn't it?"

"Yes, it does. But I don't care, right now I'm happy."

"Rozia, why don't you run away and hide? You look so much like a Gentile and your Polish is so good. I could probably get you some false papers, and you could pass for a Pole."

"I don't think I have the courage, Naftali."

"Run away with Rachel. She is planning to do it. She started to make arrangements with a friendly family from Poznan. They agreed to help. I know someone who could help. Look at it this way: your mother is dead, your father and your sister and brother are away in Russia. You're alone, you have no immediate obligations. You could go away disguised as a Polish girl together with Rachel and work for a Polish family I know in one of the larger towns. You would have a much greater chance of surviving than if you stay here. You see, I can't run away, because I have a large family and must stay with them and do the best I can under the circumstances."

Rozia was silent. When I put my arm around her waist I realized she was trembling. I held her tight, resting my head against her hair. She put her arms around me, and buried her face on my chest. We held each other like this for a long time. I started to stroke her hair. She bent her neck back and looked at me with wide eyes.

"Naftali, Naftali, I'm scared. I don't want to die."

My heart twisted inside me; the fields, the sky, the beautiful world around me went black. "No," I echoed, "we don't want to die."

"But who knows if we'll survive?"

"Yes, we will, you have to keep telling yourself that you will."

She did not seem reassured. Nor could I reassure myself. When I walked home with her, I had the feeling we had little time left.

In June, 1942, the Judenrat was ordered by Kreisshauptman Dr. Ehaus, the chief German administrator of our district, to Rzeszow for an important meeting. Eight other councils in our area were similarly summoned. At the appointed time Dr. Ehaus walked in brusquely. Without asking anyone to sit down, he started to speak.

"Good morning, Jews. I am pleased to inform you that you Jews are dirty and full of lice, and you have been spreading contagious diseases throughout this district. Therefore I have decided to levy a special tax on you, which comes to the following amounts: Rzeszow 1,000,000 zlotys, Sokolow 400,000, Blazowa 260,000, Glogow 260,000, Strzyzow 360,000, Tyczyn 200,000, and Kolbuszowa 360,000."[1]

In one week the funds had to be raised. The councilmen were to assemble at the same place with the money in hand. Should any community not fulfill its quota, a proportionate number of its councilmen would be shot. Pashek knew what it would take to raise such a sum, but he was convinced that Ehaus meant what he said. After much quarreling and complaining, the Jews in Kolbuszowa were forced to sell much of their remaining possessions, and the full amount was raised.

Leibush was present when the money was delivered, and told me what took place. Kolbuszowa was the only community which managed its full quota. Rzeszow, for example, was 25 percent short. Ehaus ordered 25 percent of the councilmen to step aside. The same procedure was followed for the other communities. Then all of the condemned men were led to the back yard of the district building, lined up against a wall, and shot.

When this had been done, Ehaus went back to the room where the surviving councilmen were assembled, and read a new decree. All taxes which any Jew owed to

---

[1] At that time a zloty was worth ¼ cent in U.S. money.

the government, covering the twenty-eight years from the first war to the present, must be paid in full. If the debtors were deceased, or had not means of paying, the Judenrat would become responsible for the money. Again, just a week was allowed, and the same punishment was prescribed for failure.

Pashek estimated that the full amount would come to about 200,000 zlotys. He gathered those Jews who still had merchandise hidden away, and black marketeers able to raise respectable sums of money, and ordered them to come up with half that amount. For the other half he would turn to the rest of the Jews in the ghetto, most of whom were already destitute.

Pashek's estimate was far off the mark. The Poles, who recognized an opportunity when they saw it, ledgers, covered with decades of dust from the town hall cellar. They listed taxes going back beyond memory. A detailed itemization was prepared, showing debts by Jews who had been dead a quarter of a century; by Jews who had emigrated years ago; by Jews who had fought with the Austrian army, alongside the Germans, during the first war, and had been killed in action. All these debts now had to be paid by a starved, half dead ghetto community.

In the end the total amounted to 900,000 zlotys, which had to be raised within a week.

Day and night the councilmen ran to each Jew in the ghetto, begging, pleading, entreating to give more to complete the sum. Nobody believed that the money would be raised. When the Judenrat left for Rzeszow they had the 900,000 zlotys for the taxes.

Again only Kolbuszowa had the full amount. From the rest of the towns the proportionate number of their councilmen were shot, while the remaining men had to watch the execution.

Ehaus came back to the same room and read a new

decree: any money owed by a Jew to a Pole must be paid in full within one week. If the Jew was unable to pay, the Judenrat would be responsible for the money. Again a week was allowed and the same punishment was prescribed for failure.

When Pashek with the Judenrat came back with the news, most of the people gave up, saying that this money would be impossible to collect. The Judenrat members also didn't believe the money could be raised. Only Pashek said that he must try, otherwise the Judenrat members would be shot.

The Poles, who recognized an opportunity when they saw it, swooped down on the ghetto like a flock of vultures. Our Polish neighbors were allowed to claim debts with no proof whatsoever. The Poles and the Jews had lived together in Kolbuszowa for generations, as was symbolized by the town seal, which showed hands clasped together, a cross on the top and the Star of David on the bottom. But now these Poles did not hesitate to invent debts to present to the German authorities. One of them, Jan Fryc from Kolbuszowa Gorna, owned a small grocery store, and had bought merchandise from my father before the war. He always owed us money. When the war broke out, he had owed over 1,000 zlotys, which he never paid back. Now he claimed my father owed him 5,000 zlotys. Since I was able to leave the ghetto, I went over to see him. He recognized me but he didn't greet me. When I asked how he had the heart to do such a thing, he yelled, "You'd better get out of here this minute or I'll raise the claim to 10,000."

The total of the claims by the Poles came to 1,100,000 zlotys, which had to be raised again within a week. Pashek exhorted the Jews to make this one last desperate sacrifice. He assured them that this was the final test, that if we passed this test we could hope to survive the war. It was a staggering amount, but if everyone did his utmost, it could be raised. Hardly anyone believed him, but we felt that at least we were buying time. Pashek had to resort this time to threats and even a few beatings. Yet, with only a day to go, the full amount was still not met. Those who had met their quota were now told they had to come up with more. By the end of the day the full amount had been raised, and the councilmen traveled to Rzeszow, their quota met. The scene there was the same as it had been the two previous weeks. Wherever the quota had not been met, a proportionate number of councilmen were shot.

Then Ehaus delivered the worst decree of all: within three days, all the Jews in the district had to leave their homes and resettle in the ghetto in Rzeszow.

Chapter 28

We did not know it at the time, but Rzeszow was the last stop on the way to the death camps. On the other hand we knew we were doomed; everything pointed in that direction, even though in our minds we could not imagine a civilized nation capable of such satanic, un-mitigated barbarity. After all, we were a community of ordinary Jews, content to live and let live, to mind our own business, to threaten no one.

We were barely able to catch our breath from raising the 2,360,000 zlotys when we had to start packing for the trek to Rzeszow. Like the Israelites of the time of Moses, we had to leave in haste; but unlike them there was no promised land. A year earlier our moving into the ghetto had produced a pathetic scene. Now it was worse still. We were going into the unknown, torn away from all that was familiar and to that degree comforting. The sick and the elderly despaired of surviving the change, even the trip itself. When I went to see my old *melamed*, my old Hebrew school teacher, Chaimche Birnbaum, born a cripple, to say goodbye he told me, "Don't wish me a good trip, Naftali, for I know I will be among the first to die today."

My family decided that all except myself would leave for Rzeszow on the first day of the deportation[1] and do their best to get settled there, while I would wait for the third day. In the interval I would take whatever possessions they were forced to leave behind to certain friendly Poles for safekeeping in the event we came back. It was understood that if none of our family survived the war to reclaim these possessions, they would be theirs to keep. Just as my family left[2] we heard shots outside the ghetto. It was not what we imagined, only SS men firing into the air to hurry the Jews along. Meanwhile Polish peasants waited expectantly, in high spirits, knowing that in the confusion they would be able to help themselves to what we left behind.

Rabbi Saul had asked me to help him smuggle the Kolbuszowa rabbi out of the ghetto. The old rabbi had been on the same death list as was my father, but he had been concealed and remained in hiding. He was completely blind, and had to be led by the hand. We cut off

---

[1] The decision to leave on this day (June 25th) was determined largely by a friendly German police officer who made that recommendation to my brother Leibush. If the ghetto area in Rzeszow filled up quickly, he warned, the Gestapo and S.S. might well kill all those yet remaining in Kolbuszowa.

[2] Twardon ordered the Mayor to summon Poles with wagons to be on hand to transport the Jews to Rzeszow. All through the night they assembled on the road leading into the ghetto. They were, Twardon ordered, to be paid by the Jews for their "services" (100 zlotys for a wagon with one horse, 200 for a wagon and two horses. Jews who could not afford these charges were ordered to turn over all their possessions to the Polish drivers.) I picked out four peasants whom I knew to take our entire family. We packed everything we could (excepting the furniture) in burlap bags which we had in abundance, for the trip. The Germans allowed everyone to take as much as they could knowing that once in Rzeszow it would be a simple matter to collect and confiscate all once the Jews had been deported.

his beard, changed his clothes, dressed him like a peasant and led him through a back way to a bend in the road where he was picked up by his family.

Most of the Jews left that first day. The police opened the ghetto gates, shouting, "Schneller, Schneller!— faster, faster!" By afternoon the wagons had been loaded, not with people but with their possessions. The people, regardless of age or health, had to walk on the right side, while the German and Polish police walked on the left. Occasionally a German policeman would allow a child or old person to ride for a time on the wagons, but not the Polish police. They were determined to exceed their German masters in severity toward the Jews. The next day the wagons returned to evacuate most of the remaining population. The ghetto gates remained open; thousands of peasants descended on the houses, removing the last sticks of furniture and whatever else they could find. To give this looting an air of legitimacy, the Germans had posted the Commandant of the Jewish police, Josel Rappaport, at the gate, where he collected a pittance from each peasant for what he took.

The wagons had scarcely gotten underway before a most grievous tragedy occurred. The Germans had ordered all Jews to walk on the right side of their wagons, but for some reason Herzl Landau started off on the left (his wife and 12-year-old son walking parallel to him but on the right side). This "violation" was noticed by Bartelmus, a young Volksdeutch from Bielsko (Poland) who promptly raised his rifle and with one shot killed Landau. But it was as if nothing had happened. The wagons continued to roll on and Landau's wife and son were prevented from going to where he lay on the road. When the wagons had left town Landau's body, clothed in a distinctive gray suit with large blue squares, and on his feet yellowish shoes most modern, was still there. Along with a friend of mine I picked up the body and placed it on a hand wagon and transported it to the Jewish cemetery for burial.[3]

By evening the gates were closed. I had managed to deposit some merchandise with friendly Poles. One agreed to store boxes of coffee beans which belonged to Leibush. So valued were the coffee beans that I considered my life and those of my family more secure because I had access to these beans. One Polish woman, with whom I placed most of the merchandise, was particularly sad to see me go. Her name was Kotulova. Her husband had been a government official before the war, but soon afterwards became ill and died. His widow came to Kolbuszowa and opened a small grocery store to support herself and two children. My father had been friends with her husband, and helped her out by selling merchandise on easy terms, and giving her first choice of scarce items. She was a short, stout, good-natured woman, with a round, pretty face and dark hair. She always wore black, both as a sign of her widowhood and her devotion to her departed husband. She prided herself on her good relations with Jews. When I came to say goodbye, I found her deeply upset about the expulsion of the Jews from our town.

"If only the Poles would realize that the Germans are no less our enemies than yours," she said, shaking her head, "we would all be much better off. We would join your people, and we would fight together. But the Germans are very clever. They succeeded in turning us against the Jews, so we could help them destroy your

---

[3] Some three weeks later I had the occasion to be at the cemetery to bury three other Jews shot after an escape attempt from a nearby labor camp. There I encountered the custodian of the cemetery wearing a gray suit with large blue squares, and unmistakably modern yellowish shoes.

people; then, when they are finished with you, they will turn on us. They will kill many of us, and those that are left will be their slaves. There will be no more Poland. We will become a province of the German Reich, our children will not be permitted a higher education, and the Master Race, to prove their superiority, will keep us ignorant and poor. But our people don't want to see this, so we all have to suffer. May God have mercy on us all." She crossed herself, and with tears in her eyes she seized my hands and said, "Naftali, go in peace, and may God be with you. I hope I will see you again."

I spent the night in the ghetto, sleeping in the same house with the few men who waited to leave on the last day of the evacuation. In the morning I packed my knapsack with provisions for the hike to Rzeszow. Before leaving, I took a stroll around the empty ghetto. It looked like a ghost town. Broken windows, gaping doors, feathers flying through the air with every gust of wind, clouds of dust stirred up—only the ghosts of the many who had lived for generations in these old, tumble-down quarters remained. I walked down the path to the synagogue, which my father and his father and his father's father had trod nearly every day of their lives. The ground was packed tight and hard as rock, as firm as their abiding faith in their Maker. Why had this happened? I looked toward the old synagogue, but no answer came. There was not much time to meditate. The wagons were lining up; someone told me to hurry. Guarded by German and Polish police, we marched to Rzeszow.

The ghetto there was a nightmarish place. Thousands of Jews from surrounding towns and villages had been crammed into the already crowded ghetto; there was no possibility of finding living quarters for all of them. Those, like my family, who had relatives in town somehow found a few square feet for themselves. Others remained in the streets, entire families camping on the sidewalks and in the narrow alleys, packed so close together that it was impossible to cross the street without stepping on someone. Lost children roamed about, looking for their parents; desperate mothers cried for their offspring. Everywhere I turned I was followed by eyes filled with exhaustion and despair.

After much searching, I found my family, now living in the cellar of a relative named Spitz. Everyone was sitting around, at a loss about what to do. I tried to cheer them up, telling them how I had salvaged some valuable merchandise which I left with friendly Poles, but nothing dispelled the gloom. Yet what we experienced was fortunate compared to the experience of other communities. In Sokolow, for example, Twardon, dead drunk, announced he was going to kill thirty Jews, kill them the way Jews koshered their meat, by sprinkling salt on their dead bodies. This way, he shouted, they could enter heaven already kosher. The Jewish police brought him thirty sick and elderly Jews who were already near death, but also several young girls that he insisted upon as well. Twardon personally shot them; after each execution he washed his hands, swigged down some more vodka, and kept shrieking, "Blood! More blood! Give me Jewish blood!" Before he finished his ghastly work forty-nine corpses lay piled up on the ground.

We were all exhausted. After a meager meal we went to sleep. The next day we heard that Twardon was in Rzeszow, looking for a hundred able-bodied men to return to Kolbuszowa to demolish all the buildings in the ghetto. Pashek was to draw up the list. Not too many were willing to go, for they worried about leaving their wives and children alone. Most of the volunteers were single. Leibush and I decided to go back, for we believed we would be able to use our contacts there to obtain food to help feed our family. My sisters accompanied us to the place of assembly. Almost all of the relatives of those who were going back were there to say goodbye, for everyone in his heart suspected this was not an ordinary goodbye. Nothing was said, but everyone felt it: *Who knows whether we will ever see each other again.*

We marched during the night, each with a knapsack on his back. In the morning we reached Kolbuszowa, and were quartered in the synagogue compound, or as it became known—the Kolbuszowa Labor Camp.

Part Six

LABOR CAMP—KOLBUSZOWA

Chapter 29

While we were at work razing the houses of the former ghetto, the S.S. and special "death squads" were busy in Rzeszow destroying our families. The full scope of the atrocities committed there became known to us only bit by bit. In July, 1942, a series of Aktionen began. In the first and largest one, 12,000 Jews were ordered to gather at the Umschlag Platz, the place of reshipment, with one bundle, not to exceed fifty pounds, of their possessions. A drunk S.S. man stood at the entrance, taking all the bundles away. Then the S.S. divided those assembled into two groups: on one side the young and healthy; on the other side the old and sick. Later that day, the second group, numbering about 6,000, was loaded on trucks and driven to a forest in the village Ruda near Glogow, where they were led to the edge of deep trenches. They were ordered to undress, lined up in front of a pit, then mowed down by machine guns. It was just like Black Sunday in Stanislawow. Many who fell into the trenches were wounded but not dead. In the evening the Germans brought bulldozers and filled the trenches with earth. Witnesses described hearing the moans of those buried alive, struggling to fight their way to the surface. A few escaped—I met one man who managed to claw his way out; he joined us later in the forest.

The Jews in the other group were alive, but their suffering was only beginning. They were told to put all their money and valuables in special boxes. Later everyone was searched; if anything of value was found he or she was shot immediately. Religious young men were singled out, beaten up, and forced to polish the boots of the Germans with their own blood. They were then beaten again until they died.[1] In the afternoon the remaining Jews were marched to the railroad station in Staroniwa. While they marched, the S.S. periodically fired into their ranks, so that by the time the group had reached the station, there were about 300 dead and 1,000 wounded. The rest were packed into freight cars and sent off to the death camp and Belzec.

The first Aktion was on July 7, the second on July 10, the third on July 14, the fourth on July 17, and the fifth on August 12. The wives and children of the Judenrat members and of the Jewish Police were taken on the fifth Aktion. After the fifth Aktion only a handful —2,000 Jews—remained in Rzeszow. My married sisters and their families and Rozia were taken in the first transport; my unmarried two sisters, Leibush's wife, her three children and my mother in the fourth on July 17.[2] Shortly before they were taken away, my

---

[1] The rabbi of Kolbuszowa was killed at this time. His two granddaughters, Malka, 18, and Rachel, 16, who accompanied him, begged the S.S. man who approached him not to kill their grandfather, the Rebbe of Kolbuszowa. Ignoring them he shot him, then killed the two girls.

[2] Rachel discovered the German she had worked for in Kolbuszowa now in Rzeszow organizing labor details. He offered her a job as his personal secretary, a position that would save her life. She would accept, she told him, only if he obtained work passes

mother sent a letter to Leibush and me. Never have I
or will I forget those words.

"I don't know what will become of us. We will, it
seems, share the fate of the whole community. But you,
Naftali, are young and strong, and your duty is to live.
Don't let orphanhood break your spirit. Stay alive,
and when the war is over, let the world know what the
Germans did, what kind of murderers they are!"

A few of us received letters from our families in
Rzeszow, telling us about the Aktion that had taken
place, and those that would follow. The letters indicated
that they knew they were being taken east. Some
guessed they would be killed, others mentioned labor
camps in the Ukraine that none of us had heard about.
At that time it was not known that the Jews were being
gassed and cremated and that their remains were used
to make soap, while their clothes were being shipped to
Germany for reuse. Who could imagine such things?
Who could believe the scale upon which it was carried
out?

Our families were gone. Many of us wished we had
stayed with them. We knew that after we finished razing
the ghetto Twardon would probably dispose of us, too.
But we were young, the instinct of living took over, and
we threw ourselves into our work. We had been there
two days when Twardon appeared. He lined us up
against the synagogue, counted us, and gave us a brief
lecture. If we did our work, we would have nothing to

for her sister Matel, her mother, Chancia, the wife of Leibush, and
their children. This he could not or would not do, so Rachel
passed up the chance to escape deportation and was shipped with
the rest to her death at Belzec. She was but one of countless examples of young people, given the opportunity to save their lives,
who nevertheless insisted upon remaining with their families and
so perished.

worry about. But if we tried to escape, ten men would be hanged for each one who escaped. He appointed Yankel Lampel, who had served as a sergeant in the Austrian army, as our drill commandant. He gave Yankel a hat that the Jewish police used to wear, and a toy pistol to carry. He was ordered to line us up every morning, drill us briefly, then march us to our place of work. In the evening, when we were done with work, we had to march back, shouldering our spades like rifles. Yankel did as he was ordered. Twardon in fact became quite pleased with us: we were his private little army. This he found amusing.

One by one the ghetto houses came down, a process as painful as the interment of my father and the others. Hundreds of years of Jewish life were being destroyed; what had been constructed and passed down from father to son and from mother to daughter was reduced to rubble. From the attics we tossed out cradles in which our great-grandparents had slept from the time they were born until they became toddlers, old beds in which they were conceived and in which they died, all of which had then been handed down through the generations in each family. We came across items attesting to the poverty of the Jews who had lived there—people so poor that nothing was ever thrown away. Kneading troughs, dented brass tubs, washboards, old rusty buckets, moldy barrels, broken crates, clusters of branches used in the steam baths, decrepit wrought iron stoves. Old junk, yes, but also an extension of ourselves. As each item crashed to the ground, throwing up clouds of dust, our hearts cried.

The most heartbreaking of all was the destruction of the holy books. Even for someone like myself, hardly pious, it was terrible sacrilege to see these old volumes, accumulated over centuries (for torn or worn books were never discarded but were stored in the attic of the synagogue and when the attic was full taken to the cemetery wrapped in prayer shawls and buried as the entire town looked on, in solemn ceremony) desecrated, discarded like junk. Because of the shortage of paper during the war, the Poles had helped themselves to many of these books; they used the pages for wrapping paper, and they converted the parchment on which the Torah was written into slippers and shopping bags. Every so often I saw pages from our prayer books scattered about in peasants' yards or along the roadsides. I was shattered once to see, when I stopped at an inn, a Jewish book in a washroom serving as toilet paper. It was a volume of "Mesillat Yesharim,"—The Path of the Upright—by the eighteenth century mystic Moses Hayyim Luzzatto, a book I had studied as a youngster, and which I revered as one of the finest books I knew on Jewish ethics.

After we had tossed everything we could out of the houses, we began taking apart the walls, roof beams, shingles, and all other structures. We came across coins and other valuables hidden by the inhabitants, in the hope of returning one day. Some of us took these; others refused, afraid of getting caught and being shot. As for the accumulated trash, everything had to be sorted and put in separate piles, so it could be reused in some way. There were piles for paper, brass, lead, and so on. The house next to the synagogue was used as a warehouse to store this material.

One day, as we were sorting and hauling some furniture, one of the S.S. mean, whom I had met before, came up and told us he needed some brass. He was a tall, strong man, half Pole, half German, well known for his viciousness. His face was red, his eyes were bloodshot, he staggered as he walked, and was clearly drunk. He was followed by his assistant, a young Pole named Vatzek, whom I also knew.

"Tough guys, eh?" he said to us contemptuously. We made no reply. He beckoned to his assistant, and pointing to one of us, a good-natured boy named Motek Weiss, said to Vatzek, in Polish, *"Wez tego chlopaka, i dupnij go az pod sama matke boska."* I understood the first part, "Take this boy," but the second part was an expression I had never heard before, but which I was to quickly understand. Vatzek took a two-by-four and began hitting Motek, following the orders of his superior, who kept directing him: "To the right, on the left, in front." Motek fell to the ground; we had to pick him up and stand him on his feet, after which Vatzek beat him again. After a time he had been beaten into a raw black pulp. We carried him into the synagogue. He died soon afterwards.

The S.S. man then said he needed someone to help him load the brass. Since I was standing next to Vatzek, who knew me, Vatzek suggested that I go. I couldn't refuse, even though I knew I could be the next victim. I was in the process of loading an old mirror onto a truck when the S.S. man ordered me to stop. "Look in the mirror," he said. "Look and see what good cannon fodder you are." I was then told to lead him into the warehouse where the brass was stored.

"Wait," he called out, after we had entered the house, "what's in there?"

"Paper," I said, "old books."

"What kind of books?"

"Religious books."

He walked into the room while I followed behind. Hundreds of books were stacked up on either side of a narrow aisle. There was a high window at the end of the aisle, through which a shaft of sunlight penetrated into the darkness, illuminating the motes of dust in the air and forming a square of light on the floor next to me. For a moment it seemed to me that this shaft of light was like the pillar of fire that the Lord set before the Israelites to lead them in the desert. The German must have had a similar thought. He placed himself in the square of light, looked up at the window, and shouted, *"Jehovah, Jehovah, wo bist du?*—Jehovah, Jehovah, where are You?"

Silence.

"Jehovah, Jehovah, warum helfst du nicht deine kinder?— Jehovah, Jehovah, why do you not help your children?"

Silence.

"You see," the German said, looking at me with his bloodshot eyes, "your Jehovah is too old. He is so old he has become completely deaf, and he can't hear a thing."

He spat on the floor and walked out. I was certain that indeed God was in the shaft of light and would punish that murderer. But nothing happened. There was silence, nothing but silence.

While we worked we wondered what had become of our families. No one knew for sure. Rumors we had in abundance. Some insisted they had been taken east to labor camps in Russia, others located them in the vicinity of Lublin. A minority held out no hope, maintaining that they had been killed en masse, but most though such a view implausible, unnecessarily extreme. When rumors circulated that Jews had been seen passing through Rava-Ruska, a town east of Rzeszow, we determined to investigate. Pooling our funds we hired a Pole (a communist who we trusted) to travel to that town and return with whatever information he could gather. Within a week he was back with nothing more than the fact that residents there had witnessed trainloads of Jews passing through. As to their destination, they could offer little.

Two weeks later we dispatched this same man on a second mission—to go beyond Rava Ruska and find

out what had become of our families and friends. A
month later he returned with the devastating news.
All had been killed, he said, gassed and burned in
Belzec. We were shattered. Most sensed they would
soon share a fate similar to those at Belzec. Still the
instinct toward survival returned among these mostly
young men. The desire to stay alive, nearly snuffed
out, rose once more.

Chapter 30

What would happen none of us knew but it was plain to see that Twardon enjoyed having us around. We were his playthings, his personal retinue, so proud of us was he. We were drilled twice a day by Yankel Lampel until we were able to parade about in smart fashion. Whenever Twardon entertained important visitors he was sure to take them to our camp where he ordered us to perform. *"Das sind meine Juden"* — Those are my Jews," was his proud boast as he stood with his guests on a reviewing stand. If we did exceptionally well, he rewarded us, usually with a horse that for some reason had to be destroyed. For a week following we feasted on horse meat.

One day Twardon arrived and asked Mund, our camp commandant, who among our group might be familiar with the merchandise piled up in the warehouse, untouched since 1939. Much of it was packed away in large crates and most of the merchandise bore the name of Isaak Saleschutz. Mund naturally informed him that two sons of Isaak Saleschutz were present and obviously were most familiar with the contents of those crates. On that same day Leibush and I were assigned to the warehouse.

Our job was to open the containers and sort out their contents. We were then to prepare packages of goods which Twardon directed us to send back to

Germany (intended, no doubt, for family members and friends). We were locked inside the warehouse each morning and then released in the evening. We were searched each day to discourage us from "stealing" (bitter irony since most of the goods belonged to us). Although we could not leave with anything, once inside we had a feast, helping ourselves to dried fruit, nuts, sugar and chocolates. We also managed to replenish the clothing of our fellow inmates. We did this by wearing their rags to work in the morning, then once inside changing into new clothes including shoes, underwear and outergarments. Each evening we would leave fully re-outfitted. We then distributed the different items upon our return. Each day we repeated the process.

One of our commandants, Yanche Rappaport, concluded that life in the warehouse was preferable to fulfilling the tasks imposed on the outside, so he had himself assigned there, replacing Leibush. He was about 38 years old, university-educated and extremely intelligent. While we were locked in together in the warehouse we had frequent interesting discussions on many subjects. Without doubt I learned a great deal from him.

Rappaport, however, was not the same man he was before the war. Something in him had given way, had snapped. Every day, he would frequently repeat the same question—"So what will be the end? What will the Germans do to us?" Because of this almost everyone in the camp avoided him. But matters became even worse for him in the warehouse. Twardon, you see, visited almost every day to observe our activities. Being there in his presence completely unnerved Rappaport. Terrified, he repeatedly bowed low, almost touching the ground each time Twardon passed close to him, all the time greeting him obsequiously—"Good

morning, good morning." Twardon was not one to
miss such a great opportunity. Each time Rappaport
bent low Twardon would step behind him and deliver
a swift kick to his rear. As Rappaport hurtled forward
Twardon could not contain himself and burst into fits
of laughter. This happened not just once but usually
several times whenever Twardon dropped in. Rappaport never uttered a word, accepted his humiliation
day after day. I felt so sorry for him.

Toward me Twardon's attitude was different. He
never abused me. With me he spoke as an equal,
as if we had known each other for years. I sensed
a danger here, that if I slipped and acted too familiarly,
it could all end tragically for me, so I attempted to
play along as tactfully as I could. Twardon most enjoyed talking about women and sex and related to me
almost every sexual encounter he had experienced
since his adolescent years. He would, moreover, keep
repeating the words of Martin Luther, words which in
German rhymed and so delighted him: *Zwei mahl in
der Woche shaded dir Weder ihr und macht in Jahre 104"*—
Twice a week wouldn't hurt you or her and in a year
would total 104. Somehow he concluded that I was a
ladies' man. There was no point in denying it, it
pleased him so, but it forced me to invent and relate
the most bizarre sexual acts with women. That's what
he expected to hear from me. For Twardon somehow
the word *"Brudlen"* meant having sex so he would
always ask me about my *"Brudlen"* and I would invariably respond with yet another scintillating amorous
tale. He was usually pleased and happy for me, laughing heartily, exposing the yellow teeth in his pig-like
head.

Twardon, however, was no fool, and he was exceptionally shrewd. For that reason I never discussed anything of substance with him, never mentioned politics,

the annihilation of the Jews or the destruction of Kolbuszowa. One day, however, he asked me up to his office, a request I could not refuse. It was, however, a most awkward situation for me because in order to enter, I had to pass numerous Polish and German secretaries. They no doubt assumed I was an informer preparing to divulge important information to him. Twardon had been quite successful in getting people, Jews and Poles alike, to spy for him. Once in his office he offered me a seat beside his desk and then opened a bottle of French liquor. Then he began inquiring why I had never asked him about what had happened to Kolbuszowa's Jews, or about my family. I didn't know how to react to this sudden and unexpected familiarity and evident personal interest, but I decided to respond in kind. I would be most interested in knowing, I assured him, and then proceeded to tell him of the death of my father, the expulsion of my family, even about Rozia. He listened attentively, asked for additional details, and grew uncommonly serious.

What followed next was even more startling. Twardon assured me that my family together with the other Jews from Kolbuszowa were deep in the Ukraine working on a communal farm. Moreover, he promised to take me to see them in the near future. Why he was sitting in front of me, trying to be so reassuring, offering to go out of his way to help, I could not understand. Of course I knew everything he said was an unmitigated lie.

Still our "friendship" continued. I could get to see him whenever I wished. When he wanted something done on "his" house (confiscated from Dr. Anderman) where he lived with his wife, baby and maid, he asked me to see to it. So in this strange and unexpected way I coexisted for a time with that beastly murderer.

Chapter 31

Summer was coming to an end. I had been living in the labor camp for two months, working for Twardon, doing as well as a prisoner at forced labor could. Then something happened which literally placed one foot of mine in the grave.

I was working in the warehouse with Yanche Rapaport. Each day we would march with the rest of the labor brigade, then we would separate and go to the warehouse. We would work until noon, then take a lunch break. On the way to lunch we would stop at the dairy, where farmers from the vicinity would bring their milk to have cheese and butter made for the Germans, and where the skim milk was distributed free of charge to the public. Each day we would receive fifty liters of the milk to take back to our kitchen. There was always a long line for the skim milk, so we made arrangements with the man in charge to let us have the milk without waiting in line—otherwise our entire lunch hour would be over just waiting for the milk. We would eat lunch, then report back to work at one o'clock. At five we were finished for the day. We were searched, and then joined the other workers at the camp in the former synagogue.

One day at the dairy a young woman standing in line called out to us to queue up and wait our turn. She was a young Polish girl, of loose morals and fairly good looks, who since the outbreak of the war was always seen in the company of Germans. Before the war she once worked as a maid for a Jewish family, but she became pregnant, and claimed that the oldest son was the father. The child was taken into the family, the girl was paid some money, and the affair was forgotten. Now she was the mistress of the current postmaster, a German.

"Get back in line," she snapped. "If Poles can do it so can Jews."

"Yes, yes," several people standing nearby quickly agreed.

"We're sorry," I said, "but we only have a half hour in which to eat lunch before we go back to work. If we wait in line, there will be no time left to eat."

"Who cares?" she said angrily. "Get back in there with the rest of us."

We ignored her and went to the front.

"If you get milk without waiting in line, I'll spill it, I swear I will."

We had our can filled. As we turned to leave, she grabbed the metal can and turned it over, spilling all fifty liters. I cursed her under my breath; we went back to the kitchen without the milk.

When we returned from work that evening, I saw a Polish commandant waiting outside the synagogue building. His name was Patek; he had a long mustache that turned upward, and he stood there curling its edges while he waited. I greeted him, wondering what he wanted.

"Did you have trouble at the dairy today?" he asked me. I told him what had happened.

"I came to tell you that the Polish police have orders from Twardon to shoot you tomorrow. I suggest that you run away tonight."

I was stunned; I didn't know what to say. Why would a Polish policeman, whom I knew only slightly, and who was not known for his fondness for Jews, alert me to danger, to help me escape?

"I'm sorry," I said after a time. "I can't do it. If I flee, ten of my friends will be hanged."

"I hope you change your mind," he said. "I'm sure your life is dear to you."

He left. I went inside, my head spinning, and found Leibush. I told him what I had just learned. His immediate reaction was that I should escape.

"How can I? They're likely to hang you, and nine others as well."

"Why don't you talk to the mayor, Naftali. He knew father quite well. He might do us a favor."

I didn't eat supper, but ran over to the mayor's office. He received me cordially, and listened to my story.

"I wish I could help you," he said, "but Twardon, well, you know that he won't listen to me. I have no business representing Jews; I'm only permitted to act in behalf of Poles." Some time ago, when I went to see him about freeing Dr. Anderman, he gave me a similar negative answer.

"But perhaps you could get to him on some pretext or other, and mention my name in passing?"

"I'm sorry, Twardon is too clever for that; it won't work." But as I was about to leave, he called out, "By the way, are you on good terms with Halitzki?"

Halitzki was a Ukrainian in charge of the Criminal Police Division. He was the scourge of the Poles, but not as harsh on Jews.

"I have no reason to complain," I replied.

"Why don't you go to see him; he may be able to help you. He's on good terms with Twardon."

I went to Halitzki. He too received me cordially. Before I could begin my story he interrupted me. He knew all about it, he said, and the only thing he could advise me to do was to escape.

"I can't—Twardon will hang ten of my friends!"

"So what do you care?" he answered. "You have to save your own skin."

It was strange to hear the chief of the Criminal Police urging me to run away, but such were the times.

"What about my brother? He'll probably be one of the first to be hanged."

"Let him escape with you."

"I can't. I won't do it."

"Then I'm afraid that tomorrow at this time you'll be a dead duck."

"Listen, Panie Halitzki, I have ten bars of fine soap from before the war. Perhaps you could give it to Twardon to save my life?"

"No, no, my friend, I'm afraid it won't work. No way." He rose and shook my hand. "Good luck," he said as I left.

Back at the camp, the rumor had already begun to spread that I was going to escape. I reassured everyone that I had no such plans. Unable to sleep, I stayed up with my best friends, discussing every conceivable subject, especially pre-war reminiscences. In the morning I shaved and dressed in my usual manner, joining the rest of the group as we marched to work. Yanche Rappaport refused to go with me that day, for fear that when the police came for me, they would take him away too. I left the group to go to the warehouse, thinking that it might very well be for the last time. Sure enough, when I reached the warehouse door, two Polish policemen were waiting.

"Come with us," one of them told me as soon as he spotted me.

"Why?" I asked.

"Don't ask questions. Just do as we say."

One of them, an older man, was known for his savagry. The other was perhaps only a little older than I. He used to court a Polish girl who had once liked me. I was sure that he had volunteered to handle my case just to settle an old score. They took me to Police Headquarters. Patek, the commandant with the curly moustache, was sitting at his desk. He seemed surprised to see me, but he naturally could not say anything, so he sat with furrowed brow. There was a shovel in the corner of the room, which the older policeman ordered me to take. We went out, a policeman on either side of me, each armed with a rifle. We walked across a field in back of the headquarters building, and arrived at an empty lot.

"Dig!" the older one ordered.

"What for?" I asked.

"Dig, don't ask questions."

I looked at the younger policeman, who was leaning on his rifle.

"Start!" the older man bellowed. "We don't have all day."

I knew very well why they wanted me to dig. As I worked, a million thoughts started racing through my mind. I recalled my childhood, my family, and Rozia. They were all gone. So many people had passed away. So I was going to join them. Did I care any longer about dying?

I was now knee deep in a hole. I thought of my brother in America, of another one in Palestine. Why must I die? There is such a big beautiful world out there, and my life has only just begun. Run away, Naftali, run away. But how? Throw a shovelful of dirt in their eyes and run. But how can I get both of them at once? And even if I did, how far would I get, when I

can be seen from the windows of Police Headquarters,
so close by?

I was up to my waist in the hole. How will it feel to
die? With two rifles it would take but a few seconds, or
will I only be wounded and then buried alive? Can I
still do something?

"Why am I digging this hole?" I asked the policemen.

"Dig!" the older one growled. "Don't ask questions,
keep digging."

"Who will be buried here?"

I was now three-quarters of the way inside the hole.
Soon it would be all over.

"Tell me the truth, is this for me?"

"Yes, the older one said, "it is."

"Are you going to shoot me?"

"Yes, we are." He smiled broadly.

"Do me one favor: if you're going to shoot me, kill
me with the first bullet. Make sure you do that."

"Don't teach me how to shoot. Just dig. I know all
about shooting."

"Grant me this one favor," I said again. "You're
going to murder me anyway. I don't know why, but as
long as you're going to do it, please one more favor, go
get Krzysia and tell her I have a very important
message for her." Krzysia Kotulecka was one of Twardon's secretaries. She was a local Polish girl, the
daughter of a lawyer. I had known her before the war.

"Don't bother us about Krzysia," the older man said.
"Keep digging. We have to get going; we have other
things to do."

"I am digging. But while I'm doing it why don't you
get her? It may be worth your while."

"No, no, we must watch you. We can't leave."

"But there are two of you. Why can't one of you go while the other stays?"

"He's right," the younger man spoke up. "It may be worth it to find out what he has to tell Krzysia. You wait and guard him, and I'll go to get her."

He left, returning in a few minutes with Krzysia trailing behind him.

"My God," she cried, "what's going on?"

"I don't know what I did to deserve it, but I'm preparing my own grave, and then I'm going to be shot."

"No!" she cried, crossing herself. "Why, what happened?"

"I don't know," I replied, "there's no use in asking questions, but you know what they're doing to the Jews."

Now she looked frightened. "Yes, yes, but why did you want to see me?"

"Is Twardon in the office?"

"Yes, yes, he is."

"Please go tell him that I have some very important information for him."

"But, but, I just can't go in and disturb him."

"Yes, you can. If you tell him that I have something that he will want to know, he'll be anxious to see me. Twardon is always eager to get information."

"Very well, I'll tell him."

"Make it fast," I added. "These men are in a hurry; they don't have time to wait."

"It's all right," the older policeman said, "we'll wait till she gets back."

I felt sure Twardon would see me. He would reason that I might know something about the underground, or about smuggling, or some matter that would be important for him to know and telling him I hoped would save my skin. Of course that would not necessarily stop him from having me shot later, or he could shoot me himself.

Krzysia soon returned, and announced that Twardon would see me. For the first time in what seemed an eternity, I drew a deep breath. Now maybe I would live—for another half an hour.

My two guards, rifle at ready, led me back to head-quarters, and to the main office on the second floor where Twardon's staff worked. Everyone looked at me, but no one said a word. A moment later Twardon stormed into the room, his face red and his eyes shooting sparks.

"Du verfluchte Jude," he shouted at me, "you damned Jew, what do you have to tell me? Don't you know how busy I am?"

At the moment I felt perfectly calm; nothing bothered or fazed me. I looked Twardon in the eye. "I have some very important things to tell you, and I believe you will want to listen. If you don't like what I say, you can always shoot me."

"All right, so what do you want to tell me? You want to inform me that all the Jews have money?"

"No, I have some serious information. But I can't speak to you here in front of everybody."

Twardon drew his revolver and pointed it at me. "You, you have a lot of nerve, you are a Jew, you have secrets from them? No secrets."

I started to laugh. "What's the difference, you're going to shoot me anyway, so what does it matter, here or there?"

There was a glint in his eye, as if he had suddenly come to terms with me. He sheathed his revolver and beckoned me into his office. After closing the door, he walked behind his desk, and said in a screeching voice, "Very well, Jew, what is it you have to say?"

"I have nothing to tell you. I want to make a deal."

"A deal?" His face was puffed as though ready to explode. His mouth was foaming. "You, a Jew, want to make a deal?"

"Yes, a deal. How much coffee beans would you like me to give you to let me go?"

"Hm?" he blurted, "coffee beans? What kind of coffee beans? You mean to tell me that the Jews have lots of coffee beans? Where? In the camp? In Rzeszow? Tell me, who has coffee beans?"

"I won't tell you anything. But I know you like good coffee, which no one around here can get. I can supply you with all that you want. My brother is an expert at roasting coffee; he can prepare it for you fresh on a special kind of wood. Think about it, fresh roasted coffee every day. I'm sure you'd like it."

"You have nerve," he sputtered, shaking his finger in my face. "You, a Jew, dare come here to bribe me?"

"What kind of bribe is that?" I protested. "If I give you the coffee, that's fine. If I don't, you can shoot me."

"How will I shoot you? You will run away."

"Oh, no, I won't. I could have done so last night, but I didn't. I knew then that I was going to be shot today."

"You what? Who told you?"

"Yesterday you must have told someone, and the word got around and eventually to me."

"Then why didn't you escape?"

"Because you told us that if one of us fled, ten would be hanged. I decided it was better for one person to die rather than ten."

"You mean to tell me you could have saved your life, but didn't?"

"Wouldn't you have done the same for your friends?"

"Sit down," he said. We sat across from each other where only recently we had shared French liquor. "So what are you offering me?"

I had a hundred kilos of coffee beans which my father had hidden with a peasant when the war broke out. I never touched it, figuring that the day might come when I could make good use of it.

"How much coffee would you like?"

"Fifty kilos."

"Fifty kilos? You couldn't find fifty kilos of coffee if you traveled all the way to Warsaw."

"How much, then?"

"I may be able to get ten kilos."

"It's not enough."

"I'll double it. Twenty kilos. But it'll take a lot of work."

"Very well." Twardon licked his lips. "Make it twenty-five kilos."

"It's a deal," I said.

He got up, and I also rose. "When can I have it?" he asked.

"Give me a week."

He called Krzysia in. "Where would you have to go to get it?" he asked.

"Rzeszow."

"Oh, you mean the Jews in the ghetto have a lot of coffee?"

"No, not the Jews. I know a lot of Polish storekeepers in Rzeszow from before the war, when I worked for my father. I can buy a little from this one, a little from that one. It'll cost plenty, too."

"Fraulein Krzysia," Twardon said, "give him a travel permit to Rzeszow for one week."

"No, no, that's no good. I may have to go to other towns in the district. You'd better make it for the entire district. Besides, one week won't be enough. Make it for six months."

"What, six months? Are you crazy?" he said, banging the table. "You must be out of your mind!"

"Make it three months, then."

"All right, three months."

He then called the policemen into his office. "We aren't going to shoot him," he said.

"What are we going to do with the grave?" the older one asked. It was well known that when the Germans had a grave dug, it never went unused.

"I'll tell you what," said Twardon. "You know that no-good Vinyarski, the sausage maker?" He came here yesterday complaining that my dog bit him. Go bring him over and shoot him instead. You," he turned to me, "you go with them and help cover the grave."

"There is one more thing," I said to Twardon. "May I see you alone a moment?" He motioned for the others to leave.

"I would like to know why you gave the order to have me killed."

"Did you have a quarrel with a certain woman in the dairy yesterday?"

"Yes, but it was nothing serious."

"Well, she went to her boyfriend, the postmaster, and told him that you had said that when the Russians came you would shoot her. He told me about it, and I had no choice but to give the order."

"And you really believed that I would say such a thing in a public place, with people all around? If I really thought the Russians would come here, would I say such a thing?"

"No, I don't think you would."

I saw that he made an entry in his notebook, "25 kilos of coffee." I then left his office.

I joined the two policemen outside. The younger one left, returning in about half an hour with Vinyarski, who did not have the slightest idea of what was happening. We all went back to the hole I had dug and there the policemen shot him. We then stuffed his body into the grave, covered it, and returned to the office.

In the office was Patek, the police commandant who had alerted me. He looked at me as though he were seeing a ghost.

"Didn't—didn't—didn't they shoot you just now?"

"No," I replied, "they killed someone else."

He looked greatly relieved—I couldn't learn why, no matter how much I thought about it. I wanted to ask him, but this was not the time nor the place.

I didn't work that day, my mind thoroughly shattered by the events of the morning. I went back to the camp at the synagogue building; only the cook, David Gerstel, and the man on cleaning duty were there. Both seemed greatly surprised to see me, since they were certain that I had been killed. At five o'clock I stood on the steps of the synagogue, waiting for my comrades to return from work. In a few minutes they appeared at the end of the street, marching in single file, with Yankel Lampel in front. When he saw me standing there, his face lit up. As he approached the steps of the synagogue, he bellowed, *"Achtung!"* They all noticed me now. Marching in place, their shovels over their shoulders, their shoes pounding the ground, they seemed to take great pride in their military posture.

Yankel roared, *"DIE AU-U-U-GE-E-E-N RECHTS!—* eyes right!" They all looked at me now, their eyes beaming with joy. After they were dismissed, they enveloped me with hugs and kisses. I couldn't stop crying for a long time.

Chapter 32

The twenty-five kilos of coffee I owed Twardon were readily available. I could have delivered them immediately, but what was the point if instead I could buy time, like Scheherezade in the *Arabian Nights*, by delaying the actual delivery for as long as possible. I presented him with about one kilo once a week, perhaps every other day. I would go to Rzeszow pretending that it was there that I obtained the coffee. Each time I brought him some, he made an entry in his notebook. He left orders that I was to be admitted to his office at any time, so anxious was he to obtain a supply of freshly roasted beans.

Rzeszow for me was now a city haunted by bitter memories. Each time I visited I saw in my mind's eye thousands of Jews, among them my mother, sisters, and the others of my family, my friends and neighbors from Kolbuszowa, being led to the railroad station for their last journey. The main ghetto had been closed, and the remnants of the Jewish population lived in what was known as the small ghetto. I was the only Jew who was permitted to drive a wagon in and out of the small ghetto, on special orders from Twardon.[1] Before

---

[1] Thanks to a contact in Rzeszow, one Regina Kraut, and my friendship with a Polish telephone operator in Kolbuszowa, Jadzia

long, I took advantage of my privileged position to smuggle in food. I fitted my wagon with a double bottom, and each time I visited Rzeszow with a load of wood, old bottles, or scrap iron, I hid bread, horse-meat, lard, sugar, and the like, underneath for the starving Jews who were still alive there.

One day on the way to Rzeszow I was stopped by a Gestapo car. Two men got out and started to search the wagon. The false bottom was filled with freshly baked bread; if they smelled the bread and discovered it in the false bottom, they would shoot me then and there. But to my surprise and great relief, out of the car stepped Twardon himself! I greeted him courteously, and he returned my greeting.

"What have you got in that wagon?" he asked.

"Junk," I replied.

"Let me see your bag."

I handed him my knapsack and opened it. He took out a small package. "What's this?"

"Walnuts."

He opened it to make sure I wasn't lying. "What are you doing with walnuts?"

"It's for my girlfriend, Herr Landskommissar."

"Aha," he cried, baring his yellow teeth with a broad smile. "So you have a girlfriend in Rzeszow, eh?"

"Of course."

"What about the walnuts?"

"Herr Landskommissar, how do you expect my girlfriend to go to bed with me if I don't bring her anything?"

"What? Oh, ha ha ha!" he burst out laughing. "Yes, yes, of course!"

Kurkiewicz, I was able to speak to Regina in Rzeszow each night at midnight, and learn of events there which might affect us in Kolbuszowa.

The other Gestapo men, disconcerted by this conversation, stopped searching the wagon.

"Go ahead," Twardon said, "tell your lady friend that the walnuts are a special present from me. And don't overindulge. You have to save some energy for work."

All of us in the labor camp felt increasingly isolated, as the extermination of Jews continued. Only a few remained, here and there. In the neighboring towns, special labor forces like ours had also been organized, and they too were engaged in either demolishing the old ghetto houses or performing other hard labor.[2] By the fall, with the razing of the ghetto in Kolbuszowa completed, the Germans assigned us to other odd jobs, such as regulating the river. But with increasingly fewer projects left for us, we assumed plans for our extermination were underway. Certainly that was the message we could reasonably receive when the wood we had collected from the demolished houses was made available, not to us, but to the Germans and Poles in the area. We were not to worry, Twardon replied when I reminded him that we would need the wood for fuel during the winter.

Even I became convinced that our end was imminent. A Polish construction auxiliary force was brought to Kolbuszowa ("Yunaki"-Bau Dienst) to begin

[2] Twardon instructed me to visit the two other work camps under his jurisdiction, one in Sokolow, the other at Glogow. No doubt he expected me (though he was too shrewd to state so openly) to "inform" on conditions there, whether for example workers had uncovered caches of valuables, or if trouble was brewing. This, of course, I never did, though I sensed, when he questioned me, an interest in uncovering such matters. My mission in going there was to make contact with inmates so that escape plans for all three camps might be coordinated.

digging a series of ditches in the woods in Nowa-Wies, near our town. What was the purpose of all this digging? I asked the man in charge of this work force. The Germans, he said, had given him none. That these ditches were soon to be our graves seemed the inescapable conclusion.

Hour after hour we discussed the situation, deliberating about what to do. Henrik Mund and Yossl Rappaport, directly responsible to the Germans for our actions, attempted to dissuade us from making any moves. If we tried to escape, they argued, the Germans would surely capture and subject us to torture before slaying us. If we had to die, better that we should meet our end painlessly. Leibush and I argued for escape. We would hide in the forest, link up with other Jews, join the underground, fight the Germans, and avenge ourselves.

Each side used every possible argument to persuade the other. But to convince everyone of the necessity to escape was almost impossible. Some were not in good health, others lacked the money and the courage. Some did not speak Polish, while others were afraid that their appearance would betray them. Many were without the contacts so necessary after a successful escape. The decision whether to try or not, usually hinged on whether one knew a friendly Pole who would be willing to hide him. Leaving our camp was easy, since we were not guarded. The problem was finding a place to hide.

Mund stopped me in the hall one night after our discussion and whispered in my ear, "Take my advice, Naftali, and forget this escape nonsense."

"I want to live," I told him.

"So do I. If you run away, I'll be the first one the Germans will hang."

"You should come along too."

"I warn you, Naftali, if you don't stop this nonsense, I'll turn you in."

I didn't say anything; there was no point in arguing.

The High Holidays were approaching, but we were preoccupied not with penitence, but survival. A handful were still observant, and tried to organize a minyan for Rosh Hashanah and Yom Kippur, but we were distracted by an unusual event. Two days before Rosh Hashanah, a truck stopped in front of our camp, from which twenty-three young Jews, fifteen girls and eight boys, all from Rzeszow, were led out by German guards. This group, we were told, was now in our care, and was our responsibility. We surveyed our charges; all were pale, starved, dirty; their clothes were tattered and infested with lice and flies; their feet were covered with scabs, bleeding sores, and boils. They told us that they had been taken from the labor camp in the nearby village of Biesiadka. That morning, instead of going to work, they reported sick, and then were loaded onto the truck and driven to our camp.

In the public bathhouse we had a large metal container installed when the ghetto was first erected, which we used for delousing clothes. After we assigned the group to their rooms, we had them undress in the bathhouse, and put their clothes into the delousing container. Next we prepared a hot bath for each of them—something that they hadn't enjoyed for months—and listened to them sigh pleasurably as they slipped into the tub. When they emerged, we gave them old but clean clothes to wear. With the medicine chest and medical instruments that I inherited from Dr. Anderman, I began to work on them, draining the boils, cleaning scabs, applying ointments and dressings to their wounds. For me this was fruitful work, touching their tender young bodies, relieving their pain, seeing the sincere expressions of thanks reflected in their eyes. In the afternoon our cook prepared a big meal, using the meat of a horse which was donated to us after it had broken its leg the day before. Our guests were thrilled—none of them had expected to enjoy the delights of a hot bath, clean clothes, and a satisfying meal ever again. We were excited that even in our lowly condition we could bring pleasure and relief to others. As we all sat talking to one another, they declared this day to have been the best they had spent since being taken from their homes. One lovely young girl took my hand and put it to her face, then kissed it. But later as I sat talking with my fellow inmates, the discussion turned to the German plans for these young people. Should we tell them of the ditches that were just prepared? Should we encourage them to escape? Could such an attempt possibly succeed? Since they were our responsibility would we not be punished for this, most likely killed? In the end we decided to say nothing, a decision which to this day still troubles me.

On the following day we gave them some light chores to do around the camp. They did everything they could to please us, so thrilled were they with their new situation. After work Twardon arrived to inspect the camp.

"Hey, Saleschutz, come over here."

"Yes, Herr Landskommissar."

"I brought you some girls, didn't I?"

"Yes, thank you Herr Landskommissar."

"You're going to put them to good use, aren't you now?"

"Of course, Herr Landskommissar."

"I brought the girls to this camp so you would be able to *Brudle*. Don't disappoint me, you hear?" He bared his yellow teeth and shook with self-satisfied laughter.

That night forty Jews were brought to Kolbuszowa from Rzeszow. Among them were all the doctors and nurses who had been working in the Rzeszow ghetto. The entire group was jailed in the town hall. Secretly, we were able to make contact with them. We learned that about two hundred Jews had been trying to get forged papers to flee to Hungary; forty were arrested and transported to our jail. The others were to be apprehended as soon as the Germans could arrange it. They begged us to alert the remaining Jews in Rzeszow before it was too late.

Avigdor Polimer and I immediately harnessed two horses to a wagon, loaded it with old iron, bottles and other junk, and in the middle of the night drove to Rzeszow to deliver the warning. After we had warned the Jews there, we returned to camp, arriving early in the morning, to find that our comrades had gone to work earlier, leaving the twenty-three newcomers to themselves. Ominously, we found Polish guards posted there, keeping an eye on them. The young people looked at us questioningly, but we could offer no explanations.

As we stood there perplexed, a truck with several S.S. men, and two machine guns mounted in the back, stopped next to us. A few S.S. men jumped out, and ordered everyone into the truck. They all obeyed quietly.

"You and you," said one of the S.S., pointing to Polimer and me, "get on the truck!"

"We don't belong to this group," I protested.

"Get on, fast!"

"I'm telling you, we're not part of this group."

"Then what are you doing here?"

"We're guarding them."

"Never mind guarding them, get on." He went for his rifle. Polimer and I got on the truck.

So this is it. This is the end. It had to happen sooner of later, and it's happening now. This is exactly how it had to happen—through a stupid mistake, for no reason at all, just a stupid mistake. So be it.

Standing on that truck with the rest of the shivering, mortally frightened fellow Jews I could think of no way to resist.

I really didn't care; I would just as soon die; there is no compelling reason to continue to live this way.

But just at that moment Twardon arrived, checking things personally as usual. What irony that I should look to this bestial murderer for my salvation.

"Herr Landskommissar! Herr Landskommissar!" I shouted. "May I talk with you for a moment?"

Twardon looked up greatly surprised. "What are you doing there," he shouted.

"They put me on this truck. They thought that Polimer and I were part of this group."

Polimer worked as Twardon's stable boy, taking care of his two beautiful riding horses. Twardon, I knew, would not readily part with someone who was so useful. As for me, I still owed him plenty of coffee.

"Let these two off," he ordered the S.S. man in charge.

"Why, sir? Two more Jews, what's the difference?" the S.S. man countered.

"I need them. Let them go."

We were let off the truck. With a sinking heart I watched the group of young people. They were happy two days earlier, their spirits buoyed by our concern. Now they were riding off to their doom. The young girl who had, the night before, kissed my hand looked at me with tears in her eyes. I looked back at her, unable to utter a word. My expression and my tears said it all. Our eyes remained fixed on each other until her truck rolled out of sight.

Later that day we heard machine gun fire from the direction of the ditches which had recently been dug by the Polish construction force, *Baudienst*. The shooting seemed endless.

About five o'clock a truck loaded with clothing stopped in front of our camp. The head of the Bau Dienst appeared. Since we knew each other, he turned quickly to relate the day's events.

"The Germans had themselves quite a massacre," he said. "They must have killed over two hundred Jews. They murdered the group they had in jail; they also brought over quite a few from Rzeszow[3] and Huta Komorowska (a sister camp of the one in Biesiadke, 15 kilometers north of Kolbuszowa). They ordered everyone to undress and line up before the pits, and then shot them. This one woman, named Rebhun was the head nurse in the hospital at Rzeszow, refused to undress. Twardon, who was in charge of the whole show, insisted, but she kept refusing. So he walked over to her to take her clothes off, and she took off her shoe, and with the pointed heel began to hit him on the face and head. You should see the blood spurt every time she connected with his bald head. He finally ripped off her clothes and shot her."

I could listen no longer. I rushed to the back of the truck and looked at the clothing. I instantly recognized some of those worn by the young boys and girls. My

---

[3] The Jews of Rzeszow, whom I had warned, went into hiding. The Germans, unable to find them, promptly rounded up 160 others.

entire body shook, my knees grew weak. I ran to the back of the synagogue building and hid in a corner where no one could see me. I cried, and beat myself like a madman. Inside of me a voice kept screaming, "I don't want to live! I don't want to live any longer!"

But another one responded, "Yes, you do want to live. It would please the Germans if you died; is that what you want? You are supposed to live and take revenge!"

It was the second day of Rosh Hashana, the Jewish New Year, 1942. There was no time to waste. I had to plan my escape and establish contact with friendly Poles on the outside.

Chapter 33

I remembered Kotulova, the Polish widow whom I had visited just before I left Kolbuszowa to be with my family in Rzeszow. I had left her with some of our belongings and merchandise. Her house was right behind the fence that surrounded the ghetto. I resolved to see her at once.

After nightfall I left the camp without telling anyone, not even my brother. I climbed over the fence and knocked on Kotulova's door.

"What's the matter?" she asked as she let me in. "You look terrible."

"I have to . . ." I couldn't finish the sentence. I cried, I pounded the table, I moaned like a wounded animal.

She looked frightened. "Naftali, what is it?"

"I—I want to live. You must help me! Please help me, do you hear?"

"Yes, yes, I will help you. Sit down, sit down and stop crying."

I finally calmed down. "I'm sorry, please forgive me."

"It's all right. Would you like something to eat?"

"No—yes, yes, thank you."

She served me some beet soup and black bread. I ate in silence. Then she poured me some wine.

"*Na Zdrowie,*" I said to her, "to health."[1]

---

[1] A common Polish toast.

"Pani Kotulova, I have to run away. I need forged papers, and I may need a place to hide."

"I will help you," she said.

"Where can I get papers?"

"I'll have to talk to the priest."

"Do I know him?"

"You should; Monsignor Dunajecki has been our parish priest for nearly twenty years."

I knew the name. I even remembered seeing him, a tall quiet man, coming to the podium of my elementary school to give the invocation at the dedication of a new stadium. Most Jews had absolutely no contact with the Catholic Church. Whenever they saw a priest coming down the street, they would cross to the other side to avoid him. The Church was deeply mistrusted and was looked upon as the spawning ground of anti-Semitism. How many plots against Jews, we wondered, were hatched in the dark halls of the old stone church buildings on the edge of town? I now had to turn to these enemies for help—such were the times.

"Yes, I know the Monsignor."

"He has all the birth records of the parish, and he may be able to give you the birth certificate of someone who died during the war."

"I had a friend in grade school, about my age, who was killed at the front in 1939. His name was Tadeusz Jadach. Maybe I could use his birth certificate."

"I'll see what I can do. Come back tomorrow night."

"Thank you, thank you for everything. God bless you."

When I returned the next evening, Kotulova handed me something more precious than gold: the birth certificate of Tadeusz Jadach, born in 1918 in Werynia, a Roman Catholic Pole. That paper gave me a new life; with that paper I might survive the war. I put my arms around the ample frame of my succoring angel, and hugged her until she protested that she couldn't breathe.

"I will be indebted to you for as long as I live," I told her.

"You would have done the same for me," she said.

"Just one more thing, my brother Leibush, I need a certificate for him—could you possibly get one for him, too?"

"I'll talk to the Monsignor."

The next day I had a birth certificate for Leibush: a Ludwig Kunefal, born in 1904, a Capucin who died in 1936. As she handed it over, she mentioned that the Monsignor wanted to see Leibush and me. To be safe, she suggested that the meeting take place in her house. I wanted to write the Monsignor a letter of thanks, I told her. She provided me with paper, pen, and ink, then helped me with the opening and closing to make it a proper letter. After all, I had never written to a priest. How, I wondered, could I ever repay his kindness?

"I know he will appreciate your letter," she said as she sealed the envelope. "As for how you can repay him, he suggested that you donate fifty zlotys to the church for a special mass." I gave her the money immediately.

A few days later Leibush and I went to her house to meet the Monsignor. Neither of us knew what to do or say; we were overwhelmed by the man's appearance. He was tall and majestic looking, his face inscrutable. We stood there embarrassed, but quickly realizing our discomfort, he extended his hand to us in greeting.

"I am Proboszcz Dunajecki," he said in a warm, disarming voice. "I am pleased to meet both of you."

We shook his hand, after which our hostess asked us to sit down to some food she had prepared for us. We were soon engaged in lively conversation.

"I would like to suggest something," Monsignor Dunajecki said after we had been chatting a while. "You, Tadeusz, you speak Polish like a Pole. But Leibush's Polish is a dead giveaway. I would suggest that Leibush not use the certificate that I made available to him. You don't have to decide now, but think about it."

We later realized that the Monsignor was correct; we never used that certificate.

Leibush was in the other room with Kotulova while the Monsignor and I continued to talk. The priest grew pensive.

"You know, Tadeusz," he said, "I have been a priest here in Kolbuszowa for almost twenty years, and I never really got to know a single Jew. I never had any dealings with Jewish organizations, and I never had the slightest idea about what was going on in the Jewish community. I never even met your rabbi. Now, in view of what's happened to the Jews here, I deeply regret not having made the effort to know your people better. What's most upsetting to me is the realization that I could have saved scores of Jewish children by placing them among my parishioners; it would have been an easy thing to do. But no one said anything to me, and I myself have been remiss for neglecting to learn what was happening under my very nose. I can't tell you how sorry I am."

I could tell that he was really sincere. I didn't know how to respond. He was blaming himself, but who was really guilty? The hierarchy of the Church, who never advised him about what could be done? The long history of anti-Semitism in Europe? The Polish aristocracy, who ground the peasants down and were glad that they had found a scapegoat in the Jews? How did this all come about? There was no simple answer. As we were about to leave, we shook hands and he wished us luck. Then he made the sign of the cross over us and bade us goodbye.

We spent the next two weeks urging the men in our camp to prepare to escape. Mund warned us repeatedly to stop, or he would turn us in to the Germans. But time was running out, and we were not going to sit idly by and wait for our destruction. We hoped to convince the others but when the time came, we were determined to leave, no matter how many or how few joined us. Each night I left camp and made contacts with neighboring Poles to conclude arrangements for the reception of those of us already planning to escape and to secure the cooperation of additional peasants, hoping that others in our group might, as a result, change their minds. I knew our escape effort would prompt Twardon to exterminate workers in the two other camps in Sokolow and Glogow. For that reason I visited them to alert my contacts there of our plans.

Returning from work one day I saw Patek, the Polish police commandant who had warned me about Twardon's order to have me shot. He was waiting outside the camp, visibly agitated.

"Good evening, *Panie Komendancie*," I greeted him.

"Good evening, Saleschutz. I have to talk with you for a moment."

I had to escape that very evening, he told me, for the Polish police had been instructed to surround the camp later that night, and to take all of us away. Whether we were to be executed or transported to a concentration camp he did not know, but either way, the crucial time had come for us. I promised to pass his warning along to the others.

"This time I hope you'll take my advice," he said. "Last time you gambled and stayed, and you were saved only through sheer luck."

There was a great commotion when I told the other men what I had just heard. Some refused to believe it; others immediately began their preparations for escape. But a friendly Polish policeman whom we contacted for confirmation of what Patek had told us, knew nothing about any plan to take us away. So plagued were we by doubt that even I lost some of my resolve. When night came I decided to visit Patek again at his home.

"Why did you come here?" Patek asked after he opened the door, evidently afraid someone might see me entering his house.

"I must make sure that what you told me was accurate."

"Come inside," he said.

I entered his home. He called to his wife, whom I had never met. She looked very sad.

"You can ask my wife; she knows all about it."

"It's true, it's all true," she said.

"I believe you; it's just that I have such a big responsibility to the others—I just wanted to be doubly certain."

"I understand," Patek said.

"Well, then, I'll be leaving tonight. Thanks for everything."

"Good luck to you," said his wife.

As I was about to leave, I turned to Patek and said, "You know, this is the second time you saved me. Can you tell me why? From what I was told, before you came here you lived in Poznan, and when the Germans approached that town you ran away, but you were caught by the Russians. The story I heard was that the

Russian officer in charge was a Jew, and you swore to pay them back the first chance you got. Why are you helping me, then?"

"I'm glad you asked," he replied. "It's an unusual story, but you ought to know it. My wife and I had a son, an only child. He attended a military academy. When the war erupted in 1939 he was killed in action. When we came to Kolbuszowa, and I saw you in your father's store, I thought for a moment that I was seeing my own son. You both look as alike as two drops of water. I went home and told my wife about it. A few days later we both went to the store to have another look at you. My wife was amazed at the resemblance. We decided then and there that, how should I put it, we would look upon you as if you were our son, and do what we could to help you, as if we were doing it for our own son."

I went back to camp. Fifty-five men had decided to escape.[2] It was November 18th, and winter was closing in. Each man packed a knapsack with warm clothes, food, and other necessities. There was an almost unbearable tension in the air, for we were venturing into the unknown, either to start a new life or to be caught and shot. It occurred to me that the Children of Israel might have felt this way on the night they fled Egypt.

It was eight o'clock. I went to the synagogue building urging some of the reluctant ones to leave. Hersch Gevirtz, the secretary of the Judenrat, the man who had given Leibush an unauthorized travel permit when I was so sick with the ear infection, told me he was too old to run; he would stay and take his chances. Moteleh

---

[2] We managed to get word to the work camp at Glogow. The same Polish messenger was instructed to inform Sokolow as well but I never learned whether or not he succeeded.

Kornblitt, an eighteen-year old boy who was very frail, looked at me with his big blue eyes and said, "Naftali, may the Divine Providence take care of me." Chaim Offen, an old friend, said, "If it is my fate to join my father and mother, so be it." They had already given up; no argument could sway them.

I had everything worked out for Leibush and myself, and for two friends. A hiding place had been arranged for a few weeks in the house of a Polish woman named Vichta, who lived with her young daughter in a nearby village. Her husband had left for Argentina before the war. She used to work for us as a maid, and knew us quite well. She was a poor woman, and could really use the money we agreed to pay for room and board. The two people who were to go with us were Noah, my best friend, and Leiser Spielman, one of Mund's assistants in policing our quarters in the synagogue. Leiser was a refugee from Germany who couldn't speak more than a few words of Polish. His only chance was to join up with someone like me. Both he and Noah were penniless, and had no place to go, so Leibush and I decided that they should join with us. Vichta agreed to hide four persons at her place. As for the necessary money, I had managed to sell a great deal of our family possessions that I kept smuggling back from Rzeszow while shuttling with my wagon to and from Kolbuszowa Leibush and I also had a few hundred American dollars, worth a fortune at that time, and we managed to deposit 100,000 zlotys with several Poles.

In accordance with my plan, I was first going to go to Kotulova's house, on the other side of the ghetto fence, taking Leiser with me. Leibush would go directly to Vichta with Noah. After a few days, Leiser and I would join the others at Vichta's house. We would stay a few weeks, then flee to the woods, where a number of Jews had already begun to gather, and we would be reunited with others from our camp.

I now found that Mund had posted two assistants at the entrance to our camp, whose duty it was not to allow anyone to escape. Ironically, one of them was Leiser. The other was Binin Rosenbaum, who, along with his father and brother-in-law, was also among those planning to leave. Mund kept scurrying around, threatening all of us; he told me directly that he was turning me in on the following day. I told him not to worry; there would be no next day.

I peered out into the cold night to assure myself that all was clear, then I turned to Leibush and told him to go first, with Noah. But at this point Noah refused. He had his younger brother with him, and didn't want to leave him behind. I begged him to leave, and explained that Vichta couldn't take a fifth person, but he wouldn't listen. Later I regretted not having taken both of them—Vichta probably would have consented under the circumstances. But now, one of Leibush's good friends, Froim Brodt, who had bragged all along about having a choice of several hiding places, admitted he had been bluffing and really had nowhere to go at all. Leibush decided to take him in Noah's place. So Leibush and his friend were the first to leave. Mund tried to stop them, but his two assistants announced that they were leaving, also, so Mund finally realized that he was defeated.

One by one the men left. I kept counting them, and with each departure I felt more encouraged. The plan was working. I decided to be the last one to go. We had agreed that in a few weeks all those who had escaped would try to establish contact and meet in the forest where, as an organized group, we had a much better chance to survive than as individuals.

I had prepared a knapsack to take with me, filled with food, medicine, clothes, money, jewelry, and most precious of all, a diary my sister Rachel had kept from the day the war began. As soon as Leibush left, I decided to take the knapsack to Kotulova's house and then come back—it would be much easier for me to know that my possessions were safe, and that I would not be encumbered when it was my turn to leave. I threw the knapsack over the fence, jumped over, and ran to Kotulova's house. I asked her if I could leave it in her attic, explaining that this was the night we were escaping. I also asked if I could bring a friend; she agreed. She would leave the door open.

I vaulted back over the fence and returned to the synagogue building, to find Leiser panic-stricken—he assumed that I had left without him. Again I kept trying to persuade one or more additional persons to leave. The men were now sitting around glumly, apparently convinced that Patek had spoken the truth. They looked at me, smiling sadly, as if to say, "What can we do? We want to live, but if we flee, we'll be caught on the first day. If we wait, maybe we'll be sent to a camp, where we can remain alive."

Everyone was now quiet. I went to Mund's quarters, there were the elite of the camp. Yantche and Joss'l Rappaport, Mund with his son and a few of their friends, all of them were sitting around a table drinking vodka. Some were already drunk. One of them remarked that if he were going to be shot, it would be better if he were drunk. They were cordial to me, offering me vodka, too; but I refused—at a time like this I needed to be in possession of all my wits. Then, unexpectedly, Mund came over, apologizing to me for all the fuss he made. He confessed that it was because he felt he and his son could not escape—they came from Cracow, and knew no one in this area—that he opposed me. He reminded me of the time when I could have left by myself, but stayed to keep ten of them from being hanged.

At about four in the morning, the two lookouts we had designated came in and told us that the Polish police were surrounding the area—if anyone wanted to leave, he had better do so now. Leiser and I were the only ones left. We waved goodbye, and departed through an exit at the other end of the synagogue. From this point we had to cross a street, then run to a warehouse. As we reached the other side, we were stopped by two Polish policemen, one of whom I knew.

"What's going on?" I asked him.

"You can't go anywhere," he said. "You're surrounded by German police on the opposite side."

"We have to go, anyway."

"You can't."

"Why not?"

"We're not supposed to let you."

"In that case, just look the other way and pretend you never saw us, and we'll be gone."

He wasn't sure of what he should do, and looked questioningly to his partner. I grabbed Leiser's arm and we made a dash for the warehouse. Once inside, we walked to the opposite end, and peered through a window. A portion of the street was occupied by German policemen, one of them with two dogs. A searchlight illuminated the street from one end to the other.

"We have to run across the street to the outhouse over there," I told Leiser. "We have to do this one at a time."

"You go first," said Leiser.

I remembered the time when the Germans first came

to Kolbuszowa, when I and another man tried to escape through a window. He went first, and the Germans saw him and killed him. This time Leiser wanted me to leave first.

"You first," I told Leiser. I figured that if I were shot he would be unable to make it, since he knew no Polish and had no place to go.

"No, you," Leiser insisted.

"Very well," I said, "I'll leave first."

I crept out of the window and crawled across the street. When I reached the outhouse I heard shots, but I could not stop to look around. I entered the outhouse and waited there for about ten minutes. Leiser never came. I could hear shouting in German, barking, shooting, then the noise receding into the distance. When the commotion seemed far enough away, I dashed out of the outhouse to the ghetto fence, leaped over it, and ran to the attic in Kotulova's house. The door was open. I fell onto the hay, exhausted, thinking ruefully about the men who stayed behind.

Part Seven

FELICIA MILASZEWSKA—CRACOW

Chapter 34

In the winter of 1942-1943, I, Manya Petranker, became Felicia Milaszewska, a character of my own invention. My loyal friend, Mundek, remained a wonderful benefactor to me. For over a month he hid me at his mother's house, taking care of all my needs. But his mother was determined that I should not stay a day longer than necessary. I can hardly blame her—if I were caught, all three of us would be shot. What Mundek did was extremely courageous; it was rare for anyone at that time to volunteer his help without any strings attached. True, there were others who saved Jews, but almost invariably they did so because they were paid. Actually Mundek, I learned later, had befriended and assisted eleven other girls to escape. He would bring them to Halitz, obtain papers for them, then move them to other towns. Sadly, none of them survived the war.

About a month after my escape from the ghetto, Mundek took a few days off from work and accompanied me to Lvov, the nearest large city. There I hoped to settle and assimilate with the population. Mundek had a cousin living there—a black marketeer who lived with his mistress in a one-room apartment. We went to visit him, and were cordially received. Despite the small size of his place, he invited me to stay. Mundek had introduced me as his fiancee, and told him that I was going to remain in Lvov and would look for employment; I was going to work until we were ready to get married and then settle down in Halitz.

I disliked Mundek's cousin from the very beginning. His manners and speech were those of the underworld, and while he tried to be accommodating, he was also overly friendly, in a lecherous sort of way. There were two studio couches in his room, one at either end. He slept with his mistress in one, and offered the other to Mundek and me. Mundek did not try to take advantage of me; he kept to his side and I kept to mine. After all the lights were extinguished, and everything was quiet, Mundek's cousin broke the silence.

"Hey, how come things are so quiet at your end of the room?"

"What do you want us to say?" Mundek replied.

"Aw, come on, I don't want you to say anything; I want you to do something."

"We're too tired," Mundek said. "We need some sleep."

"Well, I guess it's only me and you, baby," I heard our host say to his mistress. With that they proceeded to make love, accompanied by loud noises, totally indifferent to our presence.

I told Mundek the next day that I couldn't stay at his cousin's for very long. He agreed; he was no more comfortable there than I was. But where could we go? Mundek had to return to work, and I had to remain alone. The Jews of Lvov were living in a ghetto, much the same as in Stanislawow; in the Christian part of the city, I had no contacts, knew no one. I could not check into a hotel, since all of them had been taken over by the Germans. The only place I could go to was a boarding house, where beds became available from time to time.

Mundek thanked his cousin for his hospitality, but told him how unfair we felt it was to intrude upon his privacy, and inquired about a boarding house. His cousin gave me the address of one, and that evening, after saying goodbye to Mundek, I moved into the place, sharing a room with two other women and one child.

As luck would have it, that night the Ukrainian police were ordered by the Gestapo to raid all the boarding houses in the city, looking for Jews. Late in the evening there was a pounding on our door. Before we could answer, two policemen entered, focusing their flashlights on our faces. We were told to go out into the hall. The woman with the child had to carry him in her arms from the room.

We were ordered to show our papers. All I had was the little slip giving my name and the statement that I had been employed by a German firm dealing in scrap iron. The police, however, did not appear convinced. What made them suspicious, I do not know.

"You're a Jew," one of them said to me in a harsh voice, "and you'd better not deny it."

"No, I'm not," I said. "You're mistaken."

"Well, how about reciting The Lord's Prayer."

Every Christian in Poland knew The Lord's Prayer. Since I had attended a private Hebrew School through all my school years, I had never learned it. Some of my friends memorized it as they prepared to leave the ghetto to masquerade as Poles, but I never did.

"I don't know it—my family was never religious," I said.

"Get dressed," he ordered, "you're coming with us."

He turned to the woman with the child. "What about you? You must be Jewish, too."

"No," she said, "I'm a Christian."

"Have you any proof?"

"Here's my baptismal certificate," she said, showing it to him.

"You're a convert. You were Jewish before you became a Christian. I'm sorry, but according to the law I must treat you as a Jew. You'll have to come along too."

The third woman was allowed to remain. One of the policemen took the woman with the child, while I was led away by the other, the one who asked me about The Lord's Prayer. We walked through the icy, deserted streets, with their tall, massive, faceless buildings, to the Gestapo Headquarters on Platz Smolki. When I saw that building, I froze. Should I try to run for my life? It was dark; where would I run to?

"Why don't you admit that you're Jewish? If you do, I promise I'll let you go."

"Oh, sure," I said, "you want to have an easy job, don't you? All I have to do is tell you that I'm Jewish, and you'll have the Gestapo take care of me."

"You bitch," he muttered, "you dirty little bitch."

My leg, which had never healed well, began to throb. Limping along, I started to climb the steps leading up to the main entrance of the Gestapo Headquarters. It suddenly occurred to me that once I set foot inside that building, I would never come out alive. I knew I had to chance it, even though I had little confidence in the policeman's promise. I stopped and turned to him.

"All right," I said, "I am Jewish. Go ahead, shoot me; have another innocent victim on your conscience."

He sized me up a moment, his face crimson with rage. "You can go to hell! No, I won't take you in. Run along—someone else will get you sooner or later."

"May I go?"

"You'd better get out of this town fast. If I ever catch you again in Lvov, I'll shoot you on the spot, understand?"

I was free to go, but I knew that as soon as I left I could be picked up by another policeman; nor did I want to go back to the boarding house in the night.

"Look, there's a curfew, and if I leave now I'll be back from where I started. Would you please bring me to the railroad station?"

"All right, I'll take you there. But remember, don't ever let me see you in this town again!"

My mind was in a turmoil as I was escorted to the station, but miraculously, I had won this first round. Being petite, and roundfaced, wearing my hair in braids, I appeared younger than my mineteen years. I was able to play the role of a saucy, sharp-tongued adolescent and get away with it. It wouldn't work all the time, I knew, especially since the Germans spared no one, adult or child. Still, it was a good ploy that might succeed for a time.

The train station, I learned, was swarming with detectives on the lookout for Polish black marketeers. I sat on a bench in the waiting room all night, my head bowed, praying that I would be left alone. Luckily, I was. In the morning I returned to the boarding house and told the landlady I had been cleared by the police; but she refused to let me stay.

I desperately wanted to contact Mundek, to get his advice, but there was no time. I couldn't stay in Lvov another day. Several times I had heard it said that the

best place for a Jew trying to pass as a Gentile was
Cracow, the second largest city in Poland. There was,
however, no direct train to Cracow—one had to go south
to Stryj, then transfer to another one going west to
Cracow. That very afternoon I boarded the train to
Stryj. When I arrived that evening I learned that there
would be no train to Cracow until the next day. Many
Jews were trying to escape to Hungary by way of Stryj,
I discovered. Police surveillance was tight. Again, I
was trapped. I couldn't leave the station, but remaining
there involved the risk of getting caught.

I entered the restaurant inside the station, and
ordered a bowl of soup. The place was almost empty.
When the waitress brought me the soup, I compli-
mented her on a piece of attractive jewelry she was
wearing, and we started a conversation. Somehow I
felt I could trust this woman. I told her that I had a
problem: I was afraid to go to a hotel at that hour, and
I couldn't sleep in the station—did she have any sug-
gestions? She thought for a moment, then said I was
welcome to spend the night at her apartment, if I didn't
mind waiting until she was finished with her work.

The waitress was really a decent soul. I spent the
night with her, and on the next day went back to the
station. The place was now buzzing with activity. There
was a long line at the ticket window. I was about to get
on it when I noticed a young man following me. He
was unusually well dressed, considering wartime aus-
terity, and I noticed that several people waiting in the
queue tipped their hats to him. Who was he? I thought
that he was most likely an official of some kind, and it
would be best to stay out of his way.

I decided to go to the ladies' room—if he followed
me there, I knew there'd be trouble. Sure enough,
after I had locked myself into one of the toilet com-

partments, I observed his feet as he entered the room. I decided, once again, to play the role of the happy-go-lucky adolescent—perhaps it would work a second time.

I quickly unlocked the compartment and faced him as he stood near the anteroom mirror, looking embarrassed.

"Ha," I laughed, "you're in the wrong place."

"I—I made a mistake; I'm sorry."

He left quickly: I followed right behind him.

"How do you do?" he said as soon as we were outside.

"I'm doing fine, thank you," I said, all smiles. "But why are you following me? Is anything wrong?"

He showed me his badge. "Police," he said.

"Why?" I said, still smiling, "what would they want with me?"

"What's your name?"

"Felicia Milaszewska."

"That's a Polish name. Where are you going, Felicia?"

"To Cracow."

"What will you do there?"

"You see, I'm a poor girl, and I have a sick aunt in Cracow. I received a letter informing me that she was ill and could use some help, so I decided to come and stay with her."

I really did not think that he would believe that story, but he apparently did. He became very friendly. He asked if I had a ticket, and when I told him that I was about to get in line, he went directly to the window and got one for me. Then he accompanied me to the train, made sure I had a seat, and wished me bon voyage. To this day I wonder what made him act so kindly.

On the way to Cracow, the train stopped at Tarnow. Here, too, the station was occupied by the police; a search had been in progress. It was now nighttime and I had fallen asleep. A flashlight beaming in my face woke me.

"Your name?" the voice behind the light boomed out.

I hesitated at first. "Felicia Milaszewska," I said in a quavering voice.

"You're not sure, are you?"

"Yes, I'm sure," I replied.

"How come you answer in a tremulous voice?"

"Because I'm very tired. Wouldn't your speech be a bit shaky if you'd traveled for forty-eight hours?"

Apparently I convinced him. He shrugged his shoulders and went on to the next passenger. A few moments later, a Polish woman sitting next to me said, "You know, he actually thought you were Jewish?"

"Yes," I said, "isn't that strange?"

"It certainly is. I must say, it's not safe at all to travel these days."

Toward morning we arrived in Cracow. As we were getting off the train, all the passengers were inspected by the Polish police, while Gestapos stood by and watched. I learned that the search was not for Jews but for Poles with labor cards for work which was not vital to the war effort—those picked up were sent to Germany for forced labor.

When my turn came to show my papers, the Polish policeman took one look at me and announced, "This girl is Jewish."

"What? Why do you think so?" I said. "Why do you insult me?"

"You are not? Then tell me how many divinities there are."

"There is one God."

"And what else?"

"And He has one son."

"And what about the Holy Ghost?"

"What about it?"

"Never mind. Tell me, how many Apostles are there?"

"Ten," I answered.

"Try twelve."

"Very well, twelve."

"Now I am entirely convinced she is a Jew," he said to his colleague. "Look here," he said to me, "We don't have Jews living in the Cracow ghetto any more. We've sent them to the concentration camps in Plashov. But you know what? We won't even bother to send you there. We'll shoot you right here in the station."

As he was speaking, he pulled me by the arm and led me to one side of the crowd of passengers. The people were divided into two groups: those with the proper kind of labor card on one side, and those without, on the other. I was put to still another place by myself, with one policeman watching me.

I was resigned to my fate. I could no longer go on fighting the whole world. I recited the Shema Yisrael, and without fear waited for the end. Meanwhile, the Polish police had completed checking everyone's papers, and the chief Gestapo officer came over to question those who did not have the right labor cards. When he saw me, he asked the Polish policeman who had apprehended me, why I was standing there alone.

"She is a Jew, sir," the Pole said.

The Gestapo officer started firing questions at me in German. Since it served no purpose to let him know that I knew German, a language spoken more often by Jews than Poles, I told him, in Polish, that I understood no German.

He was a tall, strong man, holding, on a leash, a gigantic German Shepherd dog, who strained and panted with furious energy. "Show me your bag," he said, pointing to it with his gloved hand. I handed it to him, he looked through it, and returned it.

"You will translate," he ordered the Polish policeman. He then asked why I had come to Cracow. I told him my name, and repeated the story about my sick aunt. He wanted to know where she lived. I had never been to Cracow, and didn't know any of the street names. But it occurred to me that every city in Poland had a street named after the great national poet, Adam Mickiewicz. I told him she lived at 24 Ulitza Mickiewicza.

The German narrowed his eyes and looked at me through two small slits. *"Los,"* he shouted suddenly, *"das ist noch ein kind*—forget it, she's just a child." He motioned for me to leave.

I couldn't move—I felt as if I were nailed to the ground. I stood staring at him, wondering if he would loose his dog on me or take aim with his gun.

"What are you waiting for?" the Polish policeman growled. You should get down on your knees and kiss his feet for letting you go!"

In a trance, I turned around and started to walk, not even knowing if my feet were touching the ground, still expecting to be shot in the back at any moment. When I finally looked back, I could no longer see the station. I couldn't believe that I was really still alive.

Chapter 35

Cracow, the historical capital of Poland, was also the seat of the German occupation government, the nerve center of German operations in Poland. Everywhere the German presence was evident. Not only Germans in uniform, but also a great many civilians, including women and children, were living in the city; one heard German spoken everywhere. The Jewish community of Cracow, before the war the fourth largest in Poland, was mostly extinct, except for some remnants living in the ghetto, or hidden by Gentiles, or like myself, passing for Poles. The Polish population had been beaten into submission by the German conquerers and accepted its lot as second-class citizens. The situation was somewhat ironic—the city that symbolized Polish strength and glory was now transformed into the center for Polish abjectness and collaboration with its worst enemy.

This was the Cracow I found on Christmas Eve, 1942, when I left the main railroad station. Just as in Lvov, I needed a place to stay, but this time there was no Mundek to help me. I knew I had to find one before dark, or I might be picked up by the police. I stopped at a newspaper stand to look at the advertisements in the local paper. A few boarding houses were listed, one within walking distance. I headed for that one, and found a bald old man sitting at the entrance; I assumed that he was the custodian, and asked about any vacancies. He rose slowly and went inside to check. I followed him; there was a large dormitory, with two rows of beds lined up along the walls. allowing for very little privacy, but who could afford to be fussy. In any event there was no vacancy.

"But I must have a bed," I told the custodian. It was getting dark, and I was quite worried now.

"I'm sorry," he muttered, "I can't invent any beds."

"But surely there must be some way," I insisted.

"If you can get someone to share his bed with you," he chuckled lecherously, winking at another elderly man standing nearby, "it will be all right with me."

"I'll share my bed with her," I heard someone say. I turned to look and saw a woman, somewhat older than I, about my height, with dark eyes, reddish hair, and a beautiful creamy complexion.

"Oh, thank you very much," I said, "you don't know how grateful I am."

She smiled. "Don't mention it."

It then occurred to me that she might be Jewish, masquerading, like myself, as a Pole. At night, lying in bed with her, I asked who she was. She immediately put her finger to her lips. There were people in the room, and it was not wise to talk about it; but I felt certain that she was Jewish. In the morning, when we were alone, she told me that she was a seamstress, from Lublin; she had just been offered a job, and was going to move out. She advised me against staying at the boarding house; too many people with loose morals, she suggested. The best thing for me to do, she added, was to find a job. But how and where?

I recalled that in 1939, when the Russians came to Stanislawow, Kazimir Jerzenicki, my father's boss at the forestry agency, had escaped to Cracow with his wife. He was descended from a wealthy, noble Polish family. My father had introduced him to his wife. If I could locate him, he might be able to help. The seamstress found a telephone book: luckily he was listed. I took a streetcar to his home, which was located in a fashionable part of the city. A woman came to door, followed by two little girls and a maid. I recognized her immediately, but she appeared not to know me. I asked if I could come in.

"What for?" she asked in a stern, unfriendly voice.

I was reasonably sure she knew who I was. Yet, thinking perhaps that all the Jews in Stanislawow were dead, she might not have recognized me.

"I'm Manya Petranker," I said. "Don't you remember me?"

"Come in," she said in the same harsh voice. She motioned me to follow her into another room.

"Oh, Manya," she said as soon as we were alone, "I'm so happy to see you. You realize I couldn't talk with you in front of the maid, don't you? Oh, it's so good to see you. Do sit down."

"I came for your help," I told her. "I arrived in Cracow two days ago, and I need a place to stay and work. I don't have to tell you how difficult it is for me to deal with strangers."

"Yes, yes, of course," she said. "I understand. I would very much like to help you. I'm wondering whether, at least initially, you could stay with us . . . Well, I'll tell you what. You remain here till my husband comes home from work. If he recognizes you, it means that others can do so, then it will be too dangerous. But if he can't, then we'll do our best to have you stay with us.

When Mr. Jerzenicki arrived home, his wife introduced me to him as the new governess she had hired for her daughters.

"What do you think of her?" she asked.

"She looks like a nice little German girl," he said, apparently pleased with me.

"She is David Petranker's daughter," his wife announced.

"Why, Manya, of course, of course!" He embraced me warmly.

"I'll be honest with you," he told me later at dinner. I'm no friend of the Jews, but for David Petranker's daughter I'll do anything."

I stayed for three weeks at the Jerzenickis', and while all went well, we agreed it wasn't safe to stay at their house indefinitely. The best thing for me to do would be to find work with a German family, who would readily accept me as a Pole, and who would best be able to keep me from the suspicious eyes of the police, constantly on the lookout for Jews. Poring through the newspapers, Mrs. Jerzenicki found an advertisement by a German family for a live-in maid and governess for their three children. I applied for the position and was quickly accepted. They were so pleased to find a Polish girl who spoke their language, since they had difficulty with their former maid, who spoke Polish only.

It was a strange feeling, working for a family whose people were intent on destroying mine. I rationalized that this was a family like any other one; who just happened to be German. Still, they were the enemy— were they to discover my true identity they would almost certainly turn me in. But without them I could not survive; that was most important.

I had barely started in my position when I developed an abscess on my neck. They took me to their doctor, who urged that I be hospitalized to have the infection drained under anesthesia. In order to check into a hospital one needed a Kennkarte, — Identification Card, which I didn't have. Back in Lvov, I told my employer, I had been too young for a Kennkarte. He said he would arrange for the hospitalization without it, using his connections. He was a high ranking German official; I was admitted with no problem.

In the hospital, I began to worry. Who knew what I might say under anesthesia? Watching the nurses who went in and out of the ward, I noticed one nurse who I felt sure was Jewish. It was not her appearance or accent, or any other telltale feature—it was more a matter of my intuition. I decided to risk taking her into my confidence. I called her to my bed, told her of my circumstances, and begged her to be present at the procedure to watch over me. She denied being Jewish, but said she would make it a point to be there as I asked. I now felt even more certain that she was Jewish, and was greatly relieved.

The day before my surgery a team of doctors and nurses came to see me. They examined my neck, but also noticed my leg wound, which had never healed properly. They told me they would take care of both. After they left, one nurse remained behind and told me to undress. I immediately became suspicious, but she reassured me that every patient had to undress and get into a hospital gown before surgery. I calmed down and did as she asked.

As I lay in my gown, waiting to be wheeled into the operating room, the hospital priest entered the ward. I now remembered that each patient, prior to under-going surgery, was visited by the priest, who would hear confession. What did I know about that ritual? I decided once more to act like the happy-go-lucky young girl, hoping to wangle my way through. The priest, a young, amiable, handsome fellow, went from bed to bed, talking with each patient, and finally came to mine.

"Good morning, my child," he greeted me.

"Good morning, Father," I replied.

"I understand you're having surgery this morning."

"Oh, it's nothing, just a little abscess."

"Would you like me to hear confession?"

"Oh, Father, you don't really think I'm going to die, do you?"

"No, I don't," he chuckled, "but it's really not a question of dying."

"Oh," I said, "I'd rather forego it this time."

He nodded benignly. "I'm trying to place your accent. You're from Lvov, aren't you?"

"Yes, Father."

"I'll tell you what I'll do. I'll sing you a song about Lvov."

He had a beautiful voice. After he finished, I thanked him for the song, and assured him that I was now spiritually ready for the operation.

All went well, and after I woke I realized that I had a new roommate in the bed next to me. Her name was Kazia. She was pretty, about my age, with soft brown hair and blue eyes—a plain peasant girl who had, I soon learned, a heart of gold. She worked as a maid in a German club in the city, operated by the Carpathian Oil Company for its German employees. After we became friendly, I asked her if she thought I could find work at that club. I felt certain that my best hope for survival was to be right in the lion's den, working for an important German concern. Kazia said that there was a good chance that her boss, the director, might need some additional help. The atmosphere in the place, she observed, was generally friendly and relaxed, and she enjoyed working there. Her boss, a German named Zeidel, was short-tempered and demanding, but his bark was worse than his bite. Her coworkers were easy to get along with.

That evening one of her friends from the club came to visit. She was plain looking, and appeared to be a few years older than either of us. Kazia introduced us. She was Ukrainian; her name was Katya. I immediately recognized her as Jewish. Naturally I said nothing, but I felt strongly that Katya was also aware of my identity. This put her on guard. She confined her conversation with Kazia, mostly ignoring me.

After she left, Kazia said to me, "you know, I'm really surprised. Katya is an educated girl, and so are you. I was sure the two of you would hit it off, but apparently you didn't."

"She's probably shy with strangers," I remarked.

Before I went into the hospital, I had written Mundek and invited him to visit should he ever have the opportunity. Two days after the operation, I was happily surprised, awakening from a nap, to see Mundek sitting next to my bed, a gift package in his lap. We talked for a long time. He told me about the German defeat at Stalingrad, which he thought correctly as it turned out would be the turning point of the war. He predicted that the Russians would continue to push west against the Germans, weakened by their loss of men and materiel on the Russian front, and from low morale. He was still working on the railroad in Stanislawow. The ghetto there no longer existed; the once flourishing Jewish population was gone, murdered or shipped off to the death camps at Belzec and Maidanek.

When Mundek left, I felt terribly lonely and depressed. How was I to get through in the months ahead? The thought of surviving the war made me sad instead of raising my spirits. Mundek wanted to marry me after the war. But I was not in love with him. Tenderness, affection, love—all such joyful feelings had deserted me. Yet, I wanted to go on living.

Chapter 36

After my discharge from the hospital I immediately went to see Kazia at the club of the Carpathian Oil Company. She was happy to see me, and took me to her boss. How impressive were the club's spacious halls, the wood paneling, the deep armchairs and couches, the chandeliers! It was all such a contrast to the cramped quarters to which I had been accustomed in the past three years, to the squalor and anguish I had lived with for so long. Here was comfort, relaxation, good cheer, a world of style and dignity; a world belonging to the victors. Would I ever live this way again?

Now Zeidel, the manager, was a short, ape-like man, with long hairy hands, bowed legs, and a pot belly. I could tell at once that it was best not to arouse him to anger. To win his favor, I quickly apprised him of the fact that I spoke German fluently. Asked if I had done any heavy house cleaning and maintenance, I told him I had worked in a boarding house, and that as soon as I regained my strength I would be able to do any work he required. He grunted his approval, said he was willing to hire me, but that there was no room available in the living quarters upstairs, unless someone would share her rooms with me. Kazia immediately offered to accommodate me. I thanked her and Zeidel profusely. Moving into my new home, I began my new career as a chambermaid.

That evening I met another girl who lived on the same floor with Katya; her name was Zosha. I suspected that she, too was Jewish, but I wasn't sure. Both Zosha and Katya behaved coldly to me, which I found puzzling; only Kazia was friendly. But that night, as I was falling asleep, I felt a hand on my back. Turning, I saw Katya standing over me. She signaled me to be quiet, and to follow her out of the room. Outside in the hall she addressed me in a soft and surprisingly gentle and cordial manner.

"I didn't mean to hurt you, Fela, but when I saw you in the hospital I knew you were going to ask me if I were Jewish. I don't have to tell you how dangerous it is around here for each of us. But if we single each other out, the danger is heightened. I don't know if you're aware of it, but Zosha is also Jewish. With you on the floor that makes three of us. Any one of us can arouse the Gestapo's suspicions, and then all three of us will be caught. I think it's just as much in your interest as ours that you don't remain here."

"I'm sorry, but right now I must. I have nowhere else to go."

"Do you have any papers?" Katya asked.

"That's just the point. I have nothing to speak of."

"That's very bad," Katya observed.

"What about you? Do you have papers?"

"I have those of a Ukrainian girl who was sent to Siberia. I'm well covered."

"In that case it is much more urgent for me to stay here than for you. Of course, I realize that you came here long before I did, and I certainly don't wish to usurp your place. I'll tell you what, Katya. I'll try to obtain papers, and as soon as I do I'll move out."

She wasn't placated, but she decided to drop the matter for the time being.

"We'll have to go on pretending that we don't care for each other. But at night, when the others are asleep, you can come to my room simetimes, since I'm alone, and we can talk. I was a medical student in Lvov when the war broke out, and I know a few things." She patted my head and then walked back to her room.

I now had to obtain papers immediately. Without them, I couldn't safely leave my place of employment. Furthermore, I had to obtain a food ration card, and to get it I had to show my Kennkarte, which, of course, I didn't have.

I was beginning to settle in at the club, when I was surprised to receive a visit from the seamstress who had shared her bed with me on my first day in Cracow. She was greatly distressed, and she pleaded for my help. If anyone needed it it was I, I thought. I asked her what was troubling her, adding that I would do what I could for her. She had, she said, no papers at all, and only managed to survive because her landlady had pitied her and, in exchange for her sewing had given her food and a roof over her head. Lately the police were searching everyone, and without papers, she was certain to be caught and sent to a concentration camp.

I thought for a moment. This girl had, in effect, saved my life by taking me in that night. Her life was now in danger; it was my turn to reciprocate. But the only document I had was the one Mundek's friend had given me, which attested to the fact that I was a Roman Catholic Pole named Felicia Milaszewska, born in Wilno, and that I worked for the Scrap Iron Company. If I gave her this paper, I could get along without it for a while, but in her possession it might save her life.

However, now there would be two Felicia Milaszewskas in Cracow. I looked at her: we were both petite, with similar features. I decided to chance it.

When I gave her the paper, there were tears in her eyes. I reminded her that I was only repaying my debt to her, and that only if Jews helped fellow Jews could we hope to survive. She took the document and left. I never saw or heard about her again.

A few days after I gave away my only means of identification, Zeidel sent me with a basket of food to the Wawel Castle, the headquarters of Dr. Frank, the German Governor-General of Poland. The brother of the president of the Carpathian Oil Company was Dr. Frank's secretary; he lived with his mother at Wawel, and the two had their meals delivered to them from the club each day. As I was carrying the heavy basket up the hill to the castle I was stopped by a German guard, who asked to see my papers.

I had nothing to show him. Would I be arrested or shot? I pretended to be searching for them.

"I'm sorry," I said, "I must have left them at the club."

"I can't let you through without your papers."

"I'll go back and get them."

Luckily, the guard allowed me to return; my knees were shaking as I walked. Summoning up my courage, I went to Zeidel and told him I needed proof that I worked there in order to get into Wawel Castle. To my great relief, he did not ask any questions, and wrote out a *Bescheinigung*, a letter of employment. He then asked if I had a Kennkarte. I explained that I was too young to obtain one before I left home. He advised me to get it without delay.

To receive a Kennkarte, I needed a birth certificate, issued in the name of Felicia Milaszewska. My only possibility was to write to Mundek, and hope he would be able to find a priest who would issue such a document. I wasted no time in writing to him; to my great joy I received one from him shortly. I immediately filled out the application for a Kennkarte, submitting it to the police along with my new birth certificate. I waited impatiently for my card, but instead I received a summons to appear at the police station because of "certain irregularities" in my application. I was petrified. Should I run away? Should I go to the police and face who knows what? I decided to present myself and play the part of the innocent little girl yet again.

As it turned out, I was sent to see an old spinster, who was kind with maternal instincts toward me.

"This is very strange, Felicia," she said. "We received your birth certificate, but your priest must have been drunk when he made it out. You see here, it states that you are a Roman Catholic, but the stamp at the bottom lists Greek Orthodox."

"Oh, really?" I said, laughing. "I never heard of such a thing." Inwardly I was terribly frightened, but I tried hard to convincingly act my assumed role.

"Don't worry about it. Write to him again and ask him to send you the corrected certificate."

Greatly relieved, I dispatched another letter to Mundek. Soon there arrived a new document with the correct stamp. Now I had to have a picture taken. On Karmelicka Street I found a photographer, who took my picture for the Kennkarte. When I returned for the photo, I couldn't believe my eyes. There, in the center of his window, hung an enlargement of my portrait! There was Manya Petranker, a Jewish girl from Stanislawow, exhibited in one of the most public areas of the second largest city in Poland, where she could be readily seen by any number of people who knew her back home! I went inside and told the owner that I was flattered, but that I couldn't understand why he had chosen me for this honor.

"Oh, but my dear Miss Milaszewska, this is one of the best photographs I have ever taken. Surely you will not begrudge me your permission to exhibit it in the window?"

To pursue the matter further would, I was afraid, arouse his suspicions, so I thanked him and left. By the end of the week I became the proud recipient of a bona fide Kennkarte, the most precious of all documents under the German occupation. It meant freedom of movement, and of constant fear. I was now a person with an identity, instead of a hunted animal. I could breathe more confidently now than I had in years.

I started to go out with Kazia on our days off. Cracow had beautiful parks, historical sites, museums, and other places of interest, and Kazia too enjoyed going to visit these sights. The streetcar which was routed through the most beautiful sections of Cracow, I learned, also included a ride into the old ghetto. I was seized by a desire to see this place, and asked Kazia if she would join me. The following Sunday we took the tour. The stretch through the ghetto was brief. On either side of the tramway were high barbed wire fences separating the doomed from the outside. The ghetto was deserted—here and there I could see out of the corner of my eye, skeletal figures moving about, and my heart writhed and agonized. *Dear God, I prayed, spare them! Destroy our enemies; let us live.*

Chapter 37

With the exception of Katya, Zosha, and myself, all the girls who worked at the club were of Polish peasant stock. They were well built for cleaning and scrubbing and all the other heavy duty chores. I could not keep up with them nor really fit in with their life style, for that matter. They spoke a coarse Polish, interspersing their sentences with cursewords. Katya became aware of this, and one evening took me aside and advised me to make a point of swearing like everyone else. Otherwise I might be too conspicuous. I heeded her advice and began using language which would have caused my parents, may they rest in peace, to disown me. Despite my best efforts, I was not strong nor experienced enough to work as fast and as efficiently as they did. Zeidel, my boss, who, in the beginning, accepted my recent operation as an excuse for my slow pace, now began to grumble. One day he interrupted me in the middle of my chores.

"This work is not for you. The way you discharge your duties here, one would think that you were a guest at the club instead of an employee. I'll tell you what I'll do. Since you speak German, I'll try you out as a waitress at the bar. You will serve beer and liquor and talk with the members. This may be more in keeping with your pace."

I thanked him for his consideration, and that evening I started working as a waitress in the bar and restaurant on the main floor.

It was the end of the winter of 1943. I was now comfortably situated in a private club, my identity properly established as a Roman Catholic Pole with all my papers in order. I was able to enact my role successfully, except that it became apparent to my coworkers that I never received any mail. When this was mentioned to me, I wrote to Mundek, asking him to try to maintain a regular correspondence, advising him not to use his last name, which sounded Jewish, but to adopt a Polish name instead. I also wrote to the Hungarian Count, conveying Manya's regards and her wish to hear from him, but signing the letter Felicia Milaszewska. He took the hint, and wrote to me.

Having solved the mail problem, I encountered another. I was given a one-week vacation, and it was expected that I, like the other girls, would leave to visit family and/or friends. But I had no one with whom to spend it. I usually consulted Katya on such matters, but she had recently left the club to work as a housekeeper for a German doctor, a woman. I thought it best to see Katya and ask for her advice. I was luckier than I had expected: the doctor was leaving for a month, and Katya told me that I could enjoy my vacation with her as soon as the doctor left. But I hesitated—it seemed dangerous. What if someone from the club should recognize me in the street? Katya reassured me that I could remain in the house during the entire week. I brought up the question of food, which was rationed and barely enough for one person. But once again she reassured me that she would share her food. Jews had to help each other; none of us could neglect or fail to help the other. I embraced Katya; we held each other for a long time.

I was happy to have found a place to visit on my vacation, but the thought of being cooped up for a week was upsetting. I needed freedom of movement. But my fears were unfounded. Actually that week was one of my best ones of the entire war. For the first time in months I was able to be myself. Being alone with Katya, not having to worry who might be listening, I could enjoy the luxury of letting my hair down, saying what I wanted to say, talking freely about myself, the past, and my hopes for the future. Katya was a sympathetic listener. At one point I asked her, if we were lucky enough to survive the war, would we ever experience normal feelings again? Outwardly I appeared to be a happy-go-lucky girl — I was so convincing in this role that the Germans often called me *Sonnenstrahl,* little sunshine — but it was only a masquerade. When I laughed, it was never with joy. Could I ever feel happy again? Katya put her hand on mine. "You're lucky that you can make yourself appear carefree," she said, "Otherwise, you would be in danger, because you certainly don't look Slavic. Don't worry about the postwar. Right now, Fela, we have only one goal for which to strive: survival."

She was right. My hair was blonde and I had slightly almond-shaped brown eyes. Katya's were blue, an olive complexion, and straight brown hair; she definitely looked Ukrainian, and she also spoke the language perfectly. She told me how she had obtained the birth certificate of a Ukrainian girl. She was a native of Drohobycz, a town in the Ukraine. When the Russo-German war erupted in 1941, Katya was a medical student in Lvov. Her fiance, a dedicated Communist, escaped to Russia with the retreating Red Army; but he had some good Gentile friends who were able to procure a birth certificate for Katya. She then travelled west to Cracow.

I returned to the club shortly before Easter, to find Kazia and the other girls all looking forward with great anticipation to the holiday. Easter was the high point of the Christian year, celebrated with pomp and pageantry in all of the historical churches in Cracow. For me it was a day of gloom, mocking the fate of my people, but I dared not show my true feelings. I pretended to be swept up by the excitement around me, and since it was taken for granted by Kazia and the others that I would attend church with them, I never even thought to offer an excuse. I wore my best dress on that Sunday morning, and for the first time in my life went to church. During mass I followed Kazia's rituals and gestures as best I would, but when it came to singing the hymns I was really at a loss; I didn't know any of them. After the first hymn, Kazia, whispered in my ear, asking me why I wasn't singing. I told her I had a terrible voice, and I didn't want to spoil it for everyone else. She didn't mention it again.

After Easter I spent a great deal of time thinking about what would happen to me and my people once the war was over. One thing was certain: if the Germans won, they would hunt down every Jew, and those like myself who were living under an assumed identity would probably not want to survive. So, if Hitler was victorious, I vowed to end my life. News was reaching us at that time of the heroic uprising in the Warsaw ghetto. It was a palpable act of suicide, for the besieged human remnants in the ghetto were surrounded by German steel and fire. It was a deliberate decision to go down fighting. It left a lasting impression on me.

I kept asking myself what I, in my unique position of working for a German concern, could do to help in the war against the Germans. Kazia, my closest friend at the club, could not be of any help in this regard; but there was another girl, Yanka, whose father was a sculptor, and who evidently had received better educated than the rest of the girls—she, I suspected, might have contact with the Polish underground. Without any preliminaries, I told her directly that I was anxious to assist the Polish underground. She appeared not at all surprised, and promised to get back to me shortly. A week later she informed me that she had spoken to her contact in the clandestine movement, and that they would place my name on their list of contacts.[1] I could expect a call from a man called Tadek; she gave me his telephone number, with instructions to call him if I had any information which might be useful to the A.K., the Polish underground. It was unlikely that I would ever meet this man, at least before the war ended. With the underground under constant German surveillance, its members had to maintain strict anonymity.

In the meantime I kept encountering Jews, like myself, who had come to Cracow under assumed identities. One day, for example, I was strolling in the park with Kazia, taking advantage of the beautiful spring weather, when I recognized, a photographer from Stanislawow walking down a path. He once had his studio next to our house. He saw me, too, and I could tell that he recognized me. My heart skipped a beat. What if he called out my name? Thinking quickly, I ran over to him, threw my arms around him, and

---

[1] I became a member of the "Zelbet" Company of the A.K., whose leader was "Przemyslaw."

whispered in his ear, "My name is Felicia Milaszewska." He nodded, and smiled broadly. I introduced him to Kazia as an old friend and neighbor from my home town, Wilno. Later, when Kazia was out of hearing, he told me that his wife had been killed by the Germans, but he had managed to rescue his daughter and sister. They all obtained false papers, and now he was working at a large photography studio in the city. We exchanged addresses.

That evening Kazia mentioned, "You know, Fela, that photographer friend of yours, he's quite handsome."

"He's a widower," I replied, "and he's very lonely. If you like him, Kazia, why don't you date him?"

"Oh, but he must be at least fifteen years older than I am."

"So what, you don't have to marry him. It might be nice for both of you to go out together."

They started dating each other. One day the photographer failed to show up for a date with Kazia. She was quite upset, and asked me to try to find out what happened. I went to his place of employment, and learned that he had not shown up there for two days. I expected the worst.

Three days later, as I was waiting on patrons at the club, another waitress called me into the lobby to say there was someone there to see me. It was a young woman, a little older than I, and whom I had never met before. She asked if she could speak with me privately. I went outside with her. Her name, she said, was Julia, and informed me that I knew her brother, the photographer. He had been caught in a police raid and had been sent to the concentration camp at Plashow. Her eyes appeared anguished. I began to shudder; I felt as though I were looking into a mirror, reflecting my own fear and despair during the police raids in Stanislawow. I took her hands in mine, tried to calm her, and assured her that I would do what I could. She stopped sobbing, and told me that she was now left with her brother's eight-year old daughter, and that since he was gone, there was no way for her to support herself and the girl, nor did she have a place to stay. Her landlady had, it seems, found out about her brother and demanded that they move. Her situation, in short, was desperate. "Don't lose hope," I said. "I will try to help."

That night I told Kazia that the photographer had been caught by the police. I didn't mention that he was Jewish, but explained that he was working for the studio without papers but that his work was vital to the German war effort. I then told her that his sister and daughter were now homeless, and I wanted to help them.

"Your mother, Kazia, has eight children at home. Do you think she could take in this little girl? Her aunt could pay your mother for her upkeep from her wages."

Kazia, good soul that she was, immediately wrote to her mother, who agreed to take the girl. As for her aunt, I arranged with the clerk at the club to hire her on a trial basis to do cleaning. I explained that she spoke German, which would be a valuable asset, as most of the German personnel spoke no Polish.

All went well for a few weeks, but at the end of a month Kazia received an angry letter from her mother, which began with the words: "What did you do to me? You sent me a Jewess?" It developed that the girl, unlike her father and aunt, both of whom looked Polish, had Semitic features, and was stopped by a policeman who suspected it and arrested her. I told

Kazia there must have been some mistake, and I was
sure that the matter would be cleared up. I don't know
whether she believed me, but as luck would have it,
the girl was released. I later learned that the policeman still believed that she was Jewish, but taking pity
on her, claimed there had been a mistake, and returned
her to Kazia's mother. Julia turned out to be a rather careless woman, the kind that has a penchant
for getting into trouble. I lost a great deal of sleep
over her, worrying that my efforts to assist her increased my own vulnerability. But like her niece she
was fortunate; nothing ever happened to her.

Just as I became accustomed to my work, an unexpected development put an end to my career as a
waitress. Among my customers was a young German
salesman, about thirty years old, six feet tall, with clean
cut features, brown hair combed straight back, and big
green eyes. His name was Jurgen Rabbe. One day, as I
was serving him his usual stein of beer before dinner,
he said that he would like to see me upstairs in his
room after my work was finished. I told him I was
busy, but he persisted. He furrowed his brows and told
me that for my own good I had better come. Although
words such as these engendered all my fears, I had no
choice but to play along with him. I calmed myself by
reasoning that there were other people in adjacent
rooms, and there was not much he could do by dint of
force. As soon as I was finished with my work I went
to see him. He invited me in, asked me to sit down,
and offered me a drink. I preferred not to have it, I
said, for I was too tired. He smiled.

"I didn't think you would want to drink," he said.

"I usually wouldn't mind one," I replied, wondering
what he had in mind.

"Yes, of course, but generally speaking, Jews aren't
fond of drinking."

My heart skipped a beat, but I tried to remain non-chalant. "I wouldn't know, really."

"You wouldn't? You're Jewish, aren't you?"

Instead of waiting for a reply, he walked over to his closet and took out something, which he put on the night table in front of me. It was a picture of an old, bearded Jew.

"What do you make of this picture?"

"Nothing, really."

"It's my grandfather," he said.

"Your grandfather?"

"That's right. My grandfather was a Jew."

I waited for him to continue.

"Now look," he said with a pleading gesture, "why go on playing this pretending game? I don't want to harm you. If I did I would have gone to the Gestapo. I want to help you. You may not realize it, but you aren't safe in this club. You're not like the rest of the girls. Sooner or later someone is going to suspect you. Besides, I've spoken to Herr Zeidel, and you girls make almost nothing, besides your room and board. You may be able to do a lot better somewhere else."

I began to relax; I could tell that he was sincere.

"Suppose I were to quit my job here," I said, "where would I go? What would I do? My first problem would be to find a place to live, which is virtually impossible these days."

"Yes, I've thought about that," he responded. "A very good friend of mine, Theodor Henrici[2], is a top official in the railway authority. Some of the big construction companies in Poland depend on him for building contracts. If I asked him, he'd be glad to recommend you to one of those companies. You'll not

---

[2] His brother was a well known general, the military commandant of Berlin when Hitler committed suicide.

only be assured of a better job, but a much better salary."

"What kind of work would I do?"

"Secretarial, office work."

"I have no experience."

"Don't worry, you're well educated; you'll learn quickly."

I rose, and told Jurgen how grateful I was.

"I believe in helping people," he said, smiling. "One never knows how it will pay off, but one feels certain that it will."

I told Jurgen that I liked his offer, and he assured me he would speak with his friend immediately. The next problem was how to leave my present employment. As a Polish girl, I just couldn't walk out on a job at an important German concern. If I asked permission to leave, would it be granted? Or should I do something to get myself discharged? I hit upon an idea. The next evening, as I was ready to bring out the dishes to set on the dinner tables, I purposely rammed a tray full of china against a doorpost. The plates, which were impossible to replace in wartime, were scattered all over the kitchen floor. The sound of dishes breaking brought Zeidel running out of his office. He looked at the floor, then at me. Speechless with rage, he then slapped me across the face. Recovering his voice, he screamed in German, "Get out, you good-for-nothing! You're dismissed!"

As I looked down in feigned contrition, I felt elated. I had heard the very words I was hoping for. But later, in my room, I became apprehensive. I didn't expect my dismissal to occur so soon. I thought it would take a few careless accidents to provoke my ouster. Now that it had happened, what was I going to do?

Chapter 38

I had no recourse but to call Jurgen and tell him what I had done. He didn't appear perturbed at all. He had already spoken to his friend Theodor, who was confident that he could find a place for me at a certain construction company. I was to find a temporary place to stay, and after I received my first salary, more permanent quarters would be more feasible.

In some ways I was sorry to leave the club. I had become attached to Kazia, and was friendly with most of the other girls. I had become accustomed to the idea that the club would be my home until the war ended. But Jurgen was right—I was out of place in that job, and sooner or later trouble would develop.

Jurgen introduced me to his friend, Theodor Henrici, who, in turn, introduced me to the owner of a construction firm, a native German in his sixties named Wilhelm Langert. I was hired at once; he was probably only too happy to accommodate Theodor, since he depended on him for contracts. He offered me 1,000 zlotys a month (in the club my salary had been only 200 zlotys)—a fortune to me—to be an assistant office manager. Later I learned that I was replacing a man whom he paid 4,000 zlotys plus benefits.

Very soon after he left, I was put in charge of the office.

My new boss, Langert, was pleased with my work, but there was something about me he couldn't fathom. One day he said to me, "You must be Jewish. When you first came here you told me that you knew nothing about office work, and now in so short a time, you're running the office like an old pro."

"Well, I'm not exactly Jewish," I said, laughing. "Perhaps my maternal grandmother was Jewish.

"Oh, ho, ho!" he guffawed, holding his belly. "You have a good sense of humor!"

The construction company had two offices, a main office in Prokochim, a suburb of Cracow, which was where I worked, and a field office outside of Cracow, which employed Jewish inmates from the concentration camp at Plashow. These were provided by the Gestapo, who charged the company five zlotys per person. One day I asked Langert if he would mind taking me along with him to the field office, so I could get better acquainted with the operation of the firm. What I really wanted was an opportunity to come in contact with my people, and find out if I could help them in any way. Langert readily agreed. It was a beautiful summer day, the kind of easy, pleasant summer day that makes you want to stretch out on the grass, gaze at the sky, and forget all your woes and those of the world. My boss was in good spirits, humming a tune and rubbing his hands together.

"Fraulein Felicia," he said to me, "did I ever tell you that I have a son in Canada?"

"What's he doing in Canada?" I asked.

"He's a prisoner of war."

"Oh, I'm sorry to hear that."

"Ah, yes, he's not exactly having a picnic there, I can assure you."

"It must be difficult," I commiserated.

"Here," he said, taking out his wallet. "I just got a letter from him with a photograph that he posed for at the camp. Look."

I looked at the picture. This, I thought, is how Langert must have appeared at that age, with light blond hair and baby blue eyes. "He doesn't seem to have been mistreated; in fact he resembles a healthy and well fed young man," I commented.

"Handsome lad, isn't he? You know, Fraulein Felicia, I think I would like you as a daughter-in-law. The war will soon be over, and I have a hunch he would like you."

"I'm very flattered, Herr Langert."

"I have an idea! Why don't I arrange for you to take a trip to Germany, say, for two weeks. I would like you to meet my wife; she's a nice lady. I'm sure she would like you. What do you say?"

"I don't know, Herr Langert. I'm overwhelmed. I don't know, really; it may be premature. The war is still far from over."

"Mmmm," he muttered under his breath. His excitement gave way to apprehension. He became quiet. "You know," he said, "come to think of it, I've never heard you express any opinions about the war, or about our part in it. Doesn't any of this concern you?"

"It certainly does, but I don't care to think about it."

"Why not? Go ahead, I'd like to know what you think. Who do you think will win?"

"I'm afraid Germany will lose." I tried to sound casual.

Langert's face turned beet red. Her looked at me with such anger that I could see he was finding it difficult to restrain himself from slapping my face. When he finally got hold of himself, he said to me, in a hissing voice through clenched teeth, "I would like to

---

remind you that you are speaking to a member of the Nazi Party. For saying such things you could be sent to Montelupe."[1]

"I'm sorry. As I told you, I don't like to talk about these things."

He looked out of the window, obviously very upset.

"Please don't be angry with me," I pleaded, "I'm not a military or political expert."

"Oh, I'm not angry," he replied, forcing a smile. "Forget it."

The car came to a halt near the field office, which was a makeshift hut. We went in. A middle-aged, bespectacled man sat behind a rickety table.

"This is Dr. Berliner," Langert explained. "He is a Jewish inmate from Plashow. He is in charge of assigning work to his fellow inmates. We felt it would be best to have one of them oversee their work."

Dr. Berliner stood up and bowed.

"Herr Doktor," Langert called out in a cheerful voice, "this is my secretary, Fraulein Felicia."

"How do you do?" Dr. Berliner said to me most deferentially. Then turning to Langert, he added, "Your secretary, Herr Langert, looks just like my niece. If you hadn't told me who she was, I would swear that she was my niece."

For a moment I froze. All that Langert needed to be told now, even inferentially, was that I looked Jewish. Fortunately I recovered my wits and said jokingly, "Is your niece very pretty?"

"Oh, yes, quite, quite."

We all laughed, and Langert, fortunately, changed the subject and continued to talk shop. After that experience I no longer asked to go to the field office; it was too dangerous. Danger, in fact, lurked everywhere.

---

[1] A political prison in Cracow

One day, at the main office, I almost died of fear—even thinking about it now sends chills through me.

I was working in the office when unexpectedly a Gestapo officer in his S.S. uniform, very tall and thin, strode in holding two German Shepherd dogs on two leashes on either side of him. It immediately occurred to me—and later I learned that I was correct—that this might be the notorious killer and torturer, Muller, from the concentration camp at Plashow. Sitting at my desk, I was aware that the dogs were staring at me, and I became transfixed, in a cold dread, unable to move. I thought that this was really the end, but I prayed—*Dear God, let me calm down.* I stood up and asked the man what he wanted, still unable to take my eyes off the dogs.

He reached the desk in two strides, and told me in a curt manner that he wanted to see Herr Langert. I informed him politely that he was back at the home office in Zwiekau, Germany. Then he noticed that my eyes were riveted on the dogs.

"Don't be afraid of them," he said with a grin. "They are trained to attack Jews only. In fact," he beamed with pride, "they can smell one out a mile away."

"They must be very intelligent," I remarked. After some small talk he left. I flopped down into my seat, terribly shaken. After that he came to our office several times to collect the five zlotys each day for each Jew who worked for us.

One day Herr Langert mentioned to me, "I don't know if you realize it, but you come from a rather noble family."

I had no idea what he was up to. Looking surprised, I responded, "I do?"

"Oh, yes, There's a Milaszewska family living not far from here, who are members of the Polish nobility. You might be related to them."

I had chosen that name because it was the same as that of my favorite female author; I had no idea that it also belonged to a noble Polish family.

"Perhaps I will go and visit them," I said.

"Yes, you should go to see them. It might pay off."

I was hoping he would forget about it, but he didn't. He kept reminding me so often that I realized I would have to go to avoid making his suspicious. So one day I went.

This family consisted of two elderly women, one a spinster, the other a widow. They received me with warmth and elation. They wanted to know which branch of the family I was descended, the main line or a branch thereor. I had no idea as to what to say. I told them I was from Lvov.

"Lvov? Oh, yes, that is the side line." The spinster walked all around me, inspecting my face from all angles. There is definitely a family resemblance, she decided. They were both delighted over their new-found relative, and even invited me to live with them. I expressed my thanks, but made some excuse as to why this was not possible. They urged me to come to visit them again.

When I left their home, I heaved a sigh of relief; at the same time I was touched by their welcome and hospitality. I realized how much I yearned for a home and family. When I first started to work for Langert, I moved into a boarding house, similar to the first one in which I had stayed. Here too I encountered Jews from my home town who, like myself, had come to Cracow passing as Gentiles. There was, for example, the son and daughter-in-law of the Margoshes family, probably the richest Jewish family in Stanislawow and one of the wealthiest in all of Poland. Margoshes leather products were known throughout Europe. I recognized this man and his wife. Since we couldn't speak freely at that place, we went for a walk in the park, where we exchanged all the news we had, and related all the events that had befallen us since leaving Stanislawow. They needed certain papers, and I told them how they could get them. Then they disappeared.

I met them again at the end of the war. They apologized for vanishing, explaining that because of their great wealth they had many unpleasant experiences with Jews who tried to take advantage of them. For that reason they had to be on the move. I felt sorry for them; with all their riches they were less secure than I, who had nothing.

I remained at the boarding house for only a short time. I was then referred to a Mrs. Myszkowska, a woman of aristocratic Hungarian descent, who had a room to sublet, an expensive room, but I could afford it, and it offered me the privacy and anonymity I required. The Germans respected her noble lineage and would not bother her. She lived with her niece, who had a German fiance; he was trying to change her status to "native German" so they could get married. I had never met a woman quite as ugly as Mrs. Myszkowska. Her face was perfectly hideous, its ugliness accentuated even more by her very shapely figure. I soon learned that her character was consonant with her appearance. She was involved in all manner of shady deals. One evening she asked me if I would mind having men come to my room. If I would entertain them properly, both she and I would benefit. I couldn't believe what I was hearing. I became incensed.

"Mrs. Myszkowska, would you ask your daughter to do such a thing?"

She didn't answer, but left the room. For a few days she hardly spoke to me, then things returned to normal; she pretended that nothing had ever happened.

Winter started early that year, and like the other wartime winters it was very cold and snowy. I happened to mention to Mrs. Myszkowska that my galoshes were falling apart, and that I wasn't sure I could afford a new pair. When I came home that evening, I found a new pair of rubber boots in my room. I went to her and asked how they got there.

"It's my present to you," she said with a wink. "Use them in good health."

I thanked her, and thought no more about it. But after I went to sleep, I felt something move in my bed. I was quite drowsy. Then something touched my waist. I opened my eyes, and saw a man in my bed. I was about to scream when he put his hand over my mouth and whispered in my ear, "Be quiet. It's me, Frank." Frank was one of those dubious characters who frequented my landlady's home.

"I won't be quiet. What are you doing in my room?"

"What do you mean, what am I doing in your room? Didn't Myszkowska tell you?"

"What are you talking about?"

"She said you needed rubber boots, and if I got you a pair I could spend the night with you."

I was about to get out of bed, pick up the boots and throw them in his face, but he held me by the waist and wouldn't let go. I shouted for Myszkowska's niece, whose room was next to mine. She came in and asked what was wrong. I asked her to tell Frank to get out.

"You bitch," he snarled, slapping my face, "you really think you're something special, don't you?"

"Leave her alone," the landlady's niece said. "We would like to get some sleep around here."

He left.

Chapter 39

I kept the rubber boots, and said nothing about the incident to my scheming landlady. Rooms were not easy to find; a boarding house could be far worse than this arrangement.

One day in the late fall of 1943 I received a most unexpected invitation from the Bahnrat of the German Railroad Authority, Herr Braun, to attend a party, as his escort at the headquarters of the Deutche Reichsbahn (Railroad Authority). Every good reason dictated that I excuse myself. What need did I have to endanger myself, to incur additional risks? I was repelled by the thought of spending an evening in the company of Hitler's generals and high officials, the architects of my people's destruction. Still my company did business with the Authority and what a coup it would be for me to appear at such a glamorous event, my real identity unsuspected.

"I am flattered," I told Herr Braun, "but I don't see how it is possible. After all I am Polish, and I understand that only Germans are allowed to attend."

"Nonesense," he said, waving his hand as a gesture of discounting my reservation. "You speak German well, and no one has to know you are a Pole. You will accompany me and there won't be any questions asked."

I told him I would consider attending except that I did not own a long evening gown. No matter, he explained, any dress would do. And so on the appointed evening I put on a black sheath dress, and to brighten it up I pinned on a red velvet rose. My date called for me in his chauffeur-driven car on time and after a short ride through the cold dark streets of Cracow, we arrived at the headquarters of the Deutche Reichsbahn. At the gate, a quick check, and we were admitted. Inside Nazi flags were everywhere, as were guests splendidly attired in uniforms of all types, the women attired in long gowns and dresses. Everywhere there were ladies curtsying and men clicking their heels and giving Nazi salutes. Word circulated that the German Governor General of Poland, Dr. Hans Frank, would attend. In a little while he arrived, accompanied by several high ranking military men.

"Come, let me introduce you to Dr. Frank," my escort suddenly announced.

"You think it's safe?"

"Leave it to me." He steered me through the crowd to where the Governor General was busy greeting guests. We waited in line, and when our turn came to meet Dr. Frank, I was introduced.

"This is Felicia Milaszewska. She is a Baltic German." The Governor, wearing a charming smile, turned towards me.

"What a *pulchra rosa*," (Latin for "pretty rose") he said as his eyes fixed upon the flower I was wearing on my lapel.

"Only *pulchra?*" I said in feigned surprise, taking advantage of the Latin I had learned in gymnasium. "Why not *pulchrissima?*" (superlative for "very beautiful).

"Oh, you know Latin?" Dr. Frank said, this time most cordially. "I salute you." Raising his glass, he said, "May all the German girls be as well educated as this little Baltic German."

I could tell I was blushing so deeply that I was sure the color of my face matched that of my rose. If only I could have blurted out the truth, told him who I really was!

"You see," Herr Braun said to me in the car on the way home, "You were so worried about going to the party, yet look how good an impression you made on the Governor."

I continued to work for Langert until the summer of 1944. Things were now going badly for the Germans; the Allies had invaded France, and the Russians were slowly but steadily pushing closer to Cracow. Yet, even while the Germans were retreating, they redoubled their efforts to exterminate Jews. The company office was on a hill overlooking the Prokocim railroad station, where transports of Jews, in increasing numbers, stopped on their way to Auschwitz. One day a transport of Czech Jews stopped at Prokocim while I was having a chat in my office with a company engineer with whom I had become friendly, a young man named Kazik, who was Polish. Through the openings of the cattle cars we could hear cries and wailings, and over and over again the word "water" reached my ears. I noticed how Kazik's lips curled with a sarcastic smile as he heard those helpless souls. I tried to overlook it, but something in me rebelled. Ignoring the danger, I stepped outside, filled a pail of water, and taking it with a cup went down to the standing cattle cars. I ignored the Ukrainian policemen, and proceeded to offer the water to those wretched people. Suddenly I felt something cold and metallic touching my arm, and a voice screaming in my ear, "Beat it or I'll shoot you." It was one of the policemen. He wrenched the pail out of my hand and poured the contents on the ground. I went back to the office, where Kazik greeted me with a stern look.

"Why did you do that?" he asked.

"Because I can't bear to see anyone suffer, not even a dog."

"Tell me, Miss Fela, what will you be when the war is over?"

I knew what he meant. "I don't know," I said playfully. "I think I will be Mrs. So-and-so."

After that incident his attitude toward me changed completely.

Towards the end of June my company decided to close the office and move back to Germany. Many civilians were returning, terrified of being captured by the Russians, from whom they could expect no mercy. Among them was my benefactor, Jurgen. I had kept in touch with him for the past year. One summer night he came to my apartment.

"I'm going back to Munich next week," he told me. "I have an idea. Why don't we get married and return together?"

The tought appalled me. Marry a German, and later find out that his cousins and friends killed my family!

"It would be too dangerous right now," I said, trying to spare his feelings. "If I applied for a visa to go to Germany now they would check me thoroughly, and perhaps learn who I am. We'd better wait until the war is over."

Jurgen looked disappointed, but he couldn't fault my logic.

"I suppose you're right," he said, kneading his hands and looking down at his shoes. "This damned war. The sooner it ends the better."

"It won't be too long, I'm sure."

"Felicia," he said as he rose to leave, "I'd like you to have my ration card. You can collect my vodka and cigarettes, and tell them that I asked you to get these for me. Then you can convert it into money or whatever. One thing you must promise me, that you'll keep in touch."

I told him that I would. A week later I accompanied him to the railroad station, and bid him good-bye, as he left Poland forever.

During the last months of the war, the Germans' source of manpower was being depleted and they started to mobilize every able-bodied German male in Cracow. My construction company employed many native Germans, who were carpenters, cement, and metal workers. Our office was ordered to instruct all native German employees to report for duty with the army, to relieve as many soldiers as possible so they could be sent into active combat. Langert discussed this with me; it meant the suspension of all operations in Poland. For that reason he sent me to the office of the U.K. Stellung, which handled the recruitment of German civilians and arranged exemptions when and where appropriate. This company was staffed by members of the Gestapo and Municipal Police; it was the last place in the world to which I wanted to go. I argued with Langert that as a Pole I was not permitted to handle official business. He insisted that there was no need to reveal my identity; that all I had to do is tell them which company I represented, and use my charm to the best advantage.

I had no choice; I had to go. As I walked into the office of the U.K. Stellung, I prayed, and greeted the officer at the desk with a *Guten Tag*—good day. He waved me to a chair and asked why I had come. In some detail, I presented the problem that the recruitment of our men would create, as our company was engaged in a project vital to the war effort on the Russian front. The officer smiled politely, and asked me to wait while he conferred with his superior. He returned a few moments later with a high-ranking Gestapo officer, who asked me a few questions, then granted my request; the recruitment would be postponed. I rose and thanked them both profusely, greeting them again with *Guten Tag*. As I turned to leave, the officer called me back, and with a puzzled look asked why I had not given the Nazi salute. It now occurred to me that Langert had cautioned me that as a Pole I was not allowed to use the Nazi salute; I had forgotten that I was now supposed to be a German, and used what came naturally, *Guten Tag*. As calmly as I could, I explained that I was Polish and not permitted to use the Nazi salute. The German, turning red, demanded my boss's telephone number; shouting furiously into the telephone about this unheard of business of sending a Pole on such an assignment. What Langert said I never bothered to find out—I was just happy to get away from that place.

Since my company was now closing its operations in Cracow, I had to find a new position. Langert referred me to the manager Herr Kern of Organisation Todt[1] in Cracow. He hired me as a secretary. I worked for

---

[1] Named after Dr. Todt, one of Hitler's chief military engineers, Organisation Todt worked behind the lines, building fortifications for the Wehrmacht.

Kern for about two months, at which time the entire firm also returned to Germany. The work was not difficult, and the Germans with whom I worked were generally courteous to the Poles. Each day we were given hot soup for lunch, a rare luxury at the time. It was prepared by Russian women—mostly mistresses of the Germans, brought back by them as they evacuated Russian territory. The only exception was one German who worked in the planning department. He was always nasty and taunting. Once he asked, with a sarcastic sneer, whether I observed Sunday or Shabbat —the Hebrew word for Sabbath. I pretended not to understand him, and he stopped after a while.

We had many Poles working for the company who were forcibly recruited by the Germans for various projects. Many tried to evade the work by bribing officials. One day the chief comptroller approached me and told me that a certain watchmaker would be coming to our office with two timepieces, one for him and the other for me; I was to accept them and not record the man's name in the work log. Sure enough, as I was listing the names of the workers who presented themselves for duty assignment, a man came to the desk. To my horror, I recognized him as a watchmaker from Stanislawow, a rabid Jew Hater, who would have been delighted to turn me in without the slightest hesitation. I wasted no time at all and ran into the bathroom, locking myself in, and waited long enough for the man to leave. When I returned, the chief comptroller was there, looking altogether puzzled. I wore a pained expression.

"What happened to you?" he asked. "Why didn't you take the watches?"

"I developed terrible cramps all of a sudden," I replied, "and I had to run to the bathroom. I'm terribly sorry."

He never asked me to collaborate again.

Toward the end of the summer, when the organization started moving back to Germany, I was recommended to a Viennese construction firm, which was still operating in Cracow, the M & K Construction Company. As soon as I started to work I moved from Mrs. Myszkowska's place into this apartment here. Materially I had never been in such a good position. I ate all of my meals in the company restaurant, returning to the apartment after dinner. Here I became friendly with Lydia, the beautiful widow you met when you first arrived here. Her husband had belonged to an intellectual group in Cracow; when the Germans arrived, they liquidated all of the current Polish leaders and the potential ones. He was sent to Auschwitz. After my unpleasant association with the witch-like Mrs. Myszkowa, I was thrilled to find myself in the company of Lydia, such a lovely woman, so gentle and kind.

But although materially and socially I was in a better position than I had been for a long time, these last few months of the war were in some ways the most trying period for me. The Russian front forces had advanced all the way to Rzeszow, but there it was stalled. Rzeszow was only a two-hour train ride from Cracow; the long awaited liberation from the Germans seemed within reach. It was so very tantalizing to be that close to freedom, and yet realize that it was not at hand. Time began to drag, each day seemed an eternity. I planned to escape to the Russians on many occasions but considering the great danger I decided not to attempt it. Now Wilno, the origin of my forged birth certificate, was in Russian hands; no longer could the Germans check the records there, even if they suspected me. But I had to wait.

During the day I tried to immerse myself in my work. In the evening, for the first time, I tried to vigorously participate in the social whirl. At my job, I had met a handsome young Pole, about my age, named Cesiek Feliksik. He was the only son of the Polish Police Commissioner in Lvov. He escaped with his family to Cracow when the Russians occupied Lvov in 1939. Cesiek and I dated a few times, and he soon fell in love with me. He told me he wanted to get married after the war. When we talked about the Germans, he declared that he hated Hitler and everything that he stood for, except for one thing. Poland would always be grateful to Hitler, he said, for ridding Poland of Jews. I wasn't too surprised to hear him say that—it was a commonly held opinion among Poles. But while Cesiek was fantasizing about marrying me, I longed to see his reaction when I could ask, "You might like to know, by the way, that I'm Jewish; do you still want to marry me?"

One afternoon when I returned from work after our midday meal, Lydia greeted me at the door with a curious smile and a twinkle in her beautiful eyes. She asked how I enjoyed my dinner[2] and whether I had been able to get any food for our depleted larder. Then she asked me to follow her into the kitchen. There, to my astonishment, was our pantry, well stocked with all kinds of provisions. As I stood staring at our bounty, Cesiek came in, beaming, his hand clasping mine, wishing me, in a loud cheerful voice, a happy Saint's Day. I had no idea what he was talking about, and looked at him with a puzzled expression. I

---

[2] Dinner in Poland was the midday meal, usually eaten around two o'clock.

never knew that as a Roman Catholic Pole I was supposed to celebrate my patron saint's day, rather than my birthday. Cesiek was surprised by my unexpected reaction, and looked questioningly at Lydia. Realizing that I had made an awkward mistake, I laughed sheepishly, trying to cover up my ignorance. I bluffed, saying, of course I knew that this was my saint's day, but I was so overwhelmed by Cesiek's generosity in giving me so much food at one time when it was so scarce, that at first I couldn't figure out what had happened. Lydia had baked a marvelous cake for the celebration, and after the three of us had finished off the pastry we went to see a musical show. The star, whose stage name was Wawa, was in reality a refugee from the Warsaw uprising. It was one of my brightest days during that long nightmare from which I am only now beginning to awaken.

And that brings my story to an end. You already know how the Germans evacuated the M & K Construction Company, leaving me behind, about the call from the German field commander to blow up the dynamite-containing columns which our company had installed throughout the city. Instead I summoned the Polish underground, that brought you and your friends here even threatening to kill me. Had you somehow acted precipitously can you imagine, Naftali, how our stories might have ended?

Part Eight

THE FOREST

Chapter 40

As I listen to you, Manya, I understand only too well the many trials you faced, surrounded by the enemy and all the high-ranking German officials, having to watch your every word and every move, not knowing from one moment to the next whether you would live to see another day. At about the time you arrived in Cracow, I had escaped from the work camp, and began living in the forest. What a life that was—just as harrowing as your existence among the Germans. Sad to tell, I was betrayed more than once by Poles who professed to be my friends. Certain Poles I had known all of my life, and who offered friendship, soon plotted to kill Leibush and me. Why? Because we were Jews. No other reason was needed. But I am getting ahead of myself.

There were about fifty-five of us who escaped from the work camp. We all stayed, at first, in the attics and cellars of various Poles in the area, most of whom were well paid to provide this refuge. I was in the attic of Kotulova, asleep in the hay, into which I had burrowed. In the morning I was awakened by her voice; she had come up to learn how well we had progressed. She inquired about my friend, and I had to tell her that he had been shot in the escape attempt. I asked if she would return to the synagogue building and let me know of developments there. She did, and reported that she had seen about forty men loaded on police trucks, surrounded by guards. The trucks were about ready to leave, but no one could tell her their destination. I had no doubts about that, but I said nothing.

Kotulova brought me some bread and milk, and assured me that no one knew I was in the attic, not even her son and daughter. In the evening she returned with more news. About ten of the escapees had been found hiding in several houses around the ghetto, and were shot immediately. Within a week 20 others were killed. The police were now searching all the houses in the vicinity, so her house was no longer a safe place in which I could stay. The next day Kotulova went to Vichta's house to tell her I would be arriving to join Leibush. When she got there, Vichta, not expecting her visit, denied that anyone was there, but Leibush, overhearing the conversation through the wall, quickly let Vichta know that she should be told of his presence.

My next problem was how to get to Vichta's house undetected. I couldn't leave at night, because of the curfew and police patrols. In the daytime I ran the risk of being recognized. Kotulova brought me a wide-brimmed peasant's hat, a pair of wide breeches, and an old coat. I tied a rope around my waist, put a wood-chopper's axe, a saw and a carpenter's horse over my shoulder, and with my hat pulled over my face, walked to Vichta's house. No one paid any attention to me, and in an hour I made it to her place in the next village. There were four Jews hidden there, but only Leibush was glad to see me. The others clearly resented my intrusion, even though I had been responsible for arranging this hideout.[1] To relieve the crowding, Vichta convinced her sister to accommodate two escapees, nearby. Leibush told me that the day after we escaped, he saw from the attic window, two trucks transporting our comrades who remained behind. Because he thought he recognized me among them he cried for two days and nights, blaming himself for not persuading me to accompany him instead of waiting until the others had gone. That was why he never told Vichta that I was in hiding at Kotulova's house.

I stayed at Vichta's for about two weeks, going out at night to make contacts with friends who were hiding in various attics, barns, and stables. It was then that I made my first contact with the Jews in the forest through a friendly Pole named Franek Zawisza, who delivered merchandise to our store before the war. He had been in touch with the group of Jews in the forest for over a year now. I let them know that I had weapons and provisions, and that we were a group of strong young men who would like to join them. They sent a favorable reply, inviting us. Next I visited a peasant named Wasik, who had access to weapons and from whom I bought my first firearm, a long-barreled 45 caliber revolver, brand new, with 120 rounds of ammunition. This was to be my personal weapon, never to leave my side. I, Naftali, the Yeshiva student who couldn't bear to look when my mother killed a fish for the Sabbath, was now ready to go to war.

---

[1] Hideouts did not always work out as expected. Some Poles changed their minds and reported the Jews to authorities. Others became nervous and insisted they leave promptly. In certain instances those who had found refuge turned away others who arrived later, fearing overcrowding that would result in ultimate discovery.

About two weeks after our escape, Vichta came to us in tears. The authorities, she said, had learned that Jews were staying at her house. German police would, in a short time, arrive to conduct a search. Leibush and I agreed to leave immediately, crossing the fields to the house of Wasik. He wasn't too happy to see us, fearing that nearby German patrols might spot us. He did agree, however, to get a message to Zawisza, our peasant friend who was in touch with the Jews in the forest. Not far from Wasik's house was a wooden bridge, under which we would hide until Zawisza came. It later developed that Vichta had fooled us—she wanted us to leave to gain possession of our belongings, persuaded to do so by two Jews who had taken refuge with her sister, and used this ruse; but it really didn't matter, since we were planning to move shortly.

We shivered in our light jackets for several hours before Zawisza arrived. When he did come, we found him most obliging. We needed a place to stay for a few days before entering the forest, and he immediately offered us his stable. "I live with my mother only, there's no other family," he said. "You can stay as long as you want. I'm hardly ever there anyway. I come only to milk the cows; the rest of the time I stay at my girlfriend's. If the Germans catch you, the only other person they would seize is my mother. But she's an old woman; she's already lived long enough."

We didn't question Zawisza's reasoning, but simply followed him to his house. When the people in the forest were ready to receive us, they would contact Zawisza, and he would let us know.

Several nights later we heard Zawisza calling us in the stable. We let ourselves down by a ladder to the ground, which was covered with hay. Zawisza held a kerosene lamp, and behind him we could see the figure of another man. When Zawisza turned around, his lamp illuminated the face of a man whom I recognized as Lyba. He had owned a grocery store in a nearby village and had engaged in business with my father and Leibush. Lyba's face was dominated by a nose resembling Pinocchio's, which made all his other features shrink into insignificance. He was stocky, about my height, dressed in strange patchwork clothes. There was an alertness about him, like a deer or a fox whose ears prick up when they sense danger.

Shalom aleichem, brieder," Lyba said to us in Yiddish, "Hello, brothers." If he had chirped like a bird or wailed like a jackal, it would have been more in keeping with his appearance. He smiled at us in a shy, boyish way, revealing broken teeth. "Any time you're ready," he said. "We're ready," Leibush answered. That night we made our way into the forest, to start our new life.

Chapter 41

We followed Lyba into the woods, barely able to keep up with him. He slipped between the trees like a shadow disappearing from sight, pausing from time to time to look around, to make sure that all was clear ahead, which gave us an opportunity to catch up with him. It was so dark that I had to hold on to Lyba's jacket and Leibush to mine to be sure that we stayed together.

"Well, we've arrived," he finally said to us, taking the bundle off his back.

We looked around. In the light of early dawn all we could see was virgin forest all around us. Where were the others?

Lyba whistled, a long warble followed by three short chirps. A pine tree in front of us began to shake, and to our amazement it tilted to one side and a human head emerged. We were looking at a secret passageway leading to an underground bunker. We followed Lyba down into the bunker; the tree went back into its place. At first we found it difficult to breathe, and our eyes teared from the fumes of the kerosene lamp; but once we became accustomed to the dense air and the dim light we realized the place was crowded with people. Indeed we learned that the bunker had become too crammed, and a second one was planned. Leibush and

I volunteered to work on the digging and construction details.

During the day we remained inside the bunker. Since most of the activity took place at night, the daylight hours were utilized mostly for sleeping. I was exhausted on the first day. I kept waking, reliving all the experiences of the past months, all the killings, the fears, the terrors. I wondered for what purpose I had fled to the forest. How safe was I here? How could I survive in such hostile surroundings? But what choice did I have? Certainly I had a chance.

Most of the people there knew my brother; many had been customers at his store. There were about forty all told: three women, one infant, and the rest grown men. They were mostly Jews who had lived in the country among the peasants. When they saw their fellow Jews being rounded up, consigned to ghettos, and eventually transported to the concentration camps, they went into hiding in the forest. They knew the countryside, and they had trusted friends among the peasants and so could obtain foodstuffs. Lyba was one of them. He was a trapper by trade, an unusual occupation for a Jew. He knew the forest better than almost anyone, and this knowledge was the single most precious asset of the group. Lyba had brought with him his brother Herschel, and in their strange, makeshift clothes they were two of a kind. Then there was Big Avrum Seiden, a very tall country Jew who had taken his pregnant wife with him. She was a beautiful woman. Shortly after they arrived in the forest she gave birth to a son, who was now one year old. He always ran around without clothes, and was nicknamed "Tarzan" by the group. The unofficial leader of these people was Pinyeh Frohlich, who before the war worked as a forester for a rich Jewish family named

Vang, who owned a very large estate. Pinyeh was a man of great innate intelligence and wisdom. Whenever a dispute arose within the group, he was able to calm tempers and settle the problem in an amicable manner. Pinyeh also brought his wife, Feige, with him. She was the sister of Big Avrum, and almost as tall. Their sixteen-year old daughter, Itka, had been placed as a maid with a friendly peasant family. The third woman in the group was a woman in her seventies whom everyone called "Grandma." She worked harder than most of the men, and served as our cook. The males were all husky and fairly young; no surprise since they had survived four years of German occupation.

We started to build a second bunker, and before long we needed a third. Shortly after I arrived I was able to make contact with fifteen other escapees, and they joined us. Erecting the bunkers was a far more formidable enterprise than I had ever imagined. Our major problem was disposing of the soil we dug up; we just couldn't leave it around for it would have attracted the attention of the peasants who would occasionally wander through. The Germans never ventured into that part of the forest, but the peasants might enlist some of their friends and come after us. All the soil had to be deposited into sacks, and at night taken some ten kilometers away and dumped. I would often accompany Lyba and Leibush, who were both as strong as mules, and who would carry two sacks, one on either side, while I had my gun ready, prepared for any intruders. Night after night the sacks of soil were carried off; there seemed to be an endless amount. It was incredibly hard work, but it helped pass the time, and was therefore a blessing.

Nothing could be left lying around the bunkers; any trace of our presence could be our undoing. We had to be careful not to break off even a branch of a tree, for the slightest clue could arouse suspicions. We dared not use nearby trees to obtain wood for beams and supports for the new bunker but had to walk several kilometers away and carry them back. We made the hiding place about eighteen feet long, nine feet wide and five feet high, with an entrance of about two feet square to allow us to get in and out, plus several air vents which were camouflaged with pine needles. We made a wooden door for the entrance, covering it with soil, to which we attached a young tree, so that the entrance was well hidden, unlikely to be noticed by anyone passing by.

I most admired Lyba. In normal times I might not have noticed his remarkable qualities. Semi-literate, he was a simple soul whose appearance and manners were comical. But in the forest he was in his element. He could make his way in the dark as though he had X-ray vision; he never got lost. He would run barefooted through the forest like a deer, leaping over mounds and fallen trees, never hurting his feet. He could identify a person from a great distance, predict the weather with uncanny accuracy, and accomplish seeming miracles. Lyba and I liked each other from the first; for some unknown reason he became unusually protective of me. I was the inexperienced city boy and he was the expert woodsman; he was going to look after me and would make sure that I was as comfortable as possible.

One night Lyba returned to our hiding place, and from the look on his face I could tell he had a surprise for me. As often happened on such occasions, he stared at me with a sly, mysterious smile, not speaking a word, but clucking his tongue. Then he finally said that he had something for me. He took off his military pack, which was always slung over his shoulder, even when he slept, and pulled out a piece of rag. The way he unfolded it, one might think he had precious jewels inside. He put the rag under my nose and showed me two ripe cherries. "Take them," he said. "They're the first of the season. I just picked them off a tree, and I'd like you to enjoy them." As I ate the cherries, he watched approvingly.

He started bringing me all sorts of delicacies from his nightly forays among friendly peasants—a baked chicken liver, a homemade sausage. Whatever was scarce to come by, he saved for *Tadek*, as he and my comrades liked to call me. He also brought meat and fruit and other foodstuffs for which Leibush and I would pay him, and which we would share, as much as possible, with the others. When we asked him how much it cost, he would close his eyes, make faces as if in deep concentration, suck in his lips, then open his eyes and say, "This calf liver I bought tonight cost me seventeen zlotys, then I went to Baba, she baked it and charged me two zlotys, and fifty groshen for the salt . . . this comes to"—he would close his eyes again and move his lips—"twenty zlotys. And if that's too expensive, boys, I'll take it back." Baba was Lyba's best friend. She was an elderly peasant woman who lived by herself at the edge of a village; she let Lyba use her home as his headquarters. We never argued about price, although we knew he never paid as much as he claimed. We gladly gave him the money, both because he needed it and because his favors were worth more than he asked for. Lyba was instructing us on how to survive. On dark nights he would take me along on his hikes. He would tie a rope around his waist, and I would follow, holding on to the end of it. I soon became accustomed to the dark, and began to learn the secret passages through the forest. More important, I became acquainted with the Polish peasants whom Lyba visited, and on whom we depended for food and for places to hide while on foraging expeditions. Sometimes Lyba would walk three or four kilometers into the forest and bury a sack of potatoes under a tree. Later, even on the darkest night, he would find his way back to the tree, which to the untrained eye looked like a thousand others in the woods. He must, I thought, use his heightened sense of smell to find the place. So his huge nose was an asset after all.

It was not long, however, before I found myself emulating Lyba. One night Leibush and I faced a long trek to get food from a peasant. Lyba had not returned from a previous errand, and we had to decide whether we could find our way there and back by ourselves. The route wound through dangerous swampland. At first we hesitated, but then decided to try. To my amazement, I had no difficulty in coming or going; I had become a capable woodsman.

We lived in the forest for two months without any hostile encounters. Our extreme caution and vigilance made that possible. We had built up our small arms arsenal to the point where it contained five revolvers, one rifle, many rounds of ammunition, and a few hand grenades. Day and night I wore a leather belt under my winter jacket, and in that belt I kept my long-barreled revolver, two hand grenades, an axe, a flashlight, a bayonet, a wooden spoon, and one hundred and twenty rounds of ammunition. The peasants were forbidden by the Germans, under penalty of death, to own or carry firearms, so their weapons were limited to pitchforks, knives, and hatchets. We felt confident, for that reason, that if peasants should find us, we could defend ourselves. But we suffered a severe blow when we were least prepared for it.

It happened in the dead of winter, on a morning in January of 1943. The snow was piled two feet high in the forest. As we drew near the bunker Lyba immediately sensed that something was wrong. No guard was posted as was our custom, and broken branches were strewn all about. We drew our guns, fearing the worst. And the worst is what we discovered. It was a massacre, a sight as gruesome as one would ever see. All around were bodies (eighteen in all) mutilated and ripped open. Little "Tarzan" lay next to his mother, the heads of both split and gorey. The bodies appeared to have been attacked by ferocious wild animals. I watched in abject despair as "Lange" Avrum picked up his dead infant and knelt to kiss his lifeless wife.

No mystery surrounded the identity of the attackers. The wounds were those inflicted by axes, knives and pitchforks, precisely the "weapons" wielded by the Polish peasants. Somehow, we were never able to discover how these people from a nearby village had learned about the location of our bunker and managed, while all our armed men were away constructing a new one, to penetrate our hideout. And why had our fellow Poles turned upon defenseless Jews with such unrestrained fury? The bodies, stripped of clothes and shoes, told only part of the answer.

We placed the dead in the bunker and hurried back to tell our comrades the grisly news. Three days later we returned to conduct a brief funeral service, performed by my brother Leibush, and to provide a proper burial. We buried the bodies in an adjacent area. At least in death they would be liberated from the dark underground hole in which they had hidden for so many months, hoping and praying to survive.

Our first thought was revenge. We would follow the tracks back to their village and set fire to the homes and barns of those responsible, shooting as many as we could find. But after much discussion we realized that reprisal would bring back others, and that we should wait for a more opportune time.

We had no choice but to abandon the bunkers, the many weeks of hard work now wasted. We moved deeper into the swampland, where hardly anyone ever ventured. This time we did not build bunkers; but decided to stay above ground where we could protect ourselves by moving from place to place. The relative peace we had enjoyed prior to the massacre now came to an end. The peasants, afraid of our revenge, kept looking for us; we had to keep changing our positions. We now depended more than ever on the few friendly peasants in the nearby villages for food and supplies. Our only other source for provisions was trapping. As we travelled deeper into the forest, we became freer in our movements. We no longer feared leaving footprints, broken branches, or traces of fires. Lyba, who of course was an accomplished hunter, taught us to set traps, and almost every night we were able to snare wild rabbits. We also set traps for deer, and if we were lucky enough to catch one, we would have meat for days. Once we even caught a wild boar. In the summer we depended on the villages for water, but in winter the abundant snow provided an ample supply once heated over a fire.

But during any season we were still dependent on friendly peasants. I had deposited money and valuables with various Polish families when my family was temporarily deported to Rzeszow. Most of the merchandise and clothing had been left with Kotulova. One night I went to her, for I was in need of some clothes. I could sense that she was not too happy to see me.

"Pani Kotulova," I said to her, "I'm in desperate need of some clothes. I need boots and a jacket."

"I'm sorry," she shook her head and lowering her eyes. "I can't really help you. Your sister Rachel came here a while ago and reclaimed everything."

"No, she couldn't have. She was sent to the ghetto in Rzeszow, and from there she was taken to her death." I was shocked to hear her lie.

Then she said, "She must have sent someone. Yes, that's what it was."

"Well, let me say this to you, Pani Kotulova. You saved my life. You hid me in the attic. You helped to obtain false papers for me and Leibush. For this I shall be grateful to you for my entire life. But I also entrusted you with our merchandise, apparel and money. Now I'm in dire need, and I come to you for your aid. If you don't want to help, then don't—I won't hold it against you. But from now on we're even. I consider my debt to you paid in full. Don't expect anything else from me. I felt honored to know you before, but now you are just another person to me."

She did not say a word, and I left empty handed. I never saw her again. Fortunately I had spread my assets around among various families. I chose ten Poles whom I felt I could trust, and deposited 10,000 zlotys with each. The understanding was that if no one in our family ever came back to claim the money, they could keep it; but if one of us should ask for its return it would be forthcoming. Most of it was given back (eight out of the ten), but it wasn't easy.

The first family I went to see after the rebuff from Kotulova was a storekeeper named Drevnitzki. He used to buy provisions from my father, and they had been good friends. He lived in a secluded house, surrounded by trees and shrubs, so it was fairly easy to enter his yard unnoticed. When I approached the front door, I realized that a party was in progress at the back of the house. I debated whether to knock or come back another time, but because it was a long hike (two to three hours on a dark night) from the forest, I decided to knock. The door was opened by his wife; she looked at me as though I were a ghost. She must have assumed that all the Jews of Kolbuszowa were dead or gone. I told her I wanted to talk with her husband; she said he wasn't home.

"I must speak with him," I said.

"About what?"

"About some money I left with him, which I need now."

"But he's not here."

"I'll wait until he comes home," I told her.

"Oh, yes, I remember now. Your sister came and took the money."

"My sisters have been dead for more than a year."

She shrugged her shoulders.

"Besides," I added, "if someone came here pretending to be one of my sister, you would know it, for you knew all of my sisters well."

"My husband isn't here." Her voice was now quite shaky.

"Then let me talk with your son." Her son, Vladek, was one of my old schoolmates.

"All right, let me see if I can find my husband." She obviously had no trouble locating him, for he came to the door in a few seconds.

I could tell from his eyes that he was genuinely glad to see me alive, yet afraid a guest might see me and report him to the police. His wife went to rejoin her company, and I remained alone with him. I have come for the money, I said. He would be glad to give it to me, but he had only 2,000 zlotys on hand; it would take him a week to get the rest. I explained that I would take what he had, and be back at a future time for the rest — I didn't want to set a definite date, lest I be trapped if something went wrong. He gave me the money, and I thanked him.

"Do me a favor," I added. "Please tell your wife not to concoct stories about my sisters picking up the money. And please put the rest of it in a package, so when I come back a good deal of time can be saved."

I returned in three weeks and he gave me a package. When I got into the forest and opened it, the remaining 8,000 zlotys were there in full.

The next person I went to was a former school teacher, Mrs. Weglowska, who used to teach my sisters in the public school for girls, and whom I considered a very honest person. I chose a rainy night for this visit, for she lived in a densely populated area, where many people knew me, and where I could easily be recognized.

"My goodness, you're still alive!" she exclaimed when she saw me. I told her I had come for the money.

"For heaven sakes, go away," she said in a quavering voice, "I don't want my husband to see you."

"I gave the money to you, not to your husband. Now I need it to live on."

"But I don't have it. Why don't you come back next Wednesday and I'll have it for you."

I told her that I would return, but I couldn't say exactly when. I then asked her if she had a safety pin. When she brought it to me, I undid my jacket so as to expose my revolver, and pretended to hitch up my pants with the pin. As she stared at my gun, I asked her to have the money wrapped in a package for me, when I came back in a week or two. A month later, again on a dark rainy night, I went to her house. I could see her sitting in her living room, alone. I knocked on her door; when she saw me she went inside without saying a word, and brought me the package. I thanked her. She made no gesture of inviting me in, nor did she offer any comments. I expressed my gratitude again and left.[1]

All this money was an assurance of life, not only for me and my brother, but for the entire group, and for the friendly peasants as well. I would, for example, give twenty zlotys to Lyba to buy a loaf of bread worth seven. He would go to a poor peasant and pay him fifteen for the loaf. The peasant would then have a profit to enable him to buy provisions for his own family, and Lyba would have five zlotys for himself. Both Lyba and the peasant, in this way, became dependent on me, and I could rely on their loyalty.

Sometimes we would lie in wait at the edge of the forest for a herd of cows that the Germans had confiscated from the peasants, and were leading through the road to the nearest railroad station, to be shipped back to Germany. Lyba had taught us how to lure a cow into the forest and make away with it without being noticed. We all took turns doing this, sharing our booty with the group.

---

[1] In one instance, that involving Skowronski, a storekeeper, my efforts to recover my money almost led to my undoing. He and two others planned to attack me shortly after I arrived in his house to collect what I had left with him. Fortunately I had expected trouble, was armed and accompanied by two others who hid themselves outside. I shot and killed one of the would be attackers and we made our escape, money in hand.

Once we had abandoned our bunkers, we had difficulty finding places to sleep. Since we moved around so much, we had to improvise our sleeping facilities in the open. We cut down branches of spruce trees and made beds on the snow where the trees were packed most densely. Then we would bundle ourselves in whatever was available—clothes, newspapers, rags, blankets. In the morning we would find ourselves lying in a pit in the snow, sinking sometimes three feet from our weight and warmth. The nights were cold, but we were sheltered from the wind by the high walls of snow around our pit. At times fresh icy precipitation would fall, and we would wake up buried in a foot or more of soft snow. While we had to shake it off us, we were grateful, for it effectively covered all our tracks.

The worst weather was a wet snowfall or an icy drizzle. Then our clothes would be soaked through, or we would find ourselves encased in solid ice. When this happened we could hardly move, appearing like weird mummies, alien creatures. We were frozen, but had no change of clothes. It took an entire day of standing in front of a fire to dry out. Sometimes it would rain, or a wet snow would fall, for days. We shivered in our wet clothes, frozen, tired, unable to sleep. Yet almost miraculously no one got sick—not even with a cold. I wondered how much longer we could survive under these conditions. On such nights, those who could manage went to the homes of friendly peasants, and dried off in the stables, where we could hang our wet clothes. On those winter nights, I would constantly dream of having a hot cup of tea. If I could have had one wish granted, it would have been, without hesitation, cups and cups of hot tea. I kept telling myself that if I ever survived this, I would drink hot tea from morning to night.

Chapter 42

Most of our time was spent in either hunting for food or shuttling back and forth between our hiding places and friendly peasants, from whom we obtained bread, potatoes, vegetables, and occasionally some meat. One of them, Jan Hodur, whom I got to know well at the time, lived on a gravel road that bordered on the forest. Hodur was a tall, good looking man with light blue eyes and an aristocratic face. With a wife and seven children it was a miracle he survived. He was so poor (he wore no pants, just thick underwear), so unproductive the land he cultivated. To supplement his income he cut wood illegally in the forest nearby and sold it in town. However wretched his circumstances Hodur was a proud man, always eager to recount his military service, to speak glowingly of Poland. He loved to discuss politics but so opinionated was he, that it was virtually impossible to get him to consider any ideas that were not his own. Still, every Sunday he bought the newspaper and took great pleasure in discussing the events of the day with me.

Stefka, Hodur's wife, liked me. To her I was "Nash Tadek"—our Teddy. She was a fine woman, possessed of a beautiful voice and she loved to sing. For me she performed a most valuable service, washing and boiling my lice infested underwear. And even when there

was no food in the house she managed a few scraps for
me. Stefka moreover shopped for us. We gave her
money (usually twice the actual cost of the items) and
she brought back bread, carrots and onions. It was a
deal that both of us greatly welcomed. She had a young
daughter with whom I became friendly. The sixteen-
year old Stashka had long brown hair, blue eyes, pearly
teeth, and laughter that sounded as clear as a crystal
bell. When we visited Hodur, we always arrived early
in the morning before dawn, and hid in his stable all
day, waiting for nightfall before we would return. I
would often see Stashka while I was there, and in a way
became her confidant. I knew that in time of need I
could count on her.

My first winter in the woods was coming to an end. I
never thought I would live to see springtime, and here
it was, in all its resplendant beauty. Everything was
turning green again. Early in the morning hundreds
of birds would begin to chirp and sing, the air was
scented with fresh pine needles and the sweet smell of
the budding spruce. Soon the sun would emerge to
dissolve the filmy mist, revealing beautiful sights
painted by the invisible hand of nature. At times like
this I would sit down, leaning against a tree, and think.
Here new life begins—the trees, dormant all winter
are leafing; the birds have returned, all nature is re-
juvenated once more. Why can't nature work its magic
on people? Why can't my sisters' young children be
revived in the springtime; why doesn't God give them
another chance? I would sit for hours and ponder what
my life would be like if my sisters and Rozia and all
the people I knew returned to life. Then I would open
my eyes and see the forest and the dark reality of my
present existence. I was bitter. I cursed the entire
world, the whole human race. Why did mankind allow

the Germans to annihilate us, and did nothing to help?
I thought of my brother, his family and my Uncle Sam
in America. Do they know what is happening to us? If
I could know that they were thinking of us and really
cared, it would be easier to continue the struggle.[1]

I would go down to the edge of the forest and watch
young men and women from a nearby village go out
into the fields, singing and frolicking; I would lapse
into a melancholy mood, bewailing my wretched fate,
that of a hunted animal, whose only crime was being
born a Jew. It was still a beautiful world that God had
made; man, however, had turned it into a jungle. Why
hadn't God done a better job when he created man?

We kept moving through the forest, evading the
watchful eyes of those hostile peasants who would
destroy us. If any of them spotted us, we moved
quickly. Some of our group favored returning to a
bunker. Others considered it a lethal trap. I myself
felt terribly confined in the bunkers, and stayed out of
them as much as possible. Once we dug one under the
floor of the barn of a friendly peasant. It was considered the safest place we could find at the time, and
we moved in for the day. Unlike those in the woods,
there was no head room, and we had to crawl on all

---

[1] How could they possibly know that I was beaten by the
Germans because of my Uncle Sam in Brooklyn?! It happened
one day as I was returning home from forced labor. I was accosted
in town by a group of German soldiers, one of whom pummeled
me in a most brutal manner. Why, I asked him, was he beating me
so cruelly? He wished, he answered, to attack "Uncle Sam in
America," but unable to reach him he'd vent his anger on me.
Battered and quite confused, I returned home. How, I asked my
father, had the Germans known I had an Uncle Sam in America?
(The assault took place not long after Germany declared war on
the United States.)

fours. Each time a cow above us urinated, it would trickle down through the fissures in our makeshift ceiling. My companions did not seem to mind it, but I found it almost unbearable. When it became dark, I announced that I was leaving the bunker, come what may. The hole was stifling and hot, and I felt it was becoming my grave, in which I was doomed to lie until the Resurrection. Then I recalled that when I was digging it on Twardon's order my biggest fear was not that of being killed, but of lying alive in my grave, covered with soil and unable to breathe, and suffocating slowly. This dread, along with the stench, the lice eating away at our feet, and the stifling heat, affected me, and I rebelled. Even now, so many years later, I sometimes experience the nightmare of lying there, buried alive, unable to move or breathe, lice nibbling at my feet, with no possibility of scratching myself.

We returned to the forest, and we were now living in a swampy area, where the peasants never set foot. But we had a new problem—mosquitoes. They were the true marauders of the swamp; they ate us alive. I would pull the blanket over my head and wrap myself completely, but they would somehow get inside to bite, prompting me to cry, out of sheer frustration. Yet Lyba never seemed to mind them. I used to sit and study his nose, which was often so crowded with the creatures that it looked like a small porcupine. A mosquito, thin as a piece of black thread, would land on his nose; in a few minutes it grew into a reddish orb, and would take off, only to be replaced by another customer. Lyba would sleep through it all, totally oblivious. He snored so loudly that the noise rivaled a trumpet or a ram's horn blown in the synagogue on Rosh Hashanah. Actually, at times his staccato nasal sounds posed a danger to all of us; for example, when we were sleeping in someone's attic or barn without the owner's knowledge. I told Lyba something had to be done about his snoring. He agreed to have a string tied to his finger, and each time he started I would tug at the string. At first he would stop, but after a while he became inured to the tugging and ignored it; besides, I got very little sleep that way. He then agreed to have the string tied to a more sensitive part of his body. This time it worked.

All of us wanted to contribute as much as we could to the war effort against the Germans, but our small numbers and the lack of support of the local population severely limited this resolve. One opportunity, however, did present itself at about this time, and we took full advantage of it.

A peasant named Fronc worked in a dairy operated by the Germans, not far from Kolbuszowa. They had ordered all the peasants in the district to bring their milk to this dairy, where it was converted into butter and various cheeses, all of which were sent to Germany. In return, the peasants received a pittance. The milk that was left from the processing was sent to Kolbuszowa to be distributed among the local population. Fronc used to steal cheese from the dairy, and sell it to us at a good price. He would always tell us how angry he felt when he went to the dairy, seeing the Germans exploit the peasants so mercilessly. I had the idea that we should invade the dairy one night and destroy the machinery, which would, of course, stop the production at least temporarily. I told Fronc about my plan; he approved. One night six of us—my brother Leibush, Pinyeh the Forester, Lyba, Big Avrum, Ela Katz, and myself—left our hiding place and went to Franek Zavisha's stable, which was not far from the dairy. We hid in this place, without informing Franek. The following night—dark and foggy—we separated into three groups, and approached the dairy from three directions. Pinyeh and I were the first to get there. We knocked at the door, and when the night watchman came out we told him, at gun point, that we wouldn't hurt him if he cooperated. He nodded in agreement. Then the others arrived, and in half an hour we demolished the entire plant. After tying up the watchman, we gathered cheeses, and left by the way we came. As we made our escape toward the forest, the fog was so thick that I could hardly see Pinyeh who was just a few paces in front of me. It seemed as though I were walking on a cloud. On a night like this we felt quite safe, as no one outside our little band would be out in such a fog, for fear of getting lost. But with Pinyeh and Lyba as guides, we did not worry. Two hours later we were back in the forest. We had taken enough cheese to last us for a month. We learned soon after that when the peasants came to the dairy on the following morning with their milk, the police were waiting for them. They questioned every worker and every peasant, but they never could find out who had destroyed the plant. For a while, at least, the peasants were not obliged to turn over their milk to the Germans, and could enjoy their own butter and cheese. This successful foray encouraged me to consider more ambitious raids. Before the war the Polish peasants in our area had been well organized and had launched a spirited campaign of protest against the government. Many rallies were held in the marketplace at Kolbuszowa, the leaders even using our home for their headquarters during these mass gatherings. During the war they had organized the B.CH., *"Bataljony Chlopskie* (Peasant Battalion). It was my plan to seek out the leaders in

the area, men like Salach and Olszowy whom I knew
prior to the war, to urge them to combine their forces
with ours. I managed to attend a meeting where I was
received quite amiably. I assured them that we could
provide not only men but funds to support joint sabotage projects. Together we sang Polish patriotic songs
and swore vengeance against the hated Germans. This
most promising beginning, however, came to naught.
The reason: the A.K., they later informed me, was
already too strong and well organized in the area, even
among the peasants. To my great disappointment our
group would have to struggle on alone.

Gradually I learned of the fate of my friends with
whom I had lost contact after the escape from the work
camp. A man named David from Kupno came to us
one day. He told us that on the day before the peasants
had killed Yankel Lampl, the drill sergeant from our
labor camp. He had been in hiding with a peasant in
Widelka, but when his money was gone and he was no
longer able to pay him, this peasant together with his
friends arranged to have him killed, so that the police
would not learn about it and accuse him of harboring a
Jew. They agreed, rushed in with their axes, and
hacked Yankel to death.

My friend Charlie, the one who had the letter from
Eleanor Roosevelt, returned to his native village of
Kupno. Each Sunday we would call on a certain peasant
to obtain food, for which we would pay him, but he did
not charge Charlie because of his friendship with his
father. I went there with David one Sunday, and waited
for Charlie. He was delighted to see me, embracing
and kissing me. He had been told that I was taken
away, and was sure that I was dead. I invited him to
join us in the woods, and he gladly accepted. He had,
he told me, been in the Glogow labor camp just when

the messenger I sent arrived to tell them of our plans.
As a result he and sixteen others managed to escape.
He explained that he had no money; he was being
hidden by a girl who worked as a servant for a peasant
family, and who had known Charlie for a long time.
She hid him without the knowledge of the family for
whom she worked, but was unable to provide him with
food, hence his weekly pilgrimage to this peasant. The
barn that had served as his shelter was being emptied
during the winter, and he and the girl were afraid that
sooner or later he would be discovered. Charlie went
back to the girl and told her that he would now be
staying with some friends. He was with us in the forest
for a few months. One night, with another member of
our group he went to pick up some shoes from a
cobbler, whom we had used before. This time the man
and his friends set a trap for them; Charlie and his
companion were killed.

Gradually we moved from the swampland to the
more densely wooded area, where we erected a new
bunker. One day, in late spring, one of our guards
woke us—he had seen a group of peasants, armed with
pitchforks and axes, coming toward us into the forest.
Then a second lookout reported another band approaching from the opposite direction. They were, we
understood, staging an *oblava*, or manhunt. Only later
did we discover what had caused this. Ela Katz had left
a cow with his neighbor, Kardis, for safekeeping, but
the peasant had slaughtered the cow instead. So Ela
called on him, demanding a share of the meat, but
received no satisfaction. Apparently the peasant decided to keep the whole cow, for he gathered a group
of his friends, who were now descending on us.

Pinyeh, our leader, was away that morning. I usually
served as his second-in-command, but they were a

group of country dwellers who resented me, the "city boy," and would not follow my lead. We were near a clearing and some of the group wanted to run through there and escape into the forest on the opposite side. I disagreed; I believed our attackers wanted us to come out into the open. The best maneuver, I thought, was to run towards one of the attacking groups, shoot our way through, and then get away. But I was unable to convince them. We therefore split into two groups; one, of about thirteen men, headed for the clearing. The other, which I led, proceeded into the forest towards one of the attacking groups.

We started to advance. Lyba was the first to spot them, pointing them out with his weapon. Everyone stopped, looking at me.

"Let's go," I told them, "we mustn't stop."

We kept moving forward until we could hear them talking. Then they spotted us. I heard one of them say, "Let's go and get them." We kept advancing, though my knees were shaking. Now I could see their faces.

"Now!" I shouted. "Shoot!"

We fired, and all but one ran away. That one lay dead.

But our other group had met with disaster. The peasants were waiting for them. Somehow they disarmed our men, made them dig their graves, then hacked them to pieces. On this day we lost thirteen of our men, among them the "Langer" Avrum, Ela Katz and both Yankel and his brother, Nuchim Leibowitz. Now only a handful of us were left. We moved into a different part of the forest, close to Hodur's village. But the change brought us no better luck. We lost two more men, the Kraut brothers, our munitions experts, on whom we had depended for making bullets and maintaining our weapons.

These brothers, whom we nicknamed Kapusta—cabbage in Polish—came from a village near Pustkow, where the Germans had experimented with their rockets. Most of the peasants had been forced to leave that area, which was then taken over by the S.S. The brothers hid among the peasants who remained in the area, usually to perform chores for the S.S. Every week they came into the forest to reload our shells and repair the old, broken down guns we were able to acquire from the peasants. I learned from them that one of the S.S. men whom I encountered (the one who had Motek beaten to death and had yelled in the room full of holy books, "Jehovah, Jehovah, where are You?") was living with his Polish assistant Vatzek in a house in that area, where he administered the confiscated lands. Parties were held there almost every night, the really big ones on Saturdays and Sundays, when everyone got drunk. My yearning for revenge was rekindled. In my mind's eye I could picture myself stealing up to that house and destroying it along with everyone inside. I told the Kapusta brothers of my idea. How, they asked, could we manage it with our limited firepower?

I couldn't stop thinking about it. I received immediate support from one man who had joined the group in the forest long before I had, back in July of 1942, after escaping from under a pile of corpses during a German massacre of Jews. Before the war he had managed a nearby estate now controlled by the S.S., and so knew the area well. He was in favor of the plan, and agreed to recruit the Kapusta brothers. Unfortunately they were killed shortly after this conversation. In a pattern quite common by now, one of the peasants we had dealt with, named Klimek, for some reason turned against us, ambushed the brothers and murdered them, then sought out and killed the fiance of one of the brothers, who had been hiding in a house nearby. But soon afterward we surprised this beast and dealt him the same fate. Thus, in this way our numbers were reduced. From time to time new recruits arrived, some even brought to us by Polish benefactors no longer willing or able to harbor them. We, of course, welcomed them, knowing full well that they could not replace the many experienced comrades who had fallen.

Chapter 43

One day Pinyeh, his wife Feiga, Leibush and I were in the attic of a peasant woman named Maryna Preneta in Pinyeh's native village, Poremby Kupienskie. Maryna had gone into the town for us, to exchange American dollars for zlotys. While waiting, we heard her son-in-law, unaware of our presence, enter the house. Mazar, the *wojt* (mayor) of the village, we heard him say, had summoned all the able-bodied men to his house. We knew immediately what that meant: the villagers were preparing for a manhunt. When Maryna returned and learned what was planned, she was terribly upset, fearing for her safety. Still, we prevailed upon her to find out just what was happening.

She returned with the report that the mayor, having learned there were Jews hiding in the area, had asked each man to arm himself with a pitchfork or axe. We needed to act quickly, to warn our comrades in the forest before it was too late. Through the attic window we could see peasants running back and forth, each with a weapon in his hand. Pinyeh decided that as soon as it got dark he and his wife would go to a friendly family in the neighboring village to hide out for a few days. Pinyeh would not take Leibush along, however, insisting that this family would not accept anyone other than him and his wife. Leibush could not go anywhere alone—he didn't know the way and was sure to get caught. I asked Maryna if she would go into the forest to warn the others, but she was afraid and refused. To escape incrimination she wanted us out of her house. It was decided that I would go alone to warn the others in the forest. Pinyeh suggested that Maryna's fifteen-year old daughter, Helka, accompany me part way to make me appear less conspicuous—although I was dressed like a peasant and was confident that I would not be noticed. In the end Helka took two girl friends with her and the four of us proceeded jauntily down the road. Along the way the road wound through some fields where the natives were assembling, but no one paid any attention to us.

As soon as I reached the forest I ran to our hiding place and found our group. I suggested that we all go to a different area, but I asked Lyba to go back for Leibush. For the first time, Lyba refused. He said it would be like going into a lion's mouth; and besides, he was sure Pinyeh would not abandon Leibush. But I couldn't be sure, so leaving Lyba to direct the others, I went back to Maryna's house. They were all still there, though Pinyeh was about to leave. We shook hands, wished each other luck, and left going in opposite directions.

Leibush and I went to the house of Franek Zawisza, the man who had first contacted the group in the woods when I left Vichta's house. Franek wasn't there, but we went directly to the top of the barn and exhausted, fell into the hay. In the morning when Franek came to milk the cows we greeted him. He agreed to find out what had happened during the night. When he returned, there was no mistaking his expression. At five in the morning, he told us, the peasants under the leadership of Mazar uncovered the hideout in the woods, but found no one there. However, the *wojt*, to avoid appearing foolish, declared that two Jews were hiding nearby. (Pinyeh had been spotted the week before and the mayor had been told about it.) The peasants surrounded the house where Pinyeh and his wife had arrived just a few hours earlier and demanded that the Jews come out. Although Pinyeh had a gun and two hand grenades, he offered no resistance, apparently confident that given his former position as chief ranger, he was still respected by the community. But he was wrong. He and his wife were dragged to the mayor's barn until the Polish police arrived toward evening. They were then shot in the yard of the mayor's house, after which the peasants stripped them for their clothes. Thus Pinyeh, our leader, was taken away from us; a grievous loss indeed.

Chapter 44

The noose was tightening. The summer and fall of 1943 found us constantly on the run, our numbers dwindling, our sources of supply shrinking. With fewer and fewer friendly peasants, our existence became increasingly precarious every day. Caught between the Germans and the Poles as if in a nutcracker it followed that sooner or later we would all be crushed.

Hiding at Hodur's house one day we learned that the Germans were about to search the area. Walking through the night to a village some twelve miles away, we reached a barn of a peasant whom we knew, though we did not notify him of our presence. As we lay on the hay, we heard the noise of engines, and looking out, could see about ten trucks parked outside. Soon a whole company of *Sonderdienst* along with Polish policemen began diligently searching each house in the area. There were four of us there—Lyba, his brother Herschel, Leibush, and myself. We were well armed with revolvers and hand grenades and we were prepared to kill as many Germans as we could before we would let ourselves be captured.

A screeching noise told us that the barn door was being opened. As we lay embedded in the hay under some boards, the top of a ladder became visible, next the head of a *Sonderdienst,* who looked around.

"*Niemand is da*" (no one is here), he informed someone below. In a few minutes they were all gone.

The search, we found out later, had nothing to do with Jews. The Germans had spent the last few days rounding up peasants for forced labor back in Germany. The one in whose barn we were hiding had been siezed but managed to escape. The Germans had now come back in force to look for him. Some place for us to hide! Unable to find him they eventually left. Still, we waited in the barn for nightfall. While we did so we noticed a Polish policeman returning to the house, evidently thinking he might apprehend the owner. Finding no one in, he prepared to leave on his bicycle along a path that would take him past the barn. I suggested that we kill him and we all agreed. As he passed by two of us aimed, shot him and he fell dead. We took his rifle, revolver and the bicycle, which Lyba later traded for a calf. In reprisal for the killing, the Germans returned the following day and rounded up 100 peasants for forced labor in Germany.

A third enemy began to make its presence felt in the fall, the A.K. ("*Armya Krajowa*"), the nationalist Polish underground with headquarters in London. The A.K. had long been an organization on paper only, but now, as Germany's fortunes on the eastern front turned sour, it began to thrive. Belonging to the A.K. became synonymous with Polish patriotism, and its membership swelled. A.K. groups began to roam the forests and proved just as dangerous to us as were the Germans.

The commander of the A.K. in our district, I discovered, was one of my old classmates, a man named Stashek Augustin. His brother Yashek was a contributor to the weekly underground papers, "*Na Posterunku*" (On Guard) and "*Wiescie Rzeszowskie*" (News of the Rzeszow region). These I would read each week because Hodur's daughter, Stashka, was active in the organization.

Establishing contact with the brothers and proposing some joint operations might, I reasoned, give us a chance to fight the Germans, and perhaps a better possibility for survival. It was risky, certainly, but I thought I could count on Stashek's childhood friendship. We were very close in school, sitting next to each other year after year. Our families too had been friendly. Stashek's father, a wealthy man, had been head of a cooperative with a government monopoly of salt and other items, which my father purchased for our store. Both had served together as trustees of the local commercial bank. With Stashek as leader of the local underground, he might protect us even though the organization as a whole was openly anti-Semitic. But contacting a leader in the underground was no simple matter. No one member knew more than ten others in his immediate cell, and in each one of these only one man had contacts among the higher echelons, and so on to the very top. My possibility of getting through was not good. Still I asked Stashka to pass the word along that I wanted to see Stashek. Then I had to learn to deal with her father.

"What can I do for you?" he asked grouchily one evening.

"Oh, nothing much. May I stay here until tomorrow?"

"Yes, you can stay," he said.

"By the way, did you read the paper today?"

"No, I didn't. What did it have to say?" he asked.

"It reported that the Russians were advancing, and the Germans were on the run. You'll see. The Russians will soon be here and we'll be rid of the Germans."

"What Russians?" he shouted in anger. "What are you talking about? You sound like a Communist!"

"I'm not a Communist. I'm just telling you what I read in the paper."

"Don't believe it; it's not true. The Americans are the ones who will eventually liberate us."

"What gives you that idea?" I asked. "The Americans are on the other side of the ocean. How are they going to get here? The Russians are the ones who will push the Germans out."

"I've had enough of this," Hodur shouted. "I don't want any Communists in this house. Get out!"

He pushed me out of the door. I returned to the woods and told Lyba, who knew Hodur well, about our strange conversation.

"Why don't you go back and tell him that he's right?" Lyba suggested.

"But what he says is nonsense!"

"So what if it is, why should you care? We have to stay in his good graces."

I returned to Hodur on the following night and told him he was right, I had made a mistake. It would be the Americans who would liberate us. Hodur's face lit up.

"Now you're talking sense," he said smiling broadly. "Why don't you come inside and have something to eat?"

Afterwards I talked with Stashka about my plans. She agreed to talk to Wasik, the man who had sold me my first revolver. He was on friendly terms with Stashek's brother and could certainly relay my message.

That was in November. It wasn't until January of 1944, that I was finally reunited with my old school-mate. Wasik arranged for me and Leibush to meet him in the forest; from there he would lead me to Stashek. At the last minute I changed my mind about taking

Leibush, and decided to go alone. Wasik escorted me
to a clearing in the forest near the village of Werynia,
where I met fifteen young men, all about my age, and
of whom I had known before the war. They told me
they were waiting for an air drop of arms. At that time
these supplies were being sent in by the Polish govern-
ment-in-exile in London. Why, I wondered, were they
allowing me to witness this event, which I presumed
would be one of their best-guarded secrets?

Stashek and his brother were present, but so preoccupied with the drop, they could spend just a little
time with me. I told them of the men in my group and
of our willingness to undertake dangerous assignments. The brothers seemed interested but first wished
to meet with Leibush and me, they said, to work out
details. They were, at the moment, preparing a secret
room in a barn on an estate they occupied near Kolbuszowa; after that project was finished, they would
send for us.

After the air drop was successfully accomplished I
returned to our group and related the conversation. I
knew the danger of working with the A.K. quite well.
Only two weeks earlier I was almost killed by them,
and escaped only because of Stashka's help. Lyba and I
had gone to pick up some bread from a peasant named
Biesiadecki. Unknown to us, he had gone to the local
A.K. leader at Stashka's house and informed him that
we would be arriving that evening. Two armed men
were dispatched to Biesiadecki's house with orders to
kill us. But Stashka had overheard this conversation.
She knew that we would be coming for the bread, so as
soon as it turned dark, she hid in the bushes by the
road. Sitting in deep snow, she waited from eight in
the evening until two in the morning, when we finally

arrived. Half frozen, she emerged from her hiding place to warn Lyba and me. With tears in my eyes I kissed her frozen hands, then quickly retreated to the woods. When the A.K. men finally concluded that no one was coming, they beat Biesiadecki for lying to them and wasting their time.

After waiting impatiently for two weeks, we received word to report to Wasik, who would take us to the A.K. headquarters. After trekking through knee-deep snow for several hours, we reached the estate where the two brothers were awaiting us in the stable. They let us in and bolted the door. My old schoolmate gave me a big hug.

"Naftali," Stashek said excitedly, "I'm so happy to see you. I'm really delighted that we're going to work together. You'll see, we'll go out and kill Germans; we will pay them back for everything they've done to your people and to mine."

Yashek, his brother, nodded in agreement. "Let me show you your room," he said. "It's not a palace, but it's safe."

We walked past a row of horses. At the end of the stable was a trough, which Yashek removed, revealing a wooden door. He lifted it, and let himself down, motioning for us to follow. It was a narrow compartment, about eight feet wide, located between the stable and the adjacent barn. Stashek followed us in. The floor was covered with hay, and in one corner was a bundle of straw, which we were told was our bed. This, then, was to be our new residence for a while. He put a small kerosene lamp in the corner, and lit it.

"You will see, Naftali," Stashek went on. "It'll be great."

"I can't tell you how much we appreciate what you're doing for us," I said.

"Oh, don't be foolish. We're not doing you any favors. We're honored to have you. Right now our late fathers must be hugging and kissing each other in heaven as they look down upon us."

I was overwhelmed by this heartwarming demonstration of affection. I felt a lump in my throat.

"Take off those filthy clothes," said Stashek, pointing to our lice-infested patchwork tatters. In the woods we took off our underwear regularly and bathed in the river, but we never washed our clothes. "We'll get you some clean clothing."

We stripped. I still had on my leather belt with the revolver, bayonet, hand grenades, and flashlight—I never took them off, even when bathing.

"Hey Naftali, do you still have the revolver that Wasik sold you?" Stashek asked.

"Yes, I have it right here."

"May I see it?" I hesitated, but I had to assure them of my trust, so I handed it over.

Stashek looked at it, turning it from side to side, and hefting it in his hand. "How many bullets do you have?"

"All 120 original ones."

"You never used any of them?"

"I sure have, but from time to time I've managed to buy the same caliber bullets. We have this man who refills them with homemade slugs. Each slug can made a hole as big as my fist."

Stashek gave me back my gun, while Yashek returned with some old clothes. We dressed, then they brought in a pot with hot meat and potatoes and some vodka, and we all sat down to what to me was truly a feast.

"We certainly had good times in school," Stashek was saying as we ate, "didn't we, Naftali?"

"We sure did."

"I really looked up to you. I don't know if you knew that."

"No, I didn't," I said.

"Remember the time you sang solo in the choir? What was the song you sang that I liked so much?"

"Solo? Oh yes, I remember—the patriotic song about Pilsudski liberating Poland."

"Yes, yes, that's right. Well, fellows, get a night's good rest." The two of them left the room.

"What do you make of this?" Leibush asked me after they had gone.

"It's too good to be true. Why would they do all this for us? What's in it for them? Well, we'll soon find out. In the meantime we can get some rest, stay warm, eat some good food, and not worry about anyone coming after us."

We lay down on our straw bed in our clean underwear, without fleas and lice, and covered ourselves with a green military blanket. We were just getting comfortable when Yashek returned.

"I just spoke with someone who wants to sell a good revolver," Yashek said to me. "It's similar to the one you have, Naftali."

"Fine, I'll buy it."

"The problem is, the owner doesn't want money. He would like two suits in exchange."

"That's no problem," I said. "I have two suits I left with someone in town. I will send for it, and you can make the trade for me."

Yashek agreed, and said he'd be back in an hour. About two hours later he returned. As he walked into our compartment, I noticed that his right hand remained in his pants pocket. I asked him whether he got the gun. The man wasn't home, Yashek replied.

It was Tuesday, the day the underground newspaper always appeared. "What's new in your paper today?" I asked him.

"News?" He seemed surprised by the question. "I forgot."

It was a strange answer. "Listen, Yashek," I said, "I have this almost new pair of shoes in my knapsack which I never use, since boots are the only practical thing in the forest. I see that you wear the same size as I do; why don't you take them?"

"Fine," said Yashek, and he bent down toward the knapsack, without removing his right hand from his pocket. Instinctively I pulled out my revolver and held it under the blanket, pointing it at Yashek, but at the same moment Leibush moved a bit, pulling the blanket away and revealing the gun. Yashek looked at it as if he were hypnotized, then he retreated to the exit without a word.

"What did you do that for!" my brother said in disbelief. "Here we have two Poles who are risking their lives to save us, and you have to show them that you don't trust them!"

"Never mind, why did you have to throw off the blanket?"

"Look, Naftali, I don't want to argue with you, but what are we going to do now?"

"I don't know," I said.

"We're not safe here anymore."

"Look," I said, "why don't we go up to the attic and hide there? In this way they won't be able to trap us if they come in here."

I couldn't fall asleep. The events of the last hour kept spinning round in my mind. Why did Yashek keep his hand in his pocket the entire time? Why did he answer so peculiarly when I asked him about the news? My mind must have become hazy, for I finally fell asleep, but I was awakened by someone calling my name. It was Stashek. He entered and wished us a good day.

"I'm getting you some hot water to wash up, and my mother's preparing breakfast, so get ready to eat."

He left, then returned with his brother, carrying a hot breakfast — steaming borscht, hardboiled eggs, and bread and butter. The two of them were in high spirits, smiling and joking. No mention was made of the incident with the revolver. We told them we preferred to stay in the attic during the day, to get some light and fresh air. They obliged us by removing two boards, giving us easier access to the attic.

I had been mistaken. After so many disappointments and outright betrayals it became more difficult for me to trust anyone. We put our belongings inside a knapsack and climbed into the attic above the compartment. I had my diary with me and began entering a record of the events of the day. After I finished I made a hole in the hay so I could watch what went on below. There was some commotion with people coming and going. At about ten o'clock the brothers returned, this time carrying shovels.

"What are you doing with those?" I asked. "I didn't think you'd need them until springtime."

"Ach, you city boy! What do you know about farming?" Yashek answered in a patronizing way. "We have to dig up the horse manure and put it to one side, then we must place the cow dung on the other side so that it will ready for spring."

"Oh yes, I almost forgot," Stashek said. "I'm going to town later. If you need anything, I'll try to get it for you. I should be back at four."

"Good, I need a few items from the drugstore, and maybe you could get me the *Krakower Zeitung*, the German newspaper."

I gave him a list of the things I needed for my medical kit, and some money for payment, and he left. We went back to the attic, glad that the incident of the previous day had not been mentioned, that it appeared to be no more than a figment of my fevered imagination.

At about three o'clock we heard Stashek returning from his errand. At four he came in with the items and the newspaper. Handing us a bundle of clothing, he asked for our old clothes; his mother would boil and rid them of lice, he said. Why, I asked, had she not come to visit us? She wasn't feeling well, he responded. She would come soon. He returned with a hot supper, which I ate while reading the newspaper, so eager was I to learn of the developments on the Russian front. Stashek stood next to me the while I translated the news from German into Polish.

"Look," I said, "the Russians have reached the old Polish border. If all goes well, the war should be over in three months."

"Three months!" Stashek shouted, "my God, three months!" He jumped up and down and started to dance. He put his hands on my shoulders. "Naftali, as soon as the war is over, we'll become big wheels. You'll see."

"I just want the war to end, that's all I wish."

"Naftali, lend me your flashlight for a minute." I handed it to him. Suddenly, the kerosene lamp went out; there was total darkness. I heard three shots in quick succession, then one more. I became dizzy, and fell on my back. At first everything about me was spinning, then a calm prevailed, a strange peacefulness. If this is the end, I thought, it's just as well. I'm tired of fighting. But a second later my resolve was altered: if I'm going to die, so should he. I still had my gun. I drew it while still lying on the ground with my finger on the trigger, but it wouldn't move; it was like a piece of wood. I tried another finger; this one worked. I fired first in the air and in the glare saw Yashek standing in the entrance with drawn pistol, and Stashek off to one side, his gun aimed at Leibush. I fired once more, this time at Yashek and after the third shot I saw him lying across the entrance. In the glare I saw Stashek turn around and run, but not fast enough. My fourth shot hit him in the back and he dashed out screaming.

My hand was bleeding, and I could also feel blood running down my neck, but I was no longer dizzy.

"Stashek, Stashek," Leibush shouted, "what are you doing? Are you crazy, playing with firecrackers?"

"Leibush," I said, "no one is playing. This is for real. They started shooting at us, and I returned their fire. Leibush, are you all right?"

"Yes, but what do we do now?"

"We run away, that's what we do."

I tried to gather up our belongings, especially our boots and my medical case, but without a flashlight it was impossible. Leibush had not come up to the attic. I called for him, but there was no answer. Now I was really worried. I let go of what I had gathered, jumped down, then heard Leibush screaming. Outside of the stable were several men holding Leibush down, and two others with Stashek, who was lying in the snow close by. I pointed my revolver at the men.

"All right, I said to them, "I have three bullets left in this gun, and I never miss. If you don't get the hell out of here three of you will be dead."

All of them, including the two with Stashek, rose and dashed off. Leibush and I were both virtually naked, barefoot and wearing only winter underwear. It was late in the afternoon and almost dark. Shoeless, we ran through the snow up a hill and away from the road, until we were out of breath. Neither of us felt the cold; we were only fearful, afraid that we would be caught by the A.K. and tortured. I reloaded my gun.

"Leibush, if they surround us," I said, "we'll try to kill as many as we can; but we'll have to save the last two bullets."

We kept walking. It was really dark now, but a bright moon's reflection on the snow glittered like a myriad of diamonds. Unfortunately we had lost our sense of direction, were completely lost. If we could get to Kupno, we knew of a good hiding place there, but that village was about five miles away.

It was cold, but we were perspiring. I stopped behind a barn to check my wounds. The blood had run off from a bullet in my head, down my back and legs; I was also bleeding from my hand and index finger, but I couldn't quite determine the exact extent of my injuries because of a thick layer of coagulated blood coming from some of my wounds. It was then that I realized we had left a sanguinary trail all the way back to the stable; there was no mistaking it on the hard, frozen snow.

I remembered the six o'clock bus that ran from Rzeszow to Kolbuszowa; it was the only motor vehicle that passed in the area at that time of night. If we could spot the bus, we could locate the road and figure out the way to Kupno and Franek's place where we could hide.

At about 6:15 we saw two bright lights in the distance moving in the direction of Kolbuszowa; it could only be the bus. Finally, a stroke of good fortune. I tried to estimate just where on the road Franek's house would be, and then headed across the fields to that point. I don't know how I did it, but when I reached the road, there was Franek's house directly on the other side. We slid into the ditch by the side of the thoroughfare. It was, we discovered, easy enough to get down but quite another matter to climb up on the slippery frozen snow. I was able to manage it but not Leibush, kept falling back. I returned and asked him to stand on my shoulders while I pushed him up. After several attempts he made it. With what little strength we had left we ran into Franek's barn. We still couldn't spend the night there. A trail of footprints and blood continued to thwart us. We had to move on.

Chapter 45

As we walked to Kupno, I recalled another friendly peasant, a self-taught medicine man who was the village veterinarian, Jan Shitosh. He could examine us and bandage my wounds. We had no difficulty in finding his house. Shitosh had a watchdog who knew me and who often had shared his food with me. Fortunately he didn't bark when we approached. Now there was one further problem. Shitosh had a tenant living with him. When the Germans established their experimental rocket station, they evacuated most of the peasants in the area and placed them with other families. Shitosh had one such group living with him.

As luck would have it, it was not Shitosh but his tenant who opened the door. He looked at me, clothed only in my underwear, and his jaw dropped.

"Why are you staring?" I asked. "I've come to see Shitosh. My cow just swallowed a turnip, and I need his help immediately."

"But you could have at least put on a pair of pants and a shirt . . ."

"My cow is more important to me than appearance."

"All right, I'll get him."

Shitosh came out, recognized me, and immediately knew I was in trouble.

"Come into the barn," he said, tying the belt of his robe. "My God, look at the trail of blood and the footsteps in the snow! You're placing me and my family in great danger."

"I'm sorry. We were attacked by some Germans, and we need some medical attention."

"Germans," Shitosh repeated, visibly frightened. "Did you kill any of them?"

"Yes, we did."

"That's bad, that's bad. I can't let you stay here; it's too risky. On the other hand, you're human beings, and I must help you. What should I do? Well, I'll look at your wounds, but you can't remain here. When the Germans come I'll tell them you came into my barn, but left before I could see who it was."

He brought a pail of warm water, washed my neck and hand, then informed me of the bullet wounds in my neck, palm, and index finger. He bound them up and gave us some old clothes and shoes. One of the pairs fit me, but Leibush's feet were too large. He would remain barefoot.

"Where are you going now?" Shitosh asked, after we had thanked him and made ready to leave.

"We know somebody in Przedborz who might be able to get me to a doctor."

"I'll show you a shortcut to Przedborz, but be careful of deep snow." It was not that so much that proved troublesome, but the ice beneath it which kept giving way. Before we had gone far the broken ice had cut Leibush's feet in a most disabling manner.

We reached Hodur's house at about three in the morning. Rather than wake him, we climbed to our usual hiding place in the barn. To our astonishment we found Lyba there. We told him about everything that happened.

"My feet are killing me," said Leibush.

"Let me have a look at them," Lyba said. "My God, all the skin is off! It's all raw flesh."

Leibush's feet were a mess. He could not stand let alone walk.

"I'll fix it for you," Lyba said. He washed them, then wrapped them in pieces of material that he tore from a bed sheet. Then he made two bags out of cloth, and filled them with oat skins, which were very soft. He attached the bags to the soles of each of his feet. Now Leibush was at least able to stand, but he would not be able to walk any distance for the time being.

After attending to Leibush, Lyba went to get Stashka. We had, I told her, a shootout with Germans. Could she help me get to a doctor? Stashka was confused and wanted to consult with her mother. Then she saw the telltale signs in the snow.

"God," she said, "look at the tail of blood. This will bring the Germans right to our house."

Stashka's mother, such a good soul, was very sympathetic and agreed to take me to a physician. As soon as we left snow started to fall. Thick large wet flakes, a Godsend, for now our tracks were covered and I no longer had to worry about jeopardizing Shitosh or Hodur. We walked for a few hours through the forest to Sedziszow. I followed several hundred feet behind them, so as to avoid implicating them if I was caught. We entered the small chapel of a monastery. All of us knelt, crossed ourselves, and said our prayers. Stashka's mother and I remained in the chapel, while Stashka went to see the doctor. Posing as a member of the A.K. would, I hoped, get him to respond favorably.

After a short time she returned; I followed her to the doctor's office. After a half hour Dr. Lechowski, a middle-aged, tall man in a white gown, entered and escorted me to his office.

"I'm from Stashka's group," I told him.

"I see," the doctor said. "I'll take care of you, but I'll have to report it to the police."

"Police, my foot," I said, taking out my revolver. You'll do no such thing."

"No, of course not—I just had to say it as a routine procedure."

He removed the bandages and checked my neck, palm and finger. "You're a very lucky man," he said. "Apparently you were hit in the neck three times, but none of the bullets caused any serious damage. They penetrated the side of your neck causing only superficial wounds. After you were hit, you may have put your hand there, because the fourth bullet passed through the length of your finger without touching the bone. It probably was a small caliber weapon, which also helped. You're a very fortunate man. Now take off your pants." He took a syringe from his cabinet. "I have to give you a shot."

"What for?" I was getting suspicious.

"Don't worry," he said, "it's to prevent blood poisoning."

I pulled up my pants, thanked the doctor, and ran back to the chapel. It suddenly dawned upon me that I was lucky to be alive. In my haste to get to the doctor I hadn't paid much attention to all the activity in Sedziszow, especially along the new highway the Germans had built that stretched from there to Cracow and Vienna. All sorts of military vehicles clogged the road with soldiers everywhere in evidence. There were no signs of panic but the flow of men and equipment was mostly away from the Russian front. Unmistakably, the Germans were being pushed back.

Chapter 46

I was the ninth and last child born to my parents. I was only a few weeks old when a smallpox epidemic struck our town. Many died, children and adults. The makeshift hospital was full to overflowing, but people generally preferred to remain home if they were sick. No one, opinion had it, ever left the hospital alive.

One day a cousin brought his little girl, Ryfcia, from a small village where they lived, to see a doctor in Kolbuszowa. They placed her in the same cradle with me, unaware that she had contracted smallpox. A few days later I became very ill. After a night or two, my mother noticed that I was lying very still in my cradle. She called my father and they both checked me, listening for a heartbeat they could not hear, and putting a feather to my nose, which did not flutter. I was dead, they both agreed, and so I was placed on the floor and covered with a sheet. All night long my mother sat next to me, and together with my brothers and sisters, cried. Beseeching God, she acknowledged I was her ninth child, "but he was already here. Why," she pleaded, "couldn't he run around the house with the others?"

In the morning my father summoned Meyer the Carrier, who also served as the town's undertaker. My mother covered me with the sheet, and Meyer put me in a yeast box (it was exactly the right size for an infant) and fastened the lid. As he was about to leave, my father offered him a little schnapps.

"Why not?" Meyer said, and he placed the small coffin on the floor.

"Well, *l'chaim*," my father said, drinking with him, "may this be the end of the epidemic and may we know of no further sorrow."

Then my mother said to Meyer, "How about some egg cookies?"

"Why not?" he replied. As he took some he heard a squeak. "Reb Itche," he said, "do you have mice in your house?"

"Mice? Impossible, we have a very good cat."

Now everyone heard the squeak.

"What is it then?" Meyer asked.

My mother, my father, and Meyer began to look all over the room for the source of the sound.

"I think it's coming out of the box," Meyer said, pointing to the coffin.

As my parents stared in disbelief, Meyer opened the box and removed the sheet. There I was, lying with my eyes open, sneezing because of the yeast powder left in the box. So you see, early on I had learned about survival.

We were lucky to get a ride back to Hodur's house, but when we returned he was in a fury. He had heard the news that two of the best A.K. leaders had been murdered by Jews. When he saw me he started to yell.

I told him, however, exactly what had happened with Stashek and Yashek—how they trapped and tried to kill us. After I finished, Hodur's anger was heaped on the brothers. He felt sorry for them, but agreed that they got what they deserved. He then told us about the events that occurred after Leibush and I had fled.

A German patrol passing by had heard the shots, and came over directly. A group of partisans or bandits, they were told, had demanded money, then started firing their guns. The patrol, comprised of ordinary soldiers, believed the story, and left; but on the next day the German police investigated. Told the same story, they proved more skeptical. Searching the house and the stable, they discovered the secret door to the room and saw the wall inside smeared with blood. In the attic they found my boots, my medicine kit, and my diary, written in Yiddish, which had been started on the first day of the war by my sister Rachel. Now they knew the true story. They shot the wounded Stashek and killed him.

Hodur permitted me to stay in his house for a few days, until I could plan my next move. I was now the most wanted man in the district—the A.K. had placed a 100,000 zlotys reward on my head—and every peasant would be looking for me. I had to find a refuge for Leibush for at least a few weeks, until his feet could heal. The only peasant I felt I could trust completely was Franek Zawisza. He was a member of the A.K., and was no doubt aware of the reward, but he wouldn't betray me. With Lyba's help we got Leibush to the top of Franek's barn, where he would have to stay by himself. Franek would feed him every day until he was able to walk.

Two weeks later I returned to see Leibush. He was happy to see me, and reported that his feet were much better. Franek brought him food every evening. He told me that Franek never mentioned the Augustin brothers despite the fact that they had been friends, lived in the same village and were members of the same A.K. group. Franek, he said, kept asking when I was going to come and why we weren't together. I didn't want him to know I was there—my trust in him was becoming suspect. I hid under the hay when he arrived with food for Leibush the next evening.

"There's something going on that I don't like," Leibush said. "I see people coming and going in and out of Franek's house. I could swear too, that someone is spying on me from a window across the way."

"It's reasonable to assume," I said, "that the A.K. knows you're here, and they expect me to come to visit you, so they may have posted a watch."

"You'd better not come here anymore."

"I don't know. Let me talk to Franek."

He arrived a little later. "Hey Franek," I said, "is anything happening in the village, any trouble?"

No, nothing," he replied, "everything is very quiet."

I took out my grenades and gun and placed them on a board in front of me.

"Listen, Franek, if anyone is plotting against me, he'd better think twice. The only way is to burn down this barn, and that's something you wouldn't want, would you? Anyone coming up here will get his head blown off, no questions asked. Do you understand?"

"I understand, I understand," he said nervously. "Don't worry, no one will show up here."

I stayed with Leibush on top of the barn. Time moved slowly, uneasily. Outside a cold, bone-chilling wind was raging.

Each day at five o'clock Franek would bring Leibush a bowl of hot potato soup, but on this day five o'clock came with no sign of Franek. Six o'clock. Seven o'clock. Finally at eight Franek arrived with a bowl of cold soup.

"I don't think you should eat this," I told Leibush. "It very well might be poisoned."

"What makes you say that?"

"I didn't like the way Franek spoke. Why did it take him so long? Why is the soup cold?"

"Don't be silly," Leibush retorted. He gulped some down. His face contorted. "Naftali, it's burning."

"You stay here, I'll get some milk." I ran down to the barn, quickly milked one of the cows, and brought some up for Leibush.

"Drink it all. Good. Now put your finger down your throat and throw it all up."

After a short time Leibush felt much better. "We'd better get going," I said, collecting our possessions. Then I changed my mind. "Wait, Leibush. They must be watching for us around here. We'd better hide in the barn and wait for them. By this time they might think that we're dead. Once they show themselves, we'll have a better idea of what to do."

We hid behind a hay stack and waited. Presently four men came entered the barn. They tiptoed toward the ladder climbed up, then quickly came down and ran away. "They must have realized that we weren't there, and became scared," I told Leibush. "Come on, let's go; we're safe now."

We went back to the forest. Only a handful of us were left now. For the next two weeks I had nothing to do but think. Why was the A.K. so intent on our destruction? How had we hurt them? I recalled the priest who had given me the forged birth certificate. If he'd heard what happened to the brothers, how he would regret having given me that document. I felt an ardent desire to see him, and tell him the full story. What a ridiculous idea—why risk my life for this? But it became an obsession with me and so I set out to see him.

I arrived at his house in Kolbuszowa one night shortly after midnight. I knocked on the door and waited. After a few minutes a light appeared in the window; a servant came to the door and asked what I wanted.

"I'm a parishioner. I have to speak with Father."

"What's your name?"

"Tadeusz Jadach."

The servant returned in a moment and asked me to come in.

The priest was wearing a gown. I hadn't seen him in over a year—he seemed to have aged a great deal.

"Sit down, sit down. Would you like some hot tea?"

"Yes, thank you." He poured some out of a kettle for himself and for me.

"I notice that you're not wearing any shoes," he said. "I have two pairs, but I can wear only one at a time. Why don't you take a pair?"

"Oh, no, I couldn't."

"I insist."

"Very well, then. Thank you very much."

"Well, what brings you here, my son?"

"Do you know what happened to the Augustin brothers?"

"Oh, yes. They were killed by the Germans. We conducted a state funeral for them. They were buried in the most honored place in the cemetery. They were real heroes, those two. Such brave ones aren't born every day."

"Father, I have a confession to make."

"Go ahead."

"I killed them."

"You what?"

"I killed them in self-defense." I told him the whole story.

"This is outrageous," he said after I had finished. "It is unforgiveable to think that they lied to me and concocted the whole story about the Germans. It is painful to hear these things, for I am a man who loves the truth more than my very life. I will write to the bishop tomorrow and ask to have their bodies removed from their present graves, and have them reinterred by the wall, like common criminals."

As I rose to leave, he insisted that I take the shoes, but I refused, explaining that I had boots which I left just outside. I kissed his hand and went out into the night.

Chapter 47

In March of 1944, two months after the incident of
the Augustin brothers, I became a member of a fighting
unit of the A.K. But this group operated outside of our
area, so no one knew me. I passed for a Catholic Pole,
Tadeusz Jadach, and served under the command of a
man named Wacek. We raided a police station in
Glogow, and disarmed the police. We blew up the
railroad between Lvov and Cracow several times. We
attacked Ukrainian villages near the San River in
reprisal for the killing of some members of the A.K.

We entered village after village carrying rifles on
our shoulders, displaying red and white armbands and
wearing berets decorated with Polish eagles. We were
greeted as saviors. Villagers brought us food, offered
us vodka, while the girls gathered round to kiss us. As
Tadeusz Jadach, a Polish Christian, I was a heralded
hero whereas as a Jewish partisan fighting against the
same enemy I was regarded as a hated fugitive, hunted,
hounded, always forced to hide in fear for my life. The
contradiction was mind-boggling.

But then one night we met up with another underground group. Immediately, one of them came over to
me. "Where do I know you from?" I recognized him.
His name was Schuller, from a village near Kolbuszowa. I told him we might have met in the army before

the war. Not satisfied, he continued to study me. It was no longer safe to stay. Why wait until Schuller finally remembered who I was? I left without saying goodbye to my comrades.

Back to the forest—there were only ten of us left: Lyba and his brother Herschel, Leibush and I, and six others. I had kept in touch with them during my association with the A.K., visiting them when I was able to leave my unit. Now I had returned for good.

Never before had there been so many combat troops in our area. There could be no security for us. The Russian front was getting closer; it was rumored, in fact, that Russian partisans were already in the forest with us. Why not try to join them? Again it was Stashka who helped me. She knew where a unit of partisans were hiding out. I would have no problem finding the place; I went alone.

The voice calling me to stop and put my hands over my head was most welcome; I did as I was told. A man of about my age, a pepesha in his hand, stepped out, his gun aimed directly at me. I was a Polish partisan, I told him, looking for my counterparts among the Russians. We then walked about 500 feet into a clearing. Eighty men and as many horses were milling around. Taken to the unit commander, a short, energetic man with curly hair and a small moustache, I repeated my story to him.

"Well, he asked," what can we do for you?"

"We are a small group," I said, deliberately neglecting to tell him that we were Jewish. "We have a plan of attack which we can't implement by ourselves; I thought you might be interested in working together."

"What kind of a plan?"

"You must have heard about Pustkow, which isn't far from here. Now there's an S.S. sub-station near there, connected with that place. They've committed many atrocities against our people. On Saturday night they usually gather in one house, and we could easily surprise them and kill quite a few." (Hodur, who worked at the house, provided us with much detailed information about the layout and usual schedule of S.S. activities there.)

"I like the idea," the Russian said, "but first we'll have to go out there and look the place over."

This attack, as you know, had long been a personal dream of mine, more like an obsession. To settle accounts with a certain Scharführer who had my friend Motek beaten to death and who had, in my presence, cruelly mocked the God of Israel, would be a supreme achievement for me.

I returned to my group and explained my idea. Initial doubts gave way to enthusiasm. The next night Karol and I went back to meet with the Russians. He had managed an estate in the area before the war. I introduced him to them as our topographical expert. The commander picked two partisans to accompany us. They mounted their horses, then each of us rode on behind them. We reached the house, surveyed the scene, and returned on the same night. We went back there three more times to familiarize ourselves with the terrain. A plan of attack was prepared and a week later, on a Saturday evening, twenty-one men—fifteen Russians and six of our group—advanced upon the estate.

I couldn't contain my excitement. I felt like a lamed one who had learned to walk again. The scenario I had enacted in my mind so many times was about to become a reality.

On Saturday night we all gathered to ride to the farm. It took us about two and one-half hours to reach our destination in the pitch dark evening. I and four others wore German uniforms so as not to arouse suspicion. We were the first to get close to the farm buildings. The rest followed.

Every one of us had his assigned place and instructions. We left our horses in the woods. The five of us in German uniforms crept into the barn opposite the main farmhouse. The others surrounded the house from the rear and both sides.

Lights were on in all the four windows. I could see them sitting inside drinking and flirting with the girls. I saw a huge figure with a jowly red face and bulbous nose that I recognized as the Scharführer. He was conversing with some S.S. men.

I had little time to stare because implementing the next stage in our operation, a Russian climbed the telephone pole and cut the wires. Seconds later the five of us in German uniforms moved closer to the open windows and threw hand grenades into the house. The explosions illuminated the sky. The Germans shot from inside. The distinctive sounds of revolver shots pinged through the air. We added the rat-a-tat of the Russian submachine guns as we shot through the windows at the front and side of the house.

I had been given a submachine gun from the commander and I looked forward to using it. I fired rounds after rounds into the house. It was exhilarating. Moments later all was quiet. The Germans had stopped firing. The main building was ablaze.

After the shooting stopped, we set fire to the storage facility next to the main house and the car and motorcycles that were parked outside. We took the German horses from the stables along with us.

As the flames were still licking the sky, we left. None of them had escaped alive. Their party was over. At that moment, with the gun still hot in my hands I no longer felt like a victim. I had settled my score with the Scharführer, and my God, who had abandoned me so many times, had not forgotten me this time.

Despite an invitation from the Russian commander to join them, they evacuated the area immediately following the raid and so eluded the S.S. who, two days later, entered the forest in search of them—I declined. I returned the pepesha, we shook hands, and I returned to our group. At an earlier time I would have given anything to have been able to join such a group. Now with the front coming ever closer and the day of liberation almost at hand, to remain independent was a situation "devoutly to be wished."

Information reached us that many roads in the area were jammed with retreating German soldiers, tanks and all kinds of military vehicles and equipment. During the night we could hear cannons booming and explosions off in the distance. Each day these sounds drew closer. The Germans began concentrating their units in those villages located near the edges of the forest. It became virtually impossible to move from one place to another.

Liberation was just a matter of time now, a fact most fortunate because there were precious few friendly peasants left. We kept going from one to another, staying only a short time with each. Our group that once numbered 125, was now reduced to six. Most had been killed, not by our sworn enemies, the Germans, but by the treacherous Poles, among whom we had lived for centuries.

One night Lyba and I went to Hodur's house, but when we got there, the entire family was gone although the place was open. We couldn't understand why. It was towards the end of summer and the barn was filled with hay as we retreated to our usual hiding place there. After a time we heard cavalry moving along the road, next to the house. As they drew closer, we could hear German voices. Even worse, they stopped briefly for hay to feed their horses. The front, we now realized, would soon reach us; Hodur and his family must have gone into hiding. After the Germans left, Lyba and I vacated the barn to rejoin the others. Just as we moved from the forest and passed the place where our comrades had been murdered during the manhunt a year ago, shots rang out from opposite directions. We quickly took cover in a large haystack nearby and waited for the firing to stop.

We emerged into a moonlit night and immediately spotted a horse with two riders about 200 meters away silhouetted against the sky, and coming in our general direction.

Lyba said, "I know these men." "I even know the horse and the man who bought it from me before the war. They're peasants from the next village. You ask them where the shooting is coming from. They would recognize me immediately as a Jew, so you go."

"Are you sure you know them?"

"Did I ever steer you wrong? I even know one of their names — Posluszny."

The horse was getting closer now. I ran out and called after them, "Panie Posluszny, Panie Posluszny!"

The riders heard me, slowed down and came to a halt as I ran up to them. By the time I realized who they really were it was too late. They were two S.S. men in uniform, fully armed. Lyba, who was always reliable about such things, was wrong this time, dead wrong. One of them alit, drew his gun, and asked me who I was.

Dressed like a peasant, with bare feet, I pretended I couldn't understand a word of German, and kept telling them in Polish that I was a farmer from a nearby

village and that my wife and children had left our
home when the shooting started. Was it true that the
Russians kidnapped the women and raped them? I
started crying. I could see that one of the S.S. men
understood Polish, and was translating my blubberings
to the other. I started yelling louder.

"What should I do? What should I do? The Russians
will take my wife!"

I heard one of them say in German, "Let's take him
with us. This way we won't have to go to the next
village." He then said to me in broken Polish: "You'll
have to come with us. Then you can look for your wife
and children."

They told me to get in front. The one with the gun
replaced it in its holster and started to remount. Here
was my opportunity. Drawing my own revolver, I
emptied it into the two of them. Both fell dead. I
helped myself to their revolvers, then took the horse
by the reins, using it to shield me from the intermit-
tent firing. At the edge of the forest, I heard a voice
ordering me to stop. I could see that he was a Russian.
He directed me into the forest where a band of Russian
partisans waited. I was relieved of all four of my guns
along with the horse. After explaining that I had just
shot two Germans I was told to wait for the arrival of
the group's commander. A short time later I was
drinking vodka, and eating bread and some canned
meat (my first experience with *Swinaja Tuszonka* — mari-
nated bacon, made in America) with his comrades.

About an hour later the commander arrived. He
rode a beautiful horse, and he wore a new leather
jacket. He jumped down, shook my hand, and expressed surprise at hearing me speak Russian. I told
him I belonged to a partisan group which was on the
other side of the woods, in an area still held by the

Germans, and that I wanted to bring them over to this side. First, he congratulated me for having shot the Germans, and said that I was welcome to stay, since he needed someone who knew the area. But if I wanted to bring back the rest of my group, he would take all of us in. He cautioned me to be careful—I might not be so lucky the next time. I asked for some proof to show my people that I had actually met the Russian partisans. A submachine gun would do, I suggested. But he laughed —if I came back he would give me one. In the meantime I could have the insignia from his cap, a red enameled star with a hammer and sickle—that would be evidence enough.

Starting back I was afraid of being shot by the Russians—what if they didn't believe my story? With each step I expected to be struck down. But soon I was out of the forest into an open field. Everything was all right; they believed me.

Chapter 48

Lyba was still sitting in the haystack in the open field. He hugged me and kissed me. There were tears in his eyes.

"I'm so happy to see you," he said, very much relieved. "When I heard the shooting and you didn't come back, I realized my mistake, and I could have killed myself. Here we are, at the end of the war, and I sent you to your death."

On the way to Kupno, we passed the two S.S. men I had just killed, and relieved them of their rifles. Then we took cover in a barn belonging to Baba, an old woman and a long-time friend of Lyba. We were awakened at about five in the morning by someone entering the barn. It was a Russian soldier, himself a peasant, holding a cup into which he hoped to get some milk for his breakfast. He and his comrades, he told us, had just liberated the village from the Germans, and were now on their way to Kolbuszowa. I looked at the Russian soldier, then suddenly realized what his presence meant: I was liberated! I no longer had to hide! I was a free man at last!

"Tovarich!" I shouted. I rushed over and threw my arms around him, hugged and kissed him, and danced around the barn with him. I invited Lyba to join me in meeting more Russian soldiers, but he was hesitant.

Cautious and still afraid, he preferred to stay in hiding for at least another day.

I walked out, not through the back but through the front door, down the main road, mingling with the other people, like a normal human being. I couldn't believe after all these years what was actually happening to me, walking in the open with other people, instead of sneaking around everywhere like a hunted animal, always looking for places to hide.

I spotted a Russian captain along with his soldiers and requested permission to shake his hand, and thanked him for giving me my freedom. I was a Jew, I told him, out in the open for the first time since 1939. All of them listened to me, gave me bread, and asked me to stay. They were an artillery unit preparing to shell Kolbuszowa in the valley below while a column of T-34 tanks and infantry approached on the main road from Rzeszow.

After the bombardment began I started off to where Leibush was staying. When I came to the barn in which he and Herschel had been hiding, they were not there. They too had been liberated. I soon discovered them sitting in the kitchen like normal human beings, having tea with two Yiddish-speaking Russian women, who happened to be physicians from a nearby Russian field hospital.

One person I wished to see right away was Shitosh, who had risked his life to dress my wounds, even with a trail of blood leading up to this house. I presented him with one of my revolvers, as a token of appreciation for all that he had done for me.

"The war is over for us, Mr. Shitosh, and I won't need two guns. Do me the honor of keeping it." He was moved by my gesture, and thanked me. Leibush went off to visit Hodur and his family, all of whom were safe. He presented his revolver to Hodur along with all the hand grenades we had collected.

Lyba and Herschel decided to remain in the village, while Leibush and I chose to head for the nearest large town, Rzeszow. Returning to Kolbuszowa made me uncomfortable, even with the Germans gone. After all that I had gone through, I feared going back home. Too many of my Polish neighbors there had become the enemy, no less deadly than the Germans. In Rzeszow we hoped we might find some fellow Jews, and find safety and comfort in numbers.

How fortunate it was that we chose Rzeszow. Had we gone to Kolbuszowa we might have suffered the fate of Naftali Kanner and Leibush Nessel, two of those who had originally escaped with me and later stayed with us in the woods. As soon as Kolbuszowa was liberated they went back home, only to be stopped on the street by a few of our townsmen, members of the A.K. who had taken charge when the Germans left. Two prominent citizens of the town, one an owner of a bus line, Staszek Zielinski, the other Kisiel, the Director of the Internal Revenue in Kolbuszowa, volunteered to be their executioners. They were taken behind the Catholic cemetery, and shot. Clearly, the A.K. was intent on completing what the Germans had started.[1]

---

[1] I do know why the revenue official might have wanted to kill Leibush Nessel. When the war broke out in 1939, Nessel was a soldier in the Polish army. He was sent to the German border to defend against the invasion. Director Kisiel was a reserve officer. He also was mobilized and sent to the same regiment at the front. One night, in a small border town populated mostly by Jews, this official asked Nessel to get two civilian suits from the Jews in town so that both could desert and return home in civilian clothes. Nessel refused; he was a soldier, and would not desert. But the

The day after Nessel and Kanner were murdered, additional survivors returned, among them Pashek Rapaport, who had been the second President of the Judenrat, and his brother Yossl. They were all apprehended by the A.K. and brought to an isolated house to be killed. But a Polish woman notified the Russian authorities and a Russian officer, who happened to be Jewish, rushed to the house with some men, and disarmed the two guards. Handing his pistol to the Jewish captives, he asked them to shoot the two guards but they refused. Instead they asked to be escorted to Rzeszow, where they joined Leibush and me.

Was this then the end of centuries of Jewish life in Kolbuszowa as it was in countless towns and villages across Poland and throughout Europe as well? The roots had been broad enough but always restricted, kept from growing deep. Now all that life and culture, piety and faith was destroyed, the soil forever poisoned.

When I came to Rzeszow the city had already enjoyed freedom for several days. The few Jewish survivors gradually came out of hiding. As we were mostly unmarried, we took up residence in a house formerly occupied by the Germans, living together in a kind of commune. Only as we began to feel safe and were able to relax for the first time in years, did we begin to grasp the horrible truths, understand the scope of the cataclysmic events that so decimated us. For the first time we realized what pitiful remnants of a once vast Jewry, sensed that millions had been reduced to a comparative handful. All along we had been preoccupied with our own survival, with neither the time nor

---

officer deserted his unit, while Nessel fought the Germans and was almost killed. Whether Nessel would have exposed the Pole I don't know. His death conveniently eliminated that possibility.

energy to reflect upon the devastation wrought on Jews collectively. We were numbed by the realization that our parents, our brothers and sisters, and entire towns were dead, gone forever—all wiped out. What, many wondered, was the point of living, of carrying with them the burden of these indelible memories? But I was young, strong and even with all that bitterness inside I knew I wanted to live.

The second day in Rzeszow I went to a barber shop for a decent haircut and shave. There were about ten people waiting ahead of me. Was this a mistake? The barber could tell I was a Jew; might he then cut my throat? I was about to leave but I changed my mind— the war was over, the Germans were gone, it was time to get back to normal living. When my turn came and the barber had finished cutting my hair and was lathering my face, I thought I detected the eyes of everyone in the shop focused on me. Could it be the barber was going to kill me? Surely the others were signaling him, "He's a Jew, kill him, kill him!" I jerked his hand away, jumped out of the chiar, and with my face full of lather, ran out of the shop and all the way to the house where I was staying without stopping once. There I just sat down on my bed, completely dazed. My friends noticed my anger and confusion, then heard me shout:

"For what did we survive?" I yelled at the top of my lungs. "Why did we have to go through all this hell, living like animals, only to be killed as they murdered Kanner and Nessel? All those wonderful neighbors of ours, all those great patriotic Poles, now emerge to slay us, instead of joining with us to celebrate our liberation? Is this our reward for surviving? What's the use?"

I felt relieved after my outburst. No one in the room tried to answer. They probably all felt the same way. Then I announced in a calm voice:

"Tomorrow I'm going to join the new Polish army. I will enlist the branch that will offer me the best opportunity to kill the enemy. I'm going to fight the Germans, and take revenge."

Chapter 49

"Naftali, what are your plans? It certainly looks as if the end of the war is in sight. Will you stay in the army? Have you thought of leaving Poland?"

"A part of me asks why not stay, I, Tadeusz Zaleski. I'm respected, I hold a position of authority, my prospects are good. As a Pole and a 'Catholic' I won't always have to be looking over my shoulder. If and when I have a family, maybe they will be able to escape, as I never could, the hatred and anti-Semitism that has for so long corrupted this land."

"But would you ever really feel safe? Are you prepared to bid a permanent farewell to Naftali Saleschutz?"

"That's the problem. When I think about it clearly, that's when I seriously doubt whether I could ever do it. Remember who I really am and where I've come from. Certainly it would dishonor the memories of my dead father, mother and sisters in this way. Besides, the Jewish people deserve more from me. Hitler tried to annihilate the Jews. How could I do something that would perpetuate his monstrous plan? How can I remain here knowing that Poland is one vast Jewish cemetery, its ground soaked through with Jewish blood, much of it shed by the very people who were our neighbors?

"Besides, I am a Cohen. That makes me, a direct male descendant of Aaron, the High Priest, brother of Moses. From biblical times this traditional linkage has remained. Who am I to break the chain? Is that why God permitted me to survive? So you see, there's such a preponderance of moral issues involved that decides, 'No, this is something you cannot do, indeed dare not do.' But with you, Felicia, maybe it is different?"

"Just as I am sure you did, it's true I have thought about it. I survived because I was Felicia Milaszewska. I have now become comfortable with my new persona. But to go on this way . . . No. Because Hitler wanted to rid the world of Jews I must say to all, proudly and loudly, 'I am a Jew, I am alive! Hitler has failed.' I must bear witness to what was perpetrated. But here in Poland, even in Europe I cannot do it. I have witnessed too many atrocities, too much inhumanity to want to remain and pick up the tattered pieces of my life. Everywhere I look, even in the faces of the people here, I am reminded of the horrors I experienced, and of the loss of all those who meant everything to me. I want to heal, or at least try to reduce the pain.

"I must leave Poland as soon as I can. If the United States would have me I would go there. I know that you have many relatives in America, so it is entirely possible for you to start a new life in this country. But my fondest wish would be to be reunited with my sister Pepka, and my grandmother in Palestine. I must see them; they must be told about all that has happened."

"Yes, Felicia, there is Palestine. I've been in contact with members of the Jewish Brigade. From what they tell me there is certain to be a showdown there. We Jews are going to have to fight for this land. During the war when I was in the ghetto or in the forest, had

someone offered me the chance to fight for a homeland, even for a day, even if it meant certain death . . .
nothing would have made me happier. I'm a fighter.
Could there be any better reason to struggle?"

"It seems then that each of us is prepared to leave
Poland. So, Naftali, where do we go from here?"

"What do you mean, 'We'?"

"We, you and I."

"You and I together?"

"Perhaps."

"We! I like the sound of it."

Epilogue

The story of Norman and Amalie (her parents and friends called her Manya) does not end with their fateful encounter in Cracow. Rather, for the two of them it was just the beginning. Love blossomed and before the end of 1945 they were wed.

Manya's long held ambition to become a doctor advanced a step when she was accepted at war's end into medical school (Universytet Jagielonski) in Cracow. However, complete concentration on studies was impossible, given the pressing needs of Jewish survivors who managed to drift into Cracow. Most owned nothing more than the tattered remnants of concentration camp clothes; all were desperate. Defeat of the Germans did not result in peace and security for Poland's Jews. Reports circulated of widespread attacks on Jewish survivors by elements in the Polish population. Manya found herself devoting a great deal of energy to providing relief and support for the desperate Jews she encountered everywhere. After the transfer of Norman from Cracow to Wroclaw (Breslau) Manya resigned from medical school.

Norman remained Tadeusz Zaleski and was rewarded with a succession of army promotions until he became a figure of considerable authority in and around Cracow. As best he could, and without betraying his identity, he worked with Jewish community representatives. His timely intervention enabled many Jewish parents to recover children who had been placed in Polish homes or Catholic institutions during the war. In addition, he diverted food and other scarce supplies to those caring for Jewish orphans. He was instrumental in providing protection for groups organized to smuggle Jews out of Poland and across Europe to Palestine. At that time he also assisted in the work of an international commission headed by Hewlett Johnson, Dean of Canterbury, engaged in investigating German atrocities. In this connection Norman visited most of the concentration camps in Poland including Auschwitz, Maidanek, Treblinka and Belzec. Inveterate photographer that he was, he recorded pictorially many of the ghastly sights which the departing Germans had been unable to conceal.

When Norman was transferred to Breslau (Wroclaw) late in 1945, he and Manya found themselves involved in much of the same activities that had occupied them in Cracow. He was now deeply committed to advancing the Jewish cause in the Holy Land, and used his position to collect weapons, which were transferred to Czechoslovakia and then to those who smuggled them into Palestine. In what surely was an action of great symbolic significance, Norman assisted in the forced removal of Germans in the Breslau area back to Germany. It could not have been accidental when he ordered large groups to leave in the middle of the night, limiting them only to what they could carry.

Despite the advantages of his position, neither Norman or Manya envisioned much of a future for themselves in postwar Poland. Were his true Jewish identity to be uncovered and his efforts in behalf of Palestine revealed, enemies would surely seek his downfall. For that reason he fled across the Polish border and into Germany. Afterwards Manya would join him. While in Germany Norman resumed his involvement in the effort to get Jews out of Europe and on to Palestine. He was intent on following this route himself, but Manya cautioned against such a decision, fearing detention by the British in Cyprus. Instead they set their sights on the United States.

Entering the United States proved no easy task. Papers requested from family members in America never arrived nor were American visas forthcoming. They would not be issued until proper identifications were presented. But how could one expect Holocaust survivors to furnish such official documentation? Was this not an excess of bureaucratic rigidity? Discussion with the American consul might prompt a reconsideration of regulations, but his secretary demanded a substantial bribe before such an audience would be arranged. Desperate now, Norman and Manya decided to confront the General Consul personally on the street and explain their predicament. This they succeeded in accomplishing (thanks in part to their ability to speak English). They won him over, and in a short time the regulation was changed. Affidavits from two witnesses instead of original identification documents would henceforth be sufficient. In short order United States visas were obtained.

The wait for transportation out of Bremerhaven became an extended agonizing delay of months when a nationwide coal strike in the United States precluded American ships from crossing the Atlantic. Finally all was in readiness on board the small, cramped, Liberty Ship, the "Ernie Pyle," that was to take them and many others to America. The crowding was intolerable, conditions aboard were exacerbated due to the severe

winter storms encountered during the two-week trip.
Norman became desperately ill during the stormy
passage, despairing, so that he even prayed that his
life, spared so many times in the past, come to an end.
Such dark thoughts receded, however, when word
spread that the vessel would soon be in American
waters. All those aboard rushed to dress in their best
clothes and then waited for hours on end, eager to
catch sight of the Statue of Liberty. When at last it
came into view their joy was unbounded.

Norman and Manya were now in the United States;
their immediate prospects, however, were not bright.
They arrived with two $100 dollar bills previously
obtained in Germany. Alas, the currency proved to be
counterfeit. They were advised by a bank to destroy
them, which they did. Now they were penniless, and
without readily marketable skills. On this unpromising
note the young couple began their life in America.
Norman proceeded through a succession of menial jobs
(his first one filling ink bottles all day), none lasting
very long. Fired from some, quitting others, his fierce
independence and outspokenness generally proved to
be his undoing. Beyond that, he experienced great
difficulty adjusting to his new lowly status. Back in
Poland he had for a time wielded considerable authority, and occupied a position of power. All that was
gone in America. Fortunately Manya obtained a position as a Hebrew school teacher, and ever so slowly
they took root in the new world.

In time Norman discovered a road to success. It
involved work, hard work, indeed, but he was equal to
the task. Rising very early in his Brooklyn apartment
every morning, he packed his wares and traveled two
hours each way by all manner of conveyances to Jersey

City, to sell his merchandise. He had discovered that the life of a peddler, however difficult and demanding, could yield a comfortable income. The secret to his success was simple enough; obtain products that people wanted, like stockings, offer customers the opportunity of buying on credit, knock on a lot of doors, and speak Polish. His buyers at first were Polish-Americans living in Jersey City, and Norman would add, living mostly on the top floors of walkup apartment buildings. Up he climbed, carrying his very heavy bundles, but that's where sales were made. In time he added to his line of products and obtained many new customers through recommendations. Before long he moved up to selling furniture and home furnishings. Indisputably, the American dream was now within reach.

But none of it might have happened had Norman and Manya not made one critical decision. Shortly after arriving in the United States he had become active in a number of groups organized to aid the Jews in Palestine. He had joined with American supporters of the Haganah, even the radical Stern Gang, to lend support to their efforts. At some point he also became active in the George Washington Legion, whose members fully intended to leave the United States for Palestine and there to join with fellow Jews in their efforts to create a Jewish homeland. And then one day in 1947 word arrived; it was time to depart. Norman was ready. For a long time it had been his dream to leave for Palestine, and there to fight just as he had during the war against the Germans. He was, after all, a trained soldier, and he was young. But Manya saw things differently. She had, in her young life, already suffered too many losses, had seen all of her family in Poland killed. She opposed his departure. In the end she prevailed. The battle in Palestine would go forward, but without Norman Salsitz.

The passing years were kind to the Salsitzes. Economic gains were steady and sure. Norman entered the real estate business, became a builder, and moved from Brooklyn into a home he purchased in suburban New Jersey. And then the blessed event. A daughter, Esther, was born to Manya and Norman. The next generation of their family was thus assured. Meanwhile Norman became quite active in Jewish community affairs, giving most generously of his time and money. A devoted supporter of Israel, he has visited that country dozens of times and contributed funds for all manner of projects and activities in that land.

But success in the United States could never mean for Norman and Manya what it meant for millions of native born Americans. Enjoyment could never be complete, satisfactions at best partial. Always there were the memories of the wartime years to cloud over any sense of contentment. In the postwar period, the world seemed uninterested in being reminded of Germany's genocidal assault against the Jews. Many of the survivors themselves were loath to speak openly of those times, and often encountered skepticism when they did. It was some time, for example, before Manya's sister, Pepka, who had spent the war years in Palestine, could accept the reality of what had happened in Poland. It was not a matter that Norman and Manya could ignore, however. Although Poland was now far off, there was no forgetting those few Poles who had risked so much to assist them during those terrible times. Norman collected food and clothes and sent a seemingly endless stream of packages to them.

Word circulated regarding these activities and in a
little while he was deluged with requests from Poles
for help, most claiming that they were among those
righteous Gentiles who had assisted Jews during the
war. To many of these pleas he responded generously,
contributing thousands of dollars of his own funds for
this purpose. Norman believed that those Poles who
did not forsake the Jews should not be neglected nor
should their efforts go unrewarded. Most recently,
Manya invited Kazia Jezienicka, and Norman, Stanis-
lawa Bardzik (Stashka Hodor), both of whom provided
vital assistance to them during the war, to America as
their guests for an extended visit. Norman and Manya
have not forgotten those who did not abandon their
humanity during the war years in Poland.

With the Holocaust becoming a subject of immense
general interest, the Salsitzes have found themselves
sought after for numerous newspaper articles and in-
terviews and have been called upon to speak at an
endless array of memorial gatherings honoring the
victims of the German reign of terror. In addition,
Norman's precious albums of photographs, most related to town life in Kolbuszowa, are much in viewing
demand, copies of which are to be found in several
museums and in numerous public exhibitions.

But for them the wounds of the Holocaust can never
heal. The pain they manage to dull at times, set aside
on other occasions, never goes away. It's worse at night.
Sleep usually brings not respite but harrowing flash-
backs, nightmarish chases, screams and images terri-
fying still. But then there are the visits from their
grandchildren (they have three, Dustin, Aaron, and
Michael), the gatherings with friends, the Jewish

holidays, family festivities, and the trips to Israel. Norman and Manya have managed to create rewarding and meaningful lives for themselves. It remains their most important and precious legacy to the rest of us.

Richard Skolnick, Ph.D.